Always Love

THE TIMELESS STORY
OF GOD'S HEART FOR THE WORLD
AND WHAT IT MEANS FOR YOU

Sara Lubbers

Always Love: The Timeless Story of God's Heart for the World and What it Means for You

Photo of Sara Lubbers by Elise Hurst Photography

Published by Peregrini Press, a division of Awen Collaborative Limited

For inquiries related to this book please email: info@peregrinipress.com
or call Tel: +44-(0)7597-170650

Dedicated to my husband,
Josh.
I am yours, and you are mine.

And to my children,
Evangeline, Selah, & Joshua.
May you always be willing to be brave
and to be a part of this Story in a way you never expected.
Remember, you are His, and He is yours.

With special thanks to Elizabeth Matthews,
my book doula

Endorsements

Always Love is *accessible, engaging, illuminating*. Sara takes the reader on a captivating journey through the Bible by employing a beautiful combination of *creative prose and theological wisdom*. And, whether you are new to the Scriptures or very familiar with them, a single chapter has the power to transform you.

Jason Thomas
Executive Vice President, InterVarsity

Sara Lubbers has done a magnificent job of choosing key stories of the Bible and weaving them together with the thread of Always Love, resulting in a powerful and creative presentation of God's truth wrapped in refreshingly alive language. This is a gem not only for young readers of God's truth, but for those all of generations who retain an adventurous spirit and a love for God's Biblical narrative.

Dr. Kate R. Pocklington
Serving in Leadership Development & Missional Formation

This is a fun and creative book! Sara tackles some both well-known and more obscure sections of the Bible and weaves them into the main storyline. It would be great for reading with children, but I think every adult Christian would benefit from it, too.

Dusty Thompson
Lead Pastor at Redeemer Church in Lubbock, Texas

Sara Lubbers has written an extraordinary book about the story of salvation. Her unique and creative retelling of the old stories captures the imagination and refreshes the soul. I was challenged and encouraged by reading it and trust it will be a blessing to many of all ages and stages in their faith journey.

T.J. MacLeslie
Author of *Designed for Relationship* (and other titles)

In a time when people are asking hard questions about the character of God and how the Bible connects, Old to New, this is the book I will hand to my friends and seekers alike, with complete confidence. The timeless truth of the Gospel and the unwavering love of the Father weaves from story to story highlighting the reality that God is both just and love, and I believe readers will walk away with a greater understanding that from beginning to end, His love is always true, and that is Good News.

Paige Allen
Executive Pastor of Outreach at Church on the Rock
Founder of Pursue Missions
Author of *Road Signs*

For the young reader, for anyone taking up the Bible for the first time, or for anyone familiar with a trove of Bible stories but unsure how they all connect to its central message, I highly commend Sara Lubbers' Always Love as a companion volume to Holy Writ. With skill and insight she weaves together key biblical moments into a coherent and seamless whole. She handles large portions of Biblical literature with remarkable concision, distilling each to the essential components necessary to drive the narrative forward. It's both imaginative and faithful to the biblical texts. In my view, it's greatest strength lies in its Christocentric focus, illustrating from the outset how Jesus, prefigured in every Old Testament story, is the fulfillment of God's plan to redeem the world, and highlighting how Christ's ministry in the New Testament is the attainment of every divine promise and the realization of every human longing. If you wonder how the Bible can be understood as a single story, read Always Love. You'll be given a helpful frame upon which, for years to come, you can build a fuller understanding of the Bible's message and teaching.

Leon Fillyaw
Associate Regional Director, InterVarsity

Table of Contents

Chapter 1

The Beginning of the Story
Genesis 1:1-25
John 1:1-18

Once before there was time, there was an Author whose heart was Always Love. Eventually, His heart of Always Love overflowed into a beautifully rich Story full of everything that makes a story good—astonishing feats, unbelievable courage, wonderful surprises, wicked enemies, and valiant heroes.

Over time the Author came to be called the Word, because what He did with words was extraordinary. The way He expressed Himself with them was unique. When the Word was spoken—or rather, when this Word spoke—breathtakingly *magical* things happened! Rather than simply putting pen to paper to reveal the Story in His heart, the Word spoke into existence everything in the Story. What we see, what we don't see—everything!

Just imagine! Darkness, thick and deep—rich with both the Author's presence and so much possibility. The Word hovered closely over this dark, watery canvas, so closely it could feel His warm breath as He spoke. Slowly, softly, He began to breathe words onto it; and as He did, a soft glow of light appeared...first slowly, then more quickly until it raced onto the scene and cut through the darkness—not to challenge the darkness, not to dispel it, but in a way that made the darkness more beautiful for existing alongside it.

Darkness and light were both so beautiful—so opposite in every way; and yet they fit perfectly together. They began a beautiful dance, giving forward motion to the Story. Night and day and night and day, over and over they danced together hand-in-hand as the Story unfolded.

Darkness and light now separated, the Author began separating other things as well and putting them in their spaces. He opened His mouth and more possibilities poured out as the expanse above became wide and airy and the expanse beneath stretched wide and wet as far as the eye could see. Air and water—as opposite as light and darkness; yet they fit together perfectly! Both were empty, yet full of potential for life. Light and darkness held hands, traded places, invited air and water into the dance, made another day, and guided the Story forward with sky and sea stretching out their hands to be filled.

Rumbling over the expanse came the voice of the Word once more. Powerfully it called up from under the water something completely different than water. Where water was wet and whimsical, this new substance emerging from beneath it was dry and steadfast. As the land rose from the water, it began shouting out exuberant praise in the form of plants and trees all bursting with fruit and clapping with joy. Tall, jagged mountains and rolling hills raised their hands high into the sky to their Creator. Water and land joined hands. How opposite they were, yet how perfectly they fit together! Sky grabbed hold of land's hand and drew her into the dance, too!

Everything created was full of joy, brought to life by the sound of His voice; all swept up into this breathtaking dance. They longed to see what the Author would do next! By now they saw that they were to be the stage upon which the rest of the Author's Story would unfold. Could there be a greater joy? With expectation, they looked to Him to see what He had planned, and they were not disappointed!

The Author looked at the sky, and with an excitement He couldn't contain, He laughed a deep, joyful laugh from the depths of His heart and flung globes of light like diamonds all across the sky. The sky could hardly contain its surprise or its praise! To think the sky in all its vastness and power could be improved upon—and yet it was! Immediately, these radiant lights jumped into the dance, enhancing the beauty of all things by making them shine. Where the sky had been completely dark, it now sparkled with spheres that gave meaning to the dance of light and darkness. The permanence and power of these stars and spheres created seasons so the plants and trees on land would know when to give fruit. They infused rhythm into the way the sea and land danced together and illuminated the darkness to show the way to go. Now with stars twinkling in the heavens and light warming the land as waves crashed upon it, each element danced together around the Author, making Him look so good! Night after day after night after day, the Story continued to unfold.

Now the Word opened His mouth and a string of words burst forth, instantly filling both water and sky with glory! The water teemed with fish and sharks, whales and live plants, all manner of water creatures diving and splashing, jumping and crashing to say "Thank you!" to the one who spoke them into existence. Simultaneously, the sky above felt a tickle of joy as thousands of winged animals took to the heights, flapping and hooting, cawing and crowing their praise to the one who made them feel His pleasure as they flew!

All eyes now looked to the Word, whose eyes looked to the land. Its mountains and valleys, plants and trees suddenly became home to the myriad animals dreamed up in the Author's heart. Lumbering bears, powerful lions, swift horses, lithe reptiles, tall, towering dinosaurs, cuddly pandas, and wriggling earthworms—all, and more!—burst onto the scene to be swept into the dance, becoming friends with everything brought forth from the Author's heart. Male and female, they were as opposite as could be; yet they fit together perfectly.

Then the Word spoke above the cacophony of voices, "Friends, fill every space I've given you!"

What began as a powerful but quiet dance increased by crescendos from an orchestra of created things brought together to shout His praise and *enjoy* His Always Love! But then the Author, the Word, like a conductor with His wand, with a motion of His hands beckoned all He'd created to be still, to draw near. Filled with curiosity, they wondered what could happen next. With all spaces filled—land, sea, and sky—what more could there be to do?

Chapter 2

Image-Bearers & A Garden
Genesis 1:26-2:25

The Author squatted low to the ground, and with His strong, steady hands, scooped up a handful of dirt. He moved it this way and that, mixing it with His Always Love, and explaining to those watching, "I'm making an image-bearer."

All creation drew near, intrigued by this sudden change of rhythm in the dance, wondering what an image-bearer might be. What He fashioned from the dust began to look a lot like the Author—but it just laid there. Why didn't it join in the dance?

Gently, the Word breathed into His new creation a deep, warm, long breath, causing his chest to rise and fall, his eyes to flutter open. Then the Word, as if greeting a dear friend, offered His newly-formed creation a hand to help him up, and introduced the rest of His creation to a man He called "Adam."

A roar of applause erupted from the onlookers! To look at the Author and then at Adam was like seeing tall, majestic trees towering over a pool of water, then seeing those trees reflected so clearly in the water. There was the tree and there, in Adam, was the reflection.

Everything the Author created was so *good* because the Author Himself was so good and infused His character into

His creation. He gave Himself—His Always Love—to His creation with a simple phrase, "I am yours, and you are Mine."

But as similar as Adam was to the Author, he was also very different; and he seemed to be missing something. As Adam surveyed the endless variety of creatures gathering to meet him, he noticed each had a special friend. Yes, all creatures were friends together, but each one had a match—someone the same, but perfectly different. Somehow he knew they *belonged* together, and seeing that belonging caused a deep desire to rise in his heart. Where did Adam belong? Who was his special friend?

Adam turned to the Author, the question forming in his mind but not yet uttered in words. The Author met his gaze saying, "I want to give you what you're seeking. Lie down and sleep."

Deep sleep came over Adam, and in rest he gave up a part of himself to bring to life the crown of creation. With the precision of a master surgeon and the tenderness of a mother with her newborn child, the Author cut into the center of Adam's life as an image-bearer, where his heart beat and his lungs drew in air, where he felt his deepest emotions and found his deepest strength. Then the Author did something He hadn't done before. Rather than speak this beautiful creature into existence or shape her out of dirt, instead, from the tender strength of what it means to be an image-bearer, He drew out a woman, who now stood before her Creator, freshly fashioned, absolutely breathtaking.

Whole galaxies were flung into being to show the breadth of the Author's majesty, waterfalls birthed to continuously roar out His praise, lofty mountain peaks stretched to the heights to declare His grandeur, and vast oceans were filled with an infinitude of creativity, but nothing had prepared creation for this.

The woman burst out in laughter, caught up in the dance around her. Taken from the most tender place in Adam and written into the Story by the very hands of the Author, she was the missing piece in creation.

"Well, shall we wake him?" the Author asked her, the light in His eyes dancing, revealing the supreme happiness He felt in His heart.

Adam's eyes blinked, adjusting to the light. He slowly stood up, jaw dropping, eyes wide with wonder, he exclaimed, "She is the one I've been looking for!"

Every part of creation had its match that fit perfectly together and declared the Author's praises better because of it. Now, before him, was Eve, his match. And although he gave up part of himself to bring forth her life, in its place came to life a way of living and loving that Adam had never known before. With exuberance and passion he blurted out, "You are my equal image-bearer, my ally in life, and I love having you here! I am yours, and you are mine!"

Together they stood entirely vulnerable, completely exposed, and yet so very *safe* in the Author's Always Love.

The Author took them by the hand—male and female, Adam and Eve—looked them deeply in their eyes and from His heart of Always Love said, "My image-bearers, you were created for the Good Life, living forever in My Always Love and Always Loving each other. Now I'm giving each of you a pen, that together we might partner in this Story I'm writing for the whole world! Reflect and represent My heart in what you write. Multiply image-bearers, teaching them My Story and how to write with Me. Creation is filled to the brim with potential. With these pens, harness that potential, cultivate beauty, and turn the world into a place where I'll live with image-bearers forever! Together you reflect Me—

making you perfect for this job. And always remember that I am yours, and you are Mine!"

The two image-bearers, all creation, and the Author Himself began to laugh—uninhibited, tears-coming-to-their-eyes belly laughter—because the Story had just gotten *so good!* As they laughed, light and darkness kept dancing, hands joined together, moving the Story along from day to night to day again.

As the next morning dawned, all creation drew near—Adam and Eve in the front row wondering, "What will the Author do today?"

But today He flung no stars into the sky and created nothing new to roam the land. Instead, the Author, like a King entering His brand-new palace and establishing His Kingdom, sat down on His throne, pen in hand to rule and reign what He had created—to continue writing a Story of Always Love for His creation.

"It is finished!" the Author-King said with a smile. "Day after day, I've precisely thought out, wonderfully imagined, wholeheartedly invested Myself into creation, and invited image-bearers to partner with Me in My Story. But today is different. Today is a day of celebration. Let's enjoy My finished work by resting in all I've done."

And so they did!

But Reader, this isn't how the Story ends; for you see, sometime in the hustle and bustle of creation, the Author planted a Garden. This Garden epitomized all that creation represented—new, raw, and expectant. He gave this Garden as a gift to His image-bearers, a place to begin writing the Story with Him, a place where heaven met earth, and image-bearers enjoyed the Author's uninhibited presence.

Rivers flowed through the Garden as if watering it with the Author's very presence. The land sparkled with shiny gold, dark black stone, and glittering jewels. The fruit trees gave food for Adam and Eve to enjoy. The Garden brimmed with opportunity and potential.

On the day the Author led His image-bearers into the Garden, they wandered around it together, highlighting its beauty here and there, snacking on luscious fruit from trees as they talked. Adam and Eve listened while the Author explained His heart for the Garden. Then He listened to their excited ramblings as Adam and Eve both oozed with creative energy and fresh ideas, bolstered by the relationship of Always Love they shared together.

As they entered the middle of the Garden, the Author stopped walking and said, "My friends, I created you from My Always Love. *I am yours, and you are Mine.* I'm giving this Garden to you; but look at these two trees in the middle. They are unlike any other trees."

Quizzical expressions crept over the image-bearers' faces as they looked at the two trees. They *were* incredible. Large and beautiful, their fruit hung low. What did the Author have planned for these two trees? Why did this conversation feel so different than others they'd had that day? Had He ever before spoken with such seriousness? They drew near to catch every word.

"To the right is the Tree of Life," explained the Author. "Eat from it freely! But do not eat the fruit from the Tree of Knowledge on the left. It would end life as you know it. Do you understand?"

But perhaps, dear Reader, you are wondering why the Author would write these two trees into the Story. For the Garden was full of potential to unearth the vast treasures the Creator had hidden for them and full of invitation to make something beautiful with it. And the truest part of the Author's heart was His Always Love. Strong and fierce, and undeniably good, Always Love has one vulnerability. You see, by its very nature, Always Love cannot force itself on anyone, or it ceases to be Always Love. To ensure Always Love would forever characterize image-bearers' relationships with the Author, there had to be two trees. In all the freedoms the Creator gave His image-bearers, He also gave them freedom to reject Him and the Good Life He wanted to give them. It was all an invitation to deeply trust the Author's Always Love and live surrendered to it.

For now, the image-bearers walked away from the two trees rooted in His Always Love. But perhaps more quickly than we'd expect, the Story will wind its way past these two trees, and it's at these trees we'll begin to see the extent of the Author's Always Love.

Chapter 3

A Lie & A Promise
Genesis 3
Isaiah 14:12-15
Ezekiel 28:11-19

"Did the Author *really* say you couldn't enjoy the fruit from the trees He had created?" asked a cunning snake as he slithered his way down the branches of the Tree of Knowledge.

"Oh no," Eve laughed dismissively, "He didn't say that. We just can't eat from this one. If we even touch its fruit, our lives will end!"

The serpent broke out in a sinister laugh. "Ah yes, I thought the Author might've said that. He's like that, you know. But *I* have touched this fruit and eaten it, and life as I know it hasn't ended."

He slithered further down a branch through a few of the juiciest, lowest-hanging fruits to wrap around Adam and Eve a conversation that threatened to strangle their very lives. "You don't know the Author like I do. You see, this fruit gives you power to become like Him. Eating it is the way to the Good Life!"

At the foot of the Tree of Knowledge, the snake called into question the Author's Always Love, fooling the two image-bearers who were already as much like the Author as they could ever be. But the enemy wasn't finished. For you see, dear Reader, this villain that sneaked onto the pages of the

Story used to be the most captivating angel ever created, bright like the dawn, bedazzled with jewels, leading all other angels in worshiping the Author. Full of wisdom and flawless in beauty, one day he began to grow very jealous. He wanted a different role in the Story than the Author gave him. In fact, he wanted to *become* the Author. So he gathered an army and fought against Him.

The enemy soon found himself and his army thrown down to earth in humiliation and defeat, yet he refused to give up. He saw that he couldn't overthrow the Author; but he knew he could steal, kill, and destroy parts of the Story as it unfolded. Leaving his army behind, this time he slithered onto the Story's pages bringing just words. As the Word used words to bring forth life, the enemy would use them to bring death to image-bearers and, if he could, to the Story itself.

"Perhaps..." the serpent continued slowly, letting the gravity of his proposition sink in, "He's afraid to give you the Good Life...and you'll have to get it for yourself."

His words coiled tightly around them, challenging all they knew to be true about the Author. They couldn't deny it; the fruit looked delicious. They had noticed that much when the Author first showed them the Garden and explained the trees. Maybe the snake was right; he seemed to know things about the Author they didn't. Maybe they really did have to find the Good Life on their own.

Eve reached out, hesitantly at first, but then with renewed confidence, she grabbed a piece of the luscious fruit from the branch as a person might reach out and grab a pen. She brought the fruit to her mouth, as one might put pen to paper, and she began writing her own story. Then Adam did the same. As they chewed and swallowed the delicious fruit, they swallowed the lie into their hearts that told them they could write a better Story than the Author could—that they could secure the Good Life for themselves.

When the pleasure of the taste had passed, a wave of fear washed over their hearts for Always Love between the two image-bearers was gone. In its wake was a pool of rage, hatred, and shame. Sin—not so much what they had *done*, but who they had *become*—twisted and tangled within them, choking out life, deforming them and distorting the way they saw everything. With one single bite, they'd rejected Always Love.

The snake, beaming with pride, quickly slithered away to watch things unfold from a distance. He couldn't defeat the Author with an army; but surely he could hijack His Story. He sat celebrating his victory as Adam and Eve scrambled to protect themselves from a world that had suddenly become very threatening.

"Where are you, friends?" a voice gently called. Usually the voice brought joy to their hearts as the Author came each afternoon to enjoy their friendship, but now it deepened their shame and urge to hide themselves.

Adam called out to explain, "We heard you coming, but we'd rather not go for a walk today. We're naked and afraid, you see, and are busy clothing ourselves with leaves."

"My dear friends, who said you are naked?" the Author gently asked. *He* had always been the one to define them. *He* had always been the one to tell them who they were.

Adam stepped out from behind the bushes where he had been hiding. He walked cautiously toward his Creator, brow furrowed, searching for something. Suddenly, he found it, "It's this woman You gave me! She's the reason we're in this awful mess!"

A sadness came over the Author's face. "My daughter, what happened?" He peered behind the bush where she was hiding, took her by the hand, and drew her out into the clearing with Him. Her head hung down in shame. What could she say? Quietly she opened the same mouth that ate the fruit and muttered, "The snake deceived me. I ate the fruit." And she burst into tears.

"Snake!" the Author's voice reverberated throughout creation once more, this time not to fill the earth with life but to call forth the one who had tried to destroy it. The serpent came forth, arrogant and bitter.

"Slithering serpent, your malevolence toward Me has blinded you. You thought if you led the woman to rebel, those born to her would follow suit, and the Story would then be yours. You are forever cursed to crawl in the lowliness of that hatred of Me. But this Story will never be yours. One day, a woman will give birth to the Rescuer. My rescue plan will lead Him to death, but through death, He'll put both you and sin to death."

Keeping his mouth shut, the enemy brooded, "This isn't the last He'll hear of me. This means *war*!" and he turned to creep into the shadows.

Standing together in sorrow, the Author took His image-bearers' hands just as He had on that glorious day they first met. He looked deeply into their eyes and said, "Friends, I offered you the Good Life forever in My Always Love; yet you've rejected it, thinking you could find a better life apart from Me. Now life as you knew it has ended."

He turned to Eve, "My daughter, everything it means to be uniquely woman will be hard for you now. You were created to be like Me—to bring forth life! But in motherhood, you will know an intense pain I didn't want you to know. In marriage, you will feel a deep chasm between you and your husband that you were never meant to feel. Neither of you will know how to cross the chasm on your own."

He then turned to Adam, "My son, before I fashioned you from the dirt, I formed you in My heart, to cultivate what I created, to find joy and purpose in your work. Your choice to live apart from My Always Love means you'll now be searching for joy and purpose in all the wrong places. Work will twist its thorns around you in a way that drains your life until you return to the very dust from which you were created."

He turned to lead them once again on a journey through the Garden, tears streaming down each of their faces. As they walked, tattered leaves fell to the ground from Adam and Eve's makeshift leaf-robes, revealing how truly incompetent they were to cover up the mess they had made.

The Author led them to a clearing where there was a small flock of beautiful, spotless sheep. The Author called out a wonderful name, and the ears of one particular lamb perked up. The lamb bleated with joy and pranced toward his Maker. Through this lamb, the Author would reveal a part of His heart that we might not have expected to see. For you see, dear Reader, as long as sin is a part of this Story, the Author's Always Love must express itself toward sin as *Always Wrath*. Sin mocks the Author's heart and stands in the way of image-bearers finding life in His Always Love, but He refuses to let that define the Story.

The Author knelt on one knee, taking the head of the trusting sheep in His hand, and whispered, "My little friend, life as all creation knew it has unraveled. One day My Always Wrath against sin will destroy all evil that has come into the Story, but today, are you willing to be brave and to be a part of this Story in a way you never expected?"

The trusting sheep looked His Master in the eyes and saw nothing but Always Love. There was no selfishness, no evil in the Author's heart. The lamb knew he could trust, so he said yes. And as the sun set that day, blood was shed for the first time in this Story. But not for the last.

It was a sad twist in the Story no one had expected. How sad—and deeply curious—that the one who died that day was *not* the one who committed the wrong. The innocent gave its life for the guilty.

The guilty, now dressed in innocent lamb's clothing, turned to walk away. Too marred and stained by sin to live in the Author's presence on earth, they had to leave. Exiled from the Garden, they entered a world with an enemy on the loose, while carrying the deep sense that they had wronged the Author and were incapable of making it right. It was as the Author warned them: Life as they knew it had ended.

But it wouldn't always be this way. The Author stood at the Garden's entrance whispering a hope into the Story that would breathe life into all who believed it, "Today they forgot that I am theirs, and they are Mine, but I will never forget! I Am Who I Am, and even though it will cause Me great pain, I will Always Love them."

Then, with a sound like thunder a glorious angel appeared, blocking the entrance to the Garden, his sword aflame with the Author's Always Wrath against sin. Never again could broken image-bearers come that way into the Author's presence. But the Author would make a new way.

Chapter 4

A Boat & A Tower
Genesis 4-11:26
Acts 14:16-17
Hebrews 11:7

"Rain! What is rain? Noah, you're losing your mind!" the people laughed mockingly at Noah, for they'd never seen rain before.

But day after day, Noah and his sons continued to build their huge boat while those around him jeered and sneered. Land stretched in every direction as far as the eye could see, and the huge boat stood out from the landscape as bizarrely as Noah's friendship with the Author did, for this was a time when the Author had few friends.

Image-bearers had long ago left the Garden to fill the earth and did so in both beautiful and broken ways. Filled with the Author's creativity, they shaped the world around them, starting families, founding cities, and developing new ideas for housing, tools, and musical instruments. But deeply twisted by sin, they also used their pens to write terribly broken stories, stories in which brother killed brother, men conquered and collected women, and they sang of their violence against other image-bearers. The earth begged for comfort and rest from the sin that filled it, and the Author's Always Wrath against sin heard its plea.

Laughter continued when the boat was finished and increased while animals came from all over the earth to enter the boat, heeding the Author's voice with more faithfulness than most of His image-bearers. The jeering went on as Noah and his family followed them into the boat. Laughter filled the air even as ominous clouds rolled in from all directions, dragging deep darkness behind them.

But the sound of laughter died down as the first drops of rain fell from the dark clouds. Soon fists beat on the sides of the boat and voices begged to be let in. But the Author had shut the boat's door. How could anyone else open it? It was a twist in the Story no one would've imagined, and now it was too late for rescue.

Forty days and nights of relentless rain drowned the voices of Noah's mockers. What remained was the boat, Noah's friendship with the Author, and an invitation to start a new chapter in the Story.

"Go on, little friend," Noah whispered to the dove one day after months of floating on the water. He leaned out the window of the massive boat while the dove perched on his hand. "Bring back a sign of hope," he said as he released the white dove into the blue expanse and then stood waiting and watching for its return.

For generations, Noah's family had longed for the Author's rescue from sin, and Noah's father, Lamech, knew the time must be soon. As Lamech held his newborn son in his arms long ago, he named him Noah, saying, "He will bring comfort and rest like we've never known before."

Now comfort and rest had come to the earth in a way no one would've expected, for Always Wrath against sin had had enough. In the form of water, it cracked through the earth from beneath and poured itself out from above like big, wet tears all over the Author's manuscript. It wiped clean the unmentionable ways His image-bearers had distorted His Story trying to wrestle His pen from His hand.

But Always Love remained, offering comfort and rest in the form of an invitation to build a boat and carry into it all the hope that remained on the earth. Hope now floated with Noah and his family inside while the earth rested from the violence that had filled it for so long.

"A leafy branch!" exclaimed Noah as the dove returned carrying a new sign of hope. "The water is receding!" And he ran below to share the good news with his family.

Before long, Noah's family heard the Author's voice inviting them, "Friends, come out of the boat! Bring everything and everyone with you!" And for the first time in a full year, image-bearers walked on dry land as they exited the boat and walked down the mountain it rested on.

As Noah's feet touched dry ground he was overwhelmed by the Author's Always Love that rescued them, and his response to the Author's Always Love was to worship. He built an altar, stone by stone, and soon innocent animal blood flowed to show once again that rescue from Always Wrath against sin doesn't come without a cost.

But it was a cost the Author was always willing to pay, and He proved this to His friend Noah when He met him at the altar with a similar invitation He'd given His first image-bearers. "You were created for the Good Life," He said, "living forever in My Always Love and Always Loving each other. You each have pens to partner with Me in My Story, so reflect and represent My heart in what you write. Spread out, fill the earth with image-bearers, teaching them My Story and how to write with Me."

Then, at this beginning of all things made new, the Author took His pen and colored a beautiful rainbow in the sky. Wrapping vivid colors from one end of the earth to the other, He invited His image-bearers to remember that when all things are dark, and it seems like all hope is lost, the Author still has His pen in hand and is writing a good Story.

Walking away from the altar, Noah and his family carried the hope of Always Love with them into this new world. But before long, it was clear they'd brought something else with them into this new world—something dark and twisted and buried deep in their hearts. It was never more apparent than when Noah found himself in a garden, his vineyard. As happened the first time the Story wove its way through a garden, its fruit snared another image-bearer. Perhaps looking for comfort or rest from life in a broken world, Noah drank too much wine from the fruit of his vines and then cursed his youngest son, Ham, for grossly sinning against him while he was drunk. It became clear that Noah and his family, image-bearers though they were, were still deeply needing a Rescuer to give them comfort and rest from sin. Though the earth had been washed of wickedness, wickedness remained in their hearts. Noah, rescuer that he was, could build a boat to rescue his family from a flood, but he couldn't rescue his family from the sin that twisted their hearts.

As years went on, image-bearers multiplied, but rather than trusting the Author's Always Love, they were suspicious of it. They believed the old lie that to get the Good Life, they had to make it for themselves. So rather than spreading out over the earth to teach image-bearers the Author's Story and how to write with Him, Noah's growing family determined to cloister together to make a name for themselves, cultivating a darkness that threatened to consume them. Bolstering their scheme was the fact that everyone spoke the same language.

But neither the Author nor His Story would be overcome by darkness, for He would never forget His Always Love. He faithfully penned into the Story even the tiniest reminders of Himself: kindness in the form of rain for their crops, food for their tables, and joy for their hearts. He was nothing if not relentless in His pursuit of them even as they turned their backs to Him. Though there was no longer a Garden to walk through, and many forgot that the Author enjoyed friendship with image-bearers, He came walking among them all the same; and one day, there before His eyes loomed a tower.

"Oh, My image-bearers," the Author sighed with sadness in His heart. "You've brought together your best minds, your best plans, your best technology, pouring it all into a tower, thinking it will connect you with power just beyond your grasp and protect you from the diversity that would come from spreading out over the earth. But that's why I created you! You were created to find the Good Life in Me as we partner in making the whole world a house for My presence."

He spoke, but no one heard. Or maybe they heard, but no one understood His voice, for they were too busy writing broken stories for themselves. He knew their broken stories would stand in the way of the Good Life He wanted to give them, so He did for them what they were afraid to do for themselves. He had rescued them in a boat once before; now He rescued them from their tower.

With a stroke of His pen, the very image-bearers who couldn't understand His voice now couldn't understand each other's either. The sounds they made seemed foreign, unintelligible. Their greatest minds could no longer collaborate. All their plans came to a screeching halt as the overseers struggled to talk through what yesterday was so clear. The loads of bricks they worked so hard to make last week now sat piled up, unmoved because no one understood what to do with them. Their best minds, grandest plans, and newest technology couldn't give them the Good Life they deeply desired.

No longer able to speak the same language, they spread out in language groups looking back on their half-finished Tower of Babel with confusion. But what seemed confusing to them was beautiful to the Author who was writing the Story of a world filled with a diversity of image-bearers shaping the earth with their creativity and friendship with Him.

Neither a boat nor a tower could give them the Good Life they longed for or rescue them from the sin that twisted their hearts; but no matter how many times image-bearers forgot the Author, He would never forget them or His promise to rescue.

Chapter 5

Suffering & Trust
Job

"He only worships You for what You give him!" the Author's enemy stood bold-faced before Him, blatantly accusing. "Who loves You simply for Your Always Love anyway? You have to bribe people to love You. Withhold all their comforts and securities, and they would reject You!"

"I disagree," the Author replied. "Job would trust Me and My Story."

"Oh, would he?" the enemy snarled sarcastically. "Why don't we see if that's true?"

Up to this point, Job was the greatest man in the East. Externally, his family, wealth, and health flourished. Internally, his heart was full of integrity. Ruthless against sin, Job was committed to the Author and did everything to ensure his family was too.

But Job was about to learn that there is more behind the Story than meets the eye. Image-bearers don't have the Author's vantage point, and sometimes the Story just doesn't seem to make sense. Sometimes it even seems wrong.

In an instant, Job's life crashed down around him. The Author's enemy blew through Job's life like a violent storm, destroying his children, wealth, and health, all with the Author's complete consent. What remained was a shell of a man covered in sores, exiled from community, stripped of honor and power, but clinging tenaciously to his integrity and to a threadbare hope that the Author would explain his misery.

"Just give up, Job! Curse the Author and die!" his despairing wife counseled him at the trash heap that Job now called home.

"Maybe she's right," Job thought, grabbing a piece of broken pottery and scraping it over the sores on his legs. Pieces of dead skin flaked off, white pus accumulating on the shard. How had it come to this? What had Job done to deserve such suffering?

Weakly, his faith within him replied, "Neither my head nor my heart understands the devastation I've experienced; but surely I can trust the Author and whatever His pen writes into my chapter of this Story."

Sighing, Job's wife walked away, leaving him waiting for answers. The answers didn't come, but his friends came to comfort him, weeping for him and honoring his suffering with their silence…for Job's suffering was crushing.

Eventually, Job sighed in agony, "I wish I'd never been born."

"Job," his friend Eliphaz rebuked him mildly, "how can you say that? When all was well you were the one to comfort the discouraged. Now you're suffering and you want to give up? We live in a fair world: good people are blessed, evil people suffer. We know this is true, Job, so apply it to your own life. You must have done something to deserve this."

"Then tell me what I've done!" Job begged. "The Author knows I've done *nothing* to deserve this! My soul is overwhelmed with bitterness, and I just wish He would finish what He started. Instead, He plays target practice with me, taking shots so I die a slow, miserable death. Why has He turned against me? Doesn't He know what life is like for image-bearers and see life from our perspective?"

"Listen to yourself!" Bildad joined in, astonished. "You accuse the Author of injustice! He doesn't strengthen His enemies or weaken the blameless. You must have wronged Him, Job. But if you turn from your sin, He'll forgive you!"

"It's not that simple," moaned Job, his body aching with pain, his heart annoyed by his friends' words. "I *know* I'm innocent. My suffering is unjust; yet how could I tell the Author that? Could I stand before Him and defend myself? I wish I could!" Job's eyes teared up while his heart quietly searched for hope until it dawned on him, "I need a Rescuer! Someone to stand between the Author and me and plead my case." Job's voice trailed off as clouds rolled in over his heart. "But I'm alone. The Author knows I'm not guilty, yet I writhe in His hands with no one to rescue me! How is this Always Love?"

"This is ridiculous!" Zophar broke in. "If only the Author would show up right now and set you straight! Quit maintaining your innocence, Job. Just confess, and all this misery will melt away."

"Windbags!" Job scoffed, ferociously scraping his sores, "That's what you all are! Are these accusations really meant to comfort me? Of course, I wouldn't deny my sin if you could point it out! But no one can! The Author has set His face against me. But even if He takes my life, I want to trust Him and the Story He's writing. My only hope is that someone will rescue me, being a better friend to me than any of you!"

Tears welled up in his eyes as he continued, "Look at me! I'm nothing more than a bag of skin and bones. My wife loathes me. I've lost everything. Where is your compassion? You join the Author in striking me while I'm down. Well, that's fine!" Job said indignantly, gathering what little strength he had, struggling to stand on his feeble legs to say, "I know there is a Rescuer! In the Story's final chapter, He will return to this earth and make all things right again, and this bag of skin and bones will see Him face to face. To that end, I hope!"

"Job, sit down," Eliphaz sighed. "You're working yourself up without reason. Why would the Author let you suffer if you were innocent? Make your peace with Him, and you'll prosper once again. He is just in all He does. It's as simple as that."

But Job rebuked them, "Life is a befuddling mystery; yet you think you have it figured out! You come to me with clichés and trite comments, reducing the Author and His Story to what you can control and understand. Well, your words fall flat in the face of my pain. The Author has written something into this Story—something that we cannot understand—and you say it's my fault." Job hung his head in defeat, "I appeal to the Author Himself. Let Him come and tell me what I've done to deserve this. Then I will listen."

Elihu now spoke up, "Job, I've kept quiet so far thinking that all of you, being older, must also be wiser, but now I'm not sure. Eliphaz, Bildad, and Zophar, you've had plenty of opportunities to point out Job's guilt, but you don't. Or cannot. Perhaps Job is in fact innocent as he claims. But Job, with all due respect, you think too highly of your innocence. You say the Author denies you justice. What if this isn't a matter of *justice*? A person doesn't only suffer for wrongdoing. Sometimes the Author shapes the characters in His Story with suffering, training our hearts to run from sin. As the Author, He can write whatever He chooses, even if we don't understand. You maintain your innocence so strongly that you accuse the Author of wrongdoing. You walk a fine line, Job!"

Suddenly, a wild tempest rolled in and riding on it was the Author Himself, entering the Story to meet Job in his suffering in an unexpected way.

"Come now, Job," invited the Author, "it seems you have something to say—advice to give Me about the Story I'm writing? List your qualifications, Job. Tell Me, where were you when I penned the first lines of this Story, bringing to life the dance of creation with My very Word? Have you kept the world spinning since then? Did you make the stars to shine in wonder or bring the mountains from the heart of the sea to shout My praise? Do you sustain all living things?

"Or let's talk about justice since you think I've done you wrong," He continued. "My Story is far bigger than you, with a goodness and beauty image-bearers don't always approve of or understand. Justice is complex, Job. It's neither easy nor safe, but hand-in-hand My Always Love and Always Wrath against sin will ensure that justice will have the final say. Until then, be careful not to lose your awe of the one who holds the pen simply because the Story causes you pain."

Job sat in silence, while the Author continued. "Job, you asked if I can see life from an image-bearer's perspective. Well, do you see the Story from My vantage point? Is that why you're a competent judge of Me and My Story? If you were Me for a day, could you really do a better job? Your perspective is limited to your life's few breaths, yet I have the viewpoint of eternity. But go on, Job, plead your case. I'm listening."

But Job could not. Moments before he had longed to defend himself before the Author but now he wanted nothing more than to surrender. "I see now that I'm not the main character of this Story—or of this chapter. You are! I still don't know why I've suffered. But do I need to know as long as I know You hold the pen? My place in the Story is simply to rest in Your Always Love."

Job surrendered to what all image-bearers in this Story must learn: true wisdom is trusting the Author's Always Love, even when His Story seems confusing or causes us deep pain. Though pain and suffering have entered the plot of this Story in incomprehensible ways, dear Reader, keep reading; because the main character of this Story will enter the plot in incomprehensible ways, too. He will trust the Author unwaveringly, and by embracing suffering and submitting Himself to the Story's greatest injustice, He will make all things right once again, and everything in the Story will make sense.

Chapter 6

A Mountain & A Sacrifice
Genesis 11:27–22
Romans 4
Hebrews 11:8-12, 17-19

The mountain seemed especially steep as Abraham climbed. After all, he was more than one hundred years old now. He, his young son Isaac, and two of his servants had left home three days ago to embark on a mysterious journey with the Author. Three days had given Abraham much time to reflect on his life.

He remembered the first time he heard the Author's voice. The Author invited him to leave everything familiar in his hometown of Ur and follow Him to a foreign land. At the age of seventy-five he and his wife set out with the Author's promise driving them forward, "Abraham, I'm writing you into My Story in a special way," the Author told him. "I'm beginning My rescue plan and will turn your family into a great nation. Through your family, every family on earth can know My Always Love and enjoy the Good Life with Me!"

Then the Author led Abraham and his family far away from Ur to the foreign land of Canaan, where He excitedly told Abraham, "This is it: the land I'm giving your family! I'll make your family so big and wonderful that nations and kings will come from you, and this whole land will be theirs forever and ever!"

With simple faith in the Author's extravagant promise, Abraham responded that day to the Author's Always Love by building his first altar to Him beneath the oak tree at Shechem. At the time he didn't have any children, and it seemed an absurd promise to make to an old man and his barren wife, but faith told him he could trust the Author; so he did, resolving to follow Him in this Story He was writing.

All these decades later, Abraham still didn't own any land in Canaan, but he did have Isaac. He was learning that although the Author's Story might unfold in mysterious ways, He writes it with His faithful Always Love. Isaac was proof of that!

He turned to look at his son, remembering what his life was like without him, and how the Author promised Isaac to him. "Abraham, look up into the sky!" the Author invited. "Can you count all those stars? That's how big your family will be! For four hundred years your family will suffer outside this land; but they will be fruitful in their suffering, and I will bring them back to Canaan and give them a home. And Abraham, I will start your family by giving you and Sarah a son; for I am yours, and you are Mine!"

Now Abraham led Isaac, the miraculous beginning of that family, into an unexpected chapter in the Story. Abraham's heart wrestled as he walked. Sweat collected like beads on his forehead from the heat, yes, but also from the reality of what the Author had asked him to do. "How will my family grow to number more than the stars in the sky if Isaac dies today?" he wondered.

"Abraham," the Author had called to him a few days ago. "I gave your son Isaac to you and Sarah and now I want you to give him back to Me. Take him to Mount Moriah and sacrifice him to Me as a burnt offering."

Abraham was speechless. For over a quarter of a century, he had enjoyed the Author's friendship. Over and over the

Author had promised His Always Love to Abraham in astounding ways, and Abraham wanted to trust Him. But the Author had asked for something unimaginable: his one and only son. Now Abraham's heart was heavy, and so were his steps as he walked further and further up Mount Moriah.

But the Abraham walking up Mount Moriah wasn't the same Abraham who left Ur decades ago. He had watched the Author bring Sarah's dead womb back to life to give them a son. So if the Author had promised that Isaac would be the first of an innumerable family, then the Author could bring the dead back to life to make it happen.

"Father," Isaac called to him, breaking Abraham free from his reverie, "are we almost there?"

Abraham stopped to survey his surroundings. There it was, a little further ahead in the distance. "Yes, we are near, Isaac. Servants, stay here with the donkey. Isaac and I will go up the mountain, worship the Author together, and then return to you. We won't be long."

Abraham tied a bundle of sticks to his son's back, "We will need this for our worship. Can you carry it?"

"Yes, of course," Isaac replied, wanting to show his father his strength. "Father, we have the wood, and you have the fire to light it, but where is the offering? What will we be giving in our worship?"

Abraham looked deeply into the eyes of his only son whom he loved fiercely and simply said, "The Author will provide." With that he turned to lead his son further up the mountain, preparing his heart to worship.

They were quiet as they walked, a heaviness hovering over them both—over Abraham because he knew what lay ahead, over Isaac because he didn't. As they arrived at the place of worship, Abraham built another altar, the seventh and final altar he would build to the Author of All Life. He arranged the stones and set the wood on top. Then, with an ache in his heart and visible grief on his face, he looked at his dearly-loved son and asked, "Isaac, do you trust me?"

The young boy's eyes locked with his father's. "Yes, father, I do."

Then Abraham took his son by the hand and led him to the top of the altar.

Now Isaac understood. He was to be their offering. He laid down on the sticks he had carried up the mountain, tears pooling in the corners of his eyes, and let his father bind him to the altar with ropes. His father had told him their Story and all the Author's promises, so Isaac knew he could trust his father, just as his father trusted the one writing the Story. Isaac blinked, letting the tears fall from his eyes even as the fear rose in his heart. He watched his father raise the knife. He closed his eyes. It would all be over in a second.

"Abraham!" a voice rang out, shaking Abraham from his resolve. "Don't touch the boy! I see how deeply you trust My Always Love. You would have given Me everything you held most dear in this life, trusting the Story I'm writing."

Abraham's heart beat rapidly with shock. The Author had intervened! His shaking hands loosened the ropes around the altar, tears of relief and joy streamed down his cheeks. Then, something in the corner of his eye caught his attention. How had he not noticed it before? There, caught in a bush by its horns, was a ram struggling to get free.

"Oh Father," Isaac cried out, seeing it too, "the Author *did* provide—just as you said He would!"

Together they sacrificed the ram on the altar in Isaac's place, neither of them realizing the significance of the moment. Here, at the beginning of their family's part in the Story, the Author was showing them how deeply committed He was to giving His Always Love to Abraham's family.

Because one day—many, many chapters from now—on a similar mountain, the Author would make good on His promise to Abraham to show the world His Always Love through his family. He would lead His one and only Son up a mountain, and with His trusting Son's death would show the world the extent of His commitment to rescue the world with His Always Love. For just as Abraham's love for the Author meant he wouldn't dream of withholding his most precious possession, the Author's Always Love for Abraham's family—and the whole world—meant that He wouldn't dream of it either.

Chapter 7

A Deceiver & A Wrestling Match
Genesis 25:19-34; 27-33

"We gave him the message just as you instructed," Jacob's servants told him as they returned to his camp at the river's edge, "but now Esau is on his way to meet you with four hundred men."

A feeling of dread washed over Jacob. Fleeing an angry father-in-law who wanted to kill him brought Jacob to the edge of this river; but if he crossed it, he would have to face an angry brother who had wanted to kill him twenty years before and was now coming to meet him with a small army. His heart sank into fear as his knees sank to the ground beneath him. He cried out to the Author, "Oh Author of All Life, You were with my grandfather, Abraham, and with my father, Isaac; now be with me, just as You promised. When I left home so long ago, You said that I was Yours, and You were mine, and You promised to return me to my home safely, blessed beyond my wildest dreams, and written into Your Story in a way I never could have imagined. I am unworthy of Your Always Love, yet You lavish it on me anyway! But now I am so afraid Esau will attack us and take from me all that I hold dear—all that You have given me. Rescue us!"

Jacob sighed and stood up, blinking away the tears, looking at his large family and wealth spread out before him. He had left home with only the staff in his hand and now was returning with two wives, two concubines, eleven sons, a daughter, servants, and countless livestock. "The Author has greatly blessed me," Jacob said to himself, "but I've had to struggle for it."

"Struggle" characterized Jacob's life very well. He had struggled with his twin brother Esau even while in their mother's womb; and at birth, he grabbed Esau's heel as if trying to prevent him from being born first and receiving all the firstborn's privileges. What Jacob got at birth instead was a name that deeply shaped his life: "Jacob" or "heel-grabber"—a clever way to describe someone who deceives and takes advantage of others.

Jacob the deceiver kept "grasping at heels" all his life, taking advantage of other image-bearers in an effort to secure the Good Life for himself. Later on, knowing Esau alone would inherit his father's vast wealth, Jacob struggled with him again, wresting his birthright from him through trickery and manipulation. But Jacob wanted more. Dressed up in goat hair and Esau's cloak, he pretended to be Esau and deceived his father Isaac, stealing every last blessing Isaac meant for his firstborn son. Now, twenty years later, the Author had invited Jacob back home, but that meant facing his angry brother Esau—and his greatest fears.

"Alright, here is what we're going to do," Jacob said resolutely to his servants and his family as he explained his plan. He then proceeded to gather up an extravagant peace offering of livestock to send ahead to Esau. "Perhaps when he sees such a lavish gift, he will change his mind and not harm us," Jacob hoped against hope.

Later that night he sent the rest of his possessions across the river, his conscience striking him as he thought of how, through manipulation and trickery, he stole from his father-in-law to build up his own flocks and herds. Jacob underhandedly stole such an enormous amount of wealth from his father-in-law that he put his life in danger. He shook his head at such memories and brushed them aside, for now it was time for his family to cross the river.

His heart beat wildly from fear as he watched them cross. First went his wife, Leah, a woman he never loved but had been tricked into marrying. She crossed the river with her six sons—Reuben, Jacob's firstborn, as well as Simeon, Levi, Judah, Issachar, Zebulun, and Dinah, their daughter.

Then Rachel, his favorite wife and Leah's younger sister, crossed the river with their young son, Joseph. For so many years Rachel had struggled to get pregnant but couldn't until the Author gave her Joseph. Over and over again, Leah got pregnant and gave birth while Rachel sat back, seemingly forgotten. The jealous struggle between Rachel and Leah raged bitterly as they competed with each other for their husband's love by the number of sons they could give him. They even dragged Zilpah and Bilhah, their servants, into the struggle—giving them to Jacob to produce more sons for themselves. Now these servants, caught in the struggle, led their young sons Gad, Asher, Dan, and Naphtali to the bank on the other side of the river.

They all went across the river, leaving Jacob alone on the bank. Night had fallen around him, but it had also fallen on his heart. The future looked so bleak, so grim. Tomorrow his life could end.

He had spent his whole life trying to secure the Good Life for himself, but it had always resulted in struggle, heartache, and exile. He struggled with Esau, deceiving and tricking him, turning his brother into an enemy and having to run for his life. He struggled with his father-in-law Laban, deceiving and cheating him, turning his father-in-law into an enemy also, and again having to run for his life. Each time he ran away, the Author came to Jacob, promising life and protection, blessing and a place in His Story. But now Jacob felt caught between an enemy father-in-law behind him and an enemy brother before him, and he doubted whether the Author would show up.

"Oh, if only there were something I could do to ensure life for my family and me tomorrow! If only the Author would come to our rescue!" Jacob cried out in fear. But suddenly, something caught Jacob's attention. He swung around to see what it could be, all the hair on the back of his neck standing up.

"Who's there?" Jacob called loudly to a quickly approaching shadow. He squinted his eyes, peering into the darkness, but the Man in the shadows didn't respond. Instead, He kept coming closer.

"Well, this is one enemy I will not run from!" Jacob muttered to himself, the fear in his heart compelling him to fight rather than flee. Not even knowing if the Man intended to harm him, he ran toward the shadow, locked arms with Him, and hour after hour struggled and wrestled with more determination than he ever had before. No one, not even this Stranger, would take from Jacob the life he wanted or the story he was writing for himself.

For you see, dear Reader, as image-bearers, we love writing stories. But as *broken* image-bearers, we're suspicious of the Author's Always Love and untrusting of His pen. So we write *selfish* stories for ourselves, using other image-bearers for our advantage. What results is an intense compulsion to play tug-of-war with the Author—to believe that if we fight hard enough we can write a better story for our life.

As the wrestling match kept on through the night, suddenly Jacob realized his opponent was no stranger. He was the Author Himself—the one he'd been wrestling with all his life.

"Agh!" Jacob screamed in pain, almost losing his grip to grab hold of his throbbing hip. The Author, having come in response to Jacob's prayer to meet him in his time of need, had to disconnect his hip to connect his heart to His Always Love. Having weakened His Always Loved image-bearer, He told him, "Let go of Me! The light is dawning."

But Jacob, grimacing with pain, exhausted from a night of exerting himself, refused. "No! I will not let go until You give me what I want! Give me the Good Life!" he raged, his lungs heaving and his arms braced as he held on tight to the bitter end.

"Jacob," the Author's voice calmed the tension, and Jacob began to loosen his grip. "All your life has been a struggle with Me and other image-bearers. You can't imagine it being any other way," the Author spoke gently. "So your name no longer suits you. From now on, your name will be: 'struggle'—'Israel.'"

They stood before each other, hair disheveled, covered in dirt and sweat. Jacob glared at the Author, wondering if he could trust Him; the Author wondered if he would. Then, the Author did what He had always intended to do that night—to simply meet Jacob in his fear, remind him of His promises to Always Love Abraham's family, and to bless him.

The last wisps of darkness vanished with the morning light, and so did the Author. Jacob stood there alone, pain radiating through his hip. His name and physical body were forever changed by the struggle that night, and Reader, it seems as if his heart was too.

As a new day dawned, with it came renewed hope in Jacob's heart. "The Author let me wrestle Him…and live!"

Surprised and changed by Always Love, Jacob limped toward the river's edge to cross into his future where the Author met him, sustained him, and continued writing a beautiful Story with his life and with Abraham's growing family.

Chapter 8

A Ruler & A Rescue
Genesis 37, 39-50

"You're spies!"

The words gripped the hearts of the ten men with fear. Their lives—the very future of their family—depended on the generosity of this ruler who stood before them. Famine ravaged the nations, yet somehow Egypt had locked away enough grain to feed the world. This ruler was their only hope! But who knew he'd be so harsh?

"No! We're honest men!" the ten brothers insisted, bowing even lower as the ruler towered over them.

The ruler's eyes drew tight with a grim expression on his face. He stroked his beard as he thought to himself, "I never knew these men to be honest. They threw me into a dry well to bake in the sun while they made plans to kill me. In the end, selling me into slavery for a mere thirty pieces of silver was how they got rid of me. For almost two decades I lived as a slave, wondering how the Author could write such a Story of suffering for me, wondering what all those vivid boyhood dreams meant—dreams that never came true until now, almost three decades later."

The ruler who stood before the ten brothers questioning their honesty was their younger brother Joseph, the favorite son of their father Jacob. Decades in Egypt coupled with the Author's favor had changed Joseph dramatically from the teenage boy they threw into a well to the second-most powerful man in the world.

Joseph kept his identity a secret a little longer, unraveling a plan to see how honest his brothers had really become. After three days in custody, he sent them home—without Simeon and with a warning not to come back unless they brought their youngest brother Benjamin—Jacob and Rachel's last son.

Meanwhile, Joseph returned home heavy-hearted to his Egyptian wife and two young boys. After decades cut off from his father Jacob's love, he'd found healing in becoming a father himself. He greeted his firstborn, Manasseh, with a hug. As odd as it was to name a son "forgotten," Manasseh's life bore witness to the fact that while Joseph had felt forgotten for decades, the Author never forgot him. Instead, He breathed life into Joseph's story, and Joseph forgot his suffering.

He turned to hug his second son, Ephraim. Born to Joseph when Egypt overflowed with grain, Joseph realized that the Author had made him unbelievably fruitful in his suffering; "twice fruitful" was a fitting name for him. Famine now overwhelmed the land, but Joseph held his boys in his arms more convinced than ever that his life was part of a larger Story; and mysteriously, Joseph was playing a key role in it.

The Author had handpicked Joseph's family to give the Good Life to the whole world, but they couldn't even be good to each other. Their family was violent, immoral, and jealous. They bickered and lied and stooped so low as to become murders and human traffickers. Out of all the families in the whole world, *this* was the one the Author had picked! And in spite of their brokenness, He Always Loved them! Joseph began to see that his life in Egypt, though filled with intense suffering, was a mysterious proof of the Author's Always Love.

All those boyhood dreams of his family bowing down to him were coming true. In his youth he had flaunted the power such a position would give him, not knowing suffering would pave his path to power. Rejection by his brothers got him to Egypt where he learned to run a household and entrust his life to the Author. False accusations of wrongdoing got him thrown into an Egyptian prison where he learned to run a prison system and interpret the dreams of others. And after almost twenty years of such training, Joseph, the prison pauper, stood in the palace, making sense of dreams that were haunting Pharaoh.

"Pharaoh, the Author of All Life is offering you His Always Love," Joseph had told him. "He writes Egypt's story and the Story of the whole world, and He's giving you a glimpse of the next chapter before it unfolds. Seven years of overwhelming abundance are about to start for Egypt; but coming quickly on its heels will be seven years of severe famine. If I may be so bold, let me suggest that you appoint a ruler to store the excess food over the next seven years so there's enough to eat during the seven years of famine."

At the snap of Pharaoh's finger, Joseph's prison life was over, and he became that ruler, ready to rescue the world.

So later, when his brothers—including his younger brother, Benjamin—bowed low before him again, he pressed a little further to see how changed his brothers actually were, giving them more grain but demanding they return home without their youngest brother Benjamin.

Judah, whose idea it had been to sell Joseph as a slave all those years ago, spoke up, his voice trembling, "Sir, we cannot return without Benjamin. It would *crush* our father."

Joseph raised an eyebrow. Compassion and concern for their father? His brothers couldn't even pretend to feel those two emotions decades ago, but now those feelings drove them to their knees. Perhaps his brothers had changed after all.

Joseph could take it no longer. "Everyone leave my presence at once!" he ordered in Egyptian, and his Egyptian attendants quickly exited the room. Joseph stood before his desperate brothers, revealing the truth. He burst into tears, crying out in Hebrew, "Oh brothers, don't you see? It's *me*! I'm *Joseph*!"

His brothers looked at each other in confusion and horror. Memories of loathing Joseph for his ridiculous dreams assaulted them; yet each one of them had bowed to him after all, acknowledging his power over them. Haunting memories brought to their ears Joseph's pleas to be rescued and their roaring laughter as they ripped up his special robe from their father and dipped it in goat's blood to trick Jacob into thinking he was dead. They gasped in horror; it couldn't be!

"Come closer! Let me hug you!" Joseph said, tears flooding his eyes, love flowing from his heart as he welcomed them into his arms.

Hesitantly, they drew nearer.

Seeing dread in their faces, Joseph reassured them, "Please don't be afraid. Don't you see the beauty in the Author's Story? Everything you meant for evil has become something extravagantly good! If our family doesn't survive this famine, all the Author's promises to our family will die with us. So the Author sent me ahead of you to rescue our family and the nations! All along, it was the Author's pen ensuring our rescue even before we saw the need."

Joseph embraced his broken family, expressing the Author's mysterious Always Love, welcoming them all to Egypt so he could provide for them while the famine raged on. But more than that, Joseph pointed his family to the Rescuer whose path Joseph had so faithfully followed. Also rejected by his family, sold like a slave for thirty pieces of silver, and falsely accused, the Rescuer would descend to the lowest of lows embracing His path of suffering. But suffering would not write the Story's ending, because the Author's pen would raise Him from the pit to rule and rescue the world from the greatest famine the world had ever known.

A Reluctant Rescuer & A Powerful Pharaoh

Genesis 15:13
Exodus 1-10
Hebrews 11:23-27

"Our masters will hear his cries!" whispered Jochebed's husband. "He's simply too old for us to hide him any longer."

Jochebed hung her head in dismay, knowing that this day would come, but bitter that it was already here. She held her baby boy in her arms, surrounded by her husband, her son, and daughter and said, "I know what I have to do. I'll do it tomorrow."

Tomorrow came all too soon for Jochebed. But she was a slave and knew all too well what it was like to do something she would not have ordinarily chosen to do. She took her three-month-old baby and put him in a basket she had woven for the occasion, covering it with garments to make it look like she was headed to the river to do laundry. Then she took her daughter, Miriam, by the hand and walked out the door.

As she walked, she quietly spoke to her daughter, "Miriam, you know we are not from this land. We are the people of Israel, Hebrew people; and centuries ago, the Author promised Abraham He would give us the land of Canaan. But for more than 300 years we have lived in Egypt. I've told you of Joseph, remember? He rose to power and privilege in Egypt and rescued the world from a great famine. However, the Pharaoh on the throne today has no fear of the Joseph of 300 years ago; but he has plenty of fear of the people of Israel now."

"Why, Mommy?" asked Miriam, holding her mother's hand tightly and trying to keep up with her mother's long strides.

"The Author once promised Abraham that our people would be as numerous as the stars in the sky. And it is happening, just as the Author promised it would! But Pharaoh fears us, the Hebrew people, seeing us as a threat to his nation, thinking one day we might join with Egypt's enemies and overtake them. So the Egyptians forced our people into slavery, and since then they have treated us harshly, brutally making us work to build their cities and increase Pharaoh's power. But the more they work us, the more the Author blesses us. The more they oppress us, the more our people grow in number!"

"Is that why Pharaoh said to throw all the baby boys into the Nile River?" Miriam asked inquisitively.

"Shhh! Miriam, we're headed to the Nile River; keep your voice down," Jochebed whispered as she looked around to make sure no one had heard. Then she continued, "Pharaoh thought that if he could kill all of our baby boys, our people's Story would soon be over. But we know the Author has a purpose for your little brother, so we hid him as long as we could. And now we have no choice; we have to throw him into the Nile."

"No! What do you mean?" the frightened girl asked, suddenly stopping, unwilling to go a step further.

Jochabed urged her daughter on gently, "My daughter, keep walking. There's another story I heard as a young child. The Author told Abraham that one day, we His people, would be slaves in a foreign land for 400 years; then, the Author

Himself would rescue us and give us the land of Canaan. Miriam, my daughter, don't you see? We have been in Egypt for almost 400 years. I *know* the Author will rescue us. And *soon*."

They arrived at the bank of the great Nile River, and Miriam was more confused than ever. If the Author was going to rescue them, why did they have to throw her baby brother into the Nile? But Jochabed calmed her fears as she bent down and whispered something in her ear and then put the basket with the baby inside in the water giving it a tender push. Jochabed turned to walk away, but Miriam smiled softly, lingering in the reeds along the bank.

It wasn't long before Miriam was running toward home calling, "Mother! It worked just like you said it would! The Pharaoh's daughter came to bathe and heard baby brother crying in the basket. When she realized he was one of the Hebrew babies, I stepped out from behind the reeds and offered to find a Hebrew mother to nurse him. She named him 'Moses'! Come back to the river, mother, come talk to her!"

Before long, Jochabed was walking back home from the Nile River, her baby boy back in her arms, her daughter skipping by her side, and a huge smile on her face. She didn't know when the Author would raise up the great Rescuer of her people, but she knew that at least today she had witnessed His rescue.

Jochabed nursed and nurtured her baby boy for years, teaching him as much as she could about the Author, His Story, and His promise of a Rescuer, all while being paid by the princess to do so.

Then one day, Jochabed set out with small Moses at her side, not to launch him into a river in a basket, but to launch him into his future in an Egyptian palace. If the Author had miraculously rescued him from the Nile, surely He also had an incredible plan for Moses in the palace.

Eighty years later

"Moses, you're just making things worse!" grumbled the Israelite slaves as they turned to walk away. They were tired and overworked as it was; but now things were harsher than ever. Moses had gone to Pharaoh demanding their release, confident that the Author was about to set them free. In return, Pharaoh had doubled their workload with a mere snap of his finger.

Today had not gone as Moses thought it would. But then again, not much of his life had. Born with a death sentence over his head, his family had courageously hidden him to keep him alive. Then his rescue from the Nile River by a princess meant that he, a Hebrew boy, was brought up as Egyptian royalty. But later in life, a hasty attempt to rescue a Hebrew slave from torture by an Egyptian had left Moses scrambling to hide a murdered body in the sand. This failed attempt at rescuing his people turned Moses into an outlaw and a refugee as he fled Egypt and ran 300 miles away to Midian. After forty years as a shepherd in the desert for a Midianite priest, Moses was thoroughly humbled, disillusioned, and confident of only one thing: he could never rescue his people.

But everything about Moses' story indicated that the Author didn't agree with Moses. His timely birth and miraculous rescue, his Egyptian education, and his deep desire to rescue his people were all shaping him to play a key role in the Author's Story. Now here he was, back in Egypt—older, wiser, and with the Author's promise of rescue; yet things were not going well.

"How could you let this happen?" Moses complained to the Author. "In the desert, you came to me in the power and awe of a bush that blazed with a fire that never ended. You handpicked me to rescue Your people from Egypt because they are Yours, and You are theirs. I hesitated, wishing You would pen someone else into Your Story as the rescuer. But You showed me Your power and proved You would be with me. You said You see Your people's hardship, yet today their hardship doubled. You said You care about their suffering, yet today their suffering increased. Why did You send me here? You're only making it worse. You're not rescuing Your people at all!"

In tenderness, the Author drew near to His suffering servant, just as He had in the desert, and said, "Moses, never forget that I am yours, and you are Mine, and the same is true with all My people. This has been true for centuries and will stay true long past your lifetime. I am at work doing something bigger than you know. I will buy back each Hebrew slave. I will take each one to Myself and do more than just rescue you from Egypt and give you a good land. I will give you *Myself*. Moses, the Hebrew people are like my firstborn son. You know how important the firstborn son is—the future of the family rides on his wellbeing. Well, the future of My Story rides on the wellbeing of Israel, My firstborn. Next time you are before Pharaoh, tell him to release My firstborn son from slavery. If he refuses, he will experience My Always Wrath against sin. My Always Love will fight to the end and rescue My people in a way they will never forget!"

Back and forth, the tug of war continued as Moses demanded the release of his people, and Pharaoh hardened his heart and refused. Week after week, month after month, the Author tucked His people away in safety while He rained down His judgment on Egypt. Water turned to blood; frogs covered the land. Disgusting gnats filled the air, followed by big, black swarms of flies. Painful boils broke out over Egyptians and their livestock, tearing their skin, oozing with pus. Hail pelted their animals and crops in the fields; but still Pharaoh's heart was unrelenting. Vast clouds of locusts crept over the land, devouring anything green that remained. Thick darkness covered the land of Egypt, so tangible they could feel it.

Fueled by the enemy's hatred of the Author and a wicked determination to hijack His Story, Pharaoh willingly believed the lie that he could write a better story for the world than the Author could. His people were suffering and his country was in shambles, yet he would not surrender the pen. But this would not be how the Story ends.

Chapter 10

Passover & Rescue
Exodus 11-15:21
Hebrews 11:28-29

"I wish we didn't have to kill him, Momma. He's so cuddly and perfect in every way!" Levi whined as the children played with the year-old lamb in the courtyard. The tiny lamb chased the children making them squeal and giggle with delight. Today was the fourth day they'd enjoyed their soft, precocious pet. Their mother had warned them not to get too attached though, because the lamb would play an important but mysterious part of their rescue.

"My children, come close to me," their mother said, kneeling and drawing her children into her arms. Today is a very special day for us. Today our God, the Author of All Life, will prove Himself stronger than Pharaoh and all of the Egyptian gods. They have chosen His Always Wrath; now the Author will set us free by His Always Love! And this little lamb will protect us."

"A lamb will protect us?" her oldest child Levi, now ten years old, blurted out. His mother was not making any sense. The thought of this fluffy lamb protecting them from Pharaoh seemed absurd.

"Levi, my firstborn, the Author is writing a chapter in the Story that our people will never forget! The Author is gentle, kind, and compassionate. He has been so patient with the Egyptians, inviting them to find life in His Story of Always

Love, but Pharaoh has refused. So tonight, Pharaoh will be given no more chances, and we will be set free. That is why just now, I have been packing our bags. And, look, here comes your father, knife in hand, for it is twilight."

Their father approached them with strength and resolve. He took the lamb by the rope that had been tied around his neck and led him over to a corner of the courtyard. The children followed behind. They watched him lay the knife on the lamb's throat and then winced and covered their eyes because they just couldn't watch.

When they opened their eyes their tiny pet was not bright white any longer but stained with the red blood dripping into a bucket below him. His life was gone. When the bucket was full, the father beckoned his oldest child to follow, "Levi, come with me." Levi got up immediately and followed his father into the street. "My son, I want you to help me so that you understand the importance of this day, so your heart will know how great the Author's Always Love is for us. Take this leafy branch and dip it into this bucket of blood. Now, wipe the bloody branch on the doorposts. That's it. Good job. Brush up and down on the left side, and now come over to the right side too. Can you reach the top? Let me hold you up." He held up his boy, his firstborn son, arms shaking slightly, not because Levi was heavy but because in his heart he clung nervously to the hope that this would work.

He thought back to what Moses had told the leaders as they gathered together just days before, "In a few days, the Author will rescue us all. The Author Himself will walk through the land of Egypt at midnight, and His Always Wrath against sin will kill every firstborn son."

Each man listening thought of his own firstborn and gasped.

"But the Author has made a way to protect us from this last and terrible plague," explained Moses. "In fact, any Egyptian who wants protection may do this too! He said we must take a perfect lamb, and after four days, wipe its blood on the doorposts of our homes. That night we must stay inside and not go out. The blood will rescue us! While inside, each family must eat the roasted flesh of the lamb along with bitter herbs and bread—but just simple bread, no yeast, there will be no time to wait for it to rise. Our rescue will happen suddenly, so have your bags packed, your things ready. Begin asking your Egyptian neighbors and friends for gold, silver, and other valuables now so that you can have them packed and ready to go. We will plunder the Egyptians and be free! It will be a night to remember!"

Levi noticed how many other fathers and sons were out in the street. Up and down the tiny lane where he had grown up and played, kicked his ball and skinned his knees, families were brushing on the blood of their lambs, covering the doorposts with it, and going back inside.

Levi and his father went inside, too, silent and solemn. His mother was already beginning to roast the lamb and prepare the other dishes for dinner. The evening routine was different—everything was different. They ate their simple meal and went to sleep.

At midnight Levi suddenly sat up in bed, his heart racing. What was that awful sound that had awakened him? There it was again. Over and over, shrill screams and loud wailing broke out in the distance. Levi broke out in a cold sweat. His father, also awakened by the sounds, drew him close, putting his arm around him. Levi was alive. This must mean it worked! They were safe behind the blood that protected them from the Author's Always Wrath against sin.

Within minutes they heard a sound of fists beating on a door somewhere down the street. "Moses, come out!" called muffled voices. Pharaoh's officials had come for Moses.

Moses went with the officials, entering Pharaoh's presence to see him kneeling before a little body on a table before him. Haughty Pharaoh now looked broken and weak. Slowly Pharaoh stood up and turned around to face Moses, tears streaming down his face, fighting hard to keep from sobbing. "Cattle we can replace; crops we can replant. But my *son*? I have lost him forever! Go, Moses! Take your people and get out of my country! Go follow your Author and the Story He's writing for you and get out of here! There's not an Egyptian home that hasn't been touched by death tonight! Just go!" Pharaoh fell to his knees before Moses.

It was indeed a night to remember! The Author's Always Love hid His people behind the blood of an innocent sacrifice, and then His Always Wrath went to war with the evil that held His people captive and set them free.

Out they came, a victorious parade led by Moses into freedom, laden with silver and gold, followed by great herds and livestock, and filled with so much joy! Jacob's family had entered Egypt with fewer than one hundred members; now they were leaving more than one million strong. The Author had kept His promise!

They left Egypt headed for Canaan with the Author's presence shading them during the day like a thick cloud and guarding them at night like a blazing fire.

But soon, dust began rising behind them. Panic struck the people! They recognized the sound of Egyptian horses and chariot wheels, the sound of slave drivers and whips. "Moses, what are we going to do?" they cried in fearful desperation. They were trapped between the Egyptians and the Red Sea. "You should have just left us alone in Egypt! Our lives have only gotten worse since you came along!"

Moses encouraged them, "My people, be still! This is part of the Author's Story! Watch the Story unfold; He is not through rescuing us!"

Moses turned and faced the Red Sea. Staff in hand, he raised his arms, and a breeze began to blow until the Red Sea split in two, forming walls on each side and drying the seabed below.

Then Moses led the Israelites through the Red Sea. Sandaled feet and animals' hooves walked through the sea in a stunning turn of events that only the Author could have thought to write into the Story!

The approaching Egyptians, pursuing their fleeing slave force, rushed madly into the sea after them. But this miracle was not for them. What rescued the people of Israel destroyed the Egyptian charioteers as the walls of water crashed down on them.

As the Israelites walked away from an unforgettable rescue, smiling and laughing, Moses' sister Miriam grabbed a tambourine and gathered the women to sing and dance in praise of the Author's victorious rescue. As they danced and sang, Miriam thought back to when the Author rescued her baby brother from water by His Always Love. Now, eighty years later, by that same Always Love, she watched the Author rescue through water not just her brother, but *all of her people,* for they were His, and He was theirs.

Chapter 11

A Mountain & A Binding Promise
Exodus 19-31

Step after step, Moses climbed Mount Sinai. The Author said He'd lead His people to Canaan, the land promised to Abraham long ago; yet here in the desert, they were farther from the Promised Land than when they were in Egypt! But Moses didn't doubt the Author's leading. He had a sense that rather than leading them to a *place*, He was leading them to a *Person*—to the Person waiting for Moses on this mountaintop.

"Moses!" called the Author at the top of the mountain, like a friend greeting another friend—so warm and welcoming, yet thunderous and strong. "Of all the nations on earth, I handpicked Israel, scooping them up tenderly into My arms as a mother does with her tiny baby, rescuing you from slavery and drawing you close to My heart. Now we are alone together in this quiet desert to make a Binding Promise so you'll always know I am yours, and you are Mine. You are My *treasure*!"

Moses couldn't understand why the Author would choose Israel from all the nations on earth. Since they'd left Egypt, they hadn't done much more than grumble and complain, preferring slavery in Egypt to freedom with the Author. Yet in spite of their fearful complaining, the Author kept offering friendship to His people and giving miraculous provision of bread in the desert.

"Moses," continued the Author, "I want to show My people My heart, inviting them into a Binding Promise so they can experience the Good Life, Always Loving Me and each other, and creating a place where the world will see what friendship with Me looks like. There are Ten Words to our Binding Promise," said the Author as He took stone tablets and began writing the Ten Words upon them.

"The first four Words will teach My people how to Always Love Me," the Author began.

The First Word: I, the Author of All Life, am the only God, your Rescuer. Treasure Me.

The Second Word: Treasure Me as the only God and find the Good Life in Me. Don't be tempted to try to contain and control My vastness in an idol—a mere carving of stone. That would cut you off from My Always Love, leading only to death. Live only for Me and forsake anything else you'd turn to for life.

The Third Word: Treasure My name and reputation. If you misrepresent Me, how will the world around you know Me? You are My image-bearers, so live in ways that attractively reflect My Always Love to those around you.

The Fourth Word: Treasure rest. Work hard, giving your all for six days and then on the seventh day, the Sabbath, rest in Me. The Good Life can't be found by striving but by resting in the work I do for you.

"Now," continued the Author, "as you Always Love Me, it will overflow in Always Loving other image-bearers. Here's how," the Author continued.

The Fifth Word: Treasure your parents. They gave you life and gave their all to raise you, so don't take their sacrifice lightly.

The Sixth Word: Treasure life, for I am the Author of All Life, both giving it and taking it away. Be life-giving in the way you treat each other, never murdering another image-bearer.

The Seventh Word: Treasure marriage. Honor your binding promise to your spouse, just as I will honor this Binding Promise we're making today.

The Eighth Word: Treasure My promise to provide. Don't steal from other image-bearers, violating them and proving your heart doesn't trust Me to provide.

The Ninth Word: Treasure truth. Don't try to play Author by telling false stories about other image-bearers. I am Truth and use My Words to edify. Follow My example.

The Tenth Word: Treasure the Story I'm writing with your life—even when it looks different than the stories I write for others. Rather than wishing you had what someone else has, trust My heart to write a good story for you.

The Author handed the stone tablets containing the Ten Words back to Moses, saying, "If you mirror My image like this, the whole world will know I am yours, and you are Mine! This Binding Promise will lead you to the Good Life, so treasure it! For apart from Me, life doesn't exist."

Moses was in awe of the Author's Binding Promise. What other god tenderly drew its people out into a desert to gently shape them to know His heart and find life in Him alone?

But the Author wasn't finished. "I don't just want you to know My heart; I want to live among you to show the nations My Always Love and the beautiful Story I'm writing for the whole world! So take the gold, silver, and precious treasures you carried away from Egypt and make a beautiful

Tent to house My presence among you. Teach your brother Aaron and his sons to be priests in My Tent, representing Me to My people and representing My people to Me.

"And Moses, tell the people—and never forget!—that I am yours, and you are Mine. I will come into your world and live among you in a Tent your eyes can see so that we can be together like I've always wanted."

Filled with joy, Moses took the stone tablets and the plans for the Tent of His presence and descended the mountain to share them with His people. For the first time since the Garden of Eden, the Author would live among His people. This Binding Promise and this Tent—this moveable Garden of Eden—would make it possible for the Author to dwell among image-bearers once again!

Chapter 12

A Golden Calf & Grace
Exodus 32-40

"Moses, you're back! What took you so long?" stammered Aaron, his face growing red with shame as his younger brother approached unexpectedly.

"Aaron, what is going on?" Moses demanded, fists clenched, jaw tightened, angry pressure building up inside. "Look at the people making fools of themselves, dancing around and praising this golden calf saying it rescued them from Egypt! They mock the Author who rescued them!"

"Don't be angry, Moses," Aaron soothed and explained, "You were on the mountain for *forty days*. We thought you'd never come back! When you're here, you keep us connected to the Author, but when you left, we needed a way to remember Him. So I told everyone to bring me their gold jewelry, and then you'll never believe what happened! I threw the gold into the fire, and out popped this golden calf!"

Aaron forced a nervous laugh until Moses, still holding the stone tablets, threw them to the ground, shattering the Binding Promise that the people had already broken in their hearts. Then he ground the golden idol to dust.

As the Author was on the mountaintop making a Binding Promise with His people, they were down below already breaking it. As the Author drew up plans for them to use their plundered gold to create a beautiful place for them to live together, they were using it to craft an idol. In mere moments the gross, idolatrous partying turned into a full-on war as brother took up sword against brother, fighting and killing each other. The whole community was in shambles!

The people humbled themselves, brought low by their idolatry and shame, while Moses climbed the high mountain once again. Fresh stone tablets in hand, Moses was hopeful the Author would remember His Always Love and renew their broken Binding Promise, even though His people did not deserve it.

"They're so stubborn!" Moses cried out as he climbed, as if rehearsing a speech he would give to the Author. "They're slow to trust Him and even slower to obey. His Always Wrath against sin should destroy them. They're undeserving of what He has done for them and of the ways He is writing them into His Story. He woos them with His Always Love, yet they reject Him."

But if Moses understood anything of the Author's Always Love, he knew this mess of brokenness could turn into a tender encounter with the Author. He would forgive them, draw them nearer, and heal them with His Always Love. With that hope Moses climbed higher, moving toward the Author in the wake of their rebellion.

"It's true," Moses conceded when he reached the mountaintop, entering the Author's presence. "Your people are stubborn, love what is evil, and deserve Your Always Wrath against sin. But I beg You, remember Your Always Love. We are *nothing* without it. Trade my life for theirs! Let Me take Your Always Wrath against sin that they might get Your Always Love." Moses threw himself on the ground at the Author's feet and begged for the life of his people.

"Moses," the Author stooped down to reveal His heart to His friend. "My people sin extravagantly, but My Always Love is more extravagant still. Moses, do you know what I'm like? I am Always Love. I can never be any other way! With tender compassion, I lavish grace when it isn't deserved. With generous patience, I wait even when My Always Wrath against sin has every right to be angry and judge. I always hate sin, and one day My Always Wrath against it will do away with it for good; but even now, I've made a way to forgive."

Moses bowed even lower, in awe of the Author's heart. How could His Always Love be this good, this generous? The Author saw the way His people rejected Him, mocking Him and His rescue from Egypt. Yet here He was, moving toward His people once again, reminding Moses of His Always Love!

The Author took the new tablets from Moses' hands. "Let Me write on these again," He said. "My people have broken My Binding Promise already; but you know, Moses, they will break it again before this Story is over. However, I am committed to them and promise to see this Story through to the end. My faithfulness never depends on theirs."

Then with grace and determination, the Author once again penned the terms of the Binding Promise on the new tablets, committing Himself anew and afresh to a people He knew were incapable of mirroring the faithfulness He was showing them.

Moses' arrival in the camp below with the renewed Binding Promise in hand brought a fresh wind of hope into the community. The same hands that had brought gold to Aaron to make the golden calf now brought gold, cloth, tools, and talent to Moses to make the articles for the Tent of His presence. Generosity was their response to the grace the Author was showing them.

Day after day they worked. The same hands that had worshiped the golden calf now cut, nailed, sewed, and molded beautiful items for the Tent, each image-bearer both broken and beautiful. All the while they wondered what the finished product would look like and what it would mean for the Author to live among them…until one day, the Tent was finished.

Moses walked around inspecting everything they'd made. It was all there! The embroidered curtains of blue, purple, and scarlet linen, each hung by tiny gold clasps making the four outer walls of the Tent. The bronze altar stood ready for sacrifices, and the bronze wash basin stood filled with water to wash the priests who would enter the Author's presence.

Moses walked toward the Holy Place, a smaller Tent within the larger Tent. It, too, was made of colorful curtains. On the right side of the Holy Place was a golden table with bread to be kept on it at all times, reminding His people that their very life came from the Author alone. To the left was a large lampstand like a beautiful, golden tree of life with branches and buds and blossoms. Its light shone the way to the Author's presence.

In front of Moses hung a thick curtain, separating the Holy Place from the Most Holy Place. Before this thick curtain was a golden altar for burning incense, making the Tent not only look but also smell beautiful. Behind the curtain, inside the Most Holy Place, was an ornate box, the Chest of the Binding Promise, containing the stone tablets and serving as the throne of the Author-King among them.

Aaron and his sons tried on their new priestly garments, looking radiant as they stood before Moses. Clothed in glory and beauty, just like the Author, their vests matched the Tent's curtains as if they were small Tents themselves. Fastened onto the shoulder pieces of Aaron's priestly vest were two dark, black stones etched with the names of Jacob's twelve sons. Twelve precious stones, one for each of Israel's tribes, decorated the front of the vest. With the black stones on his shoulders and the precious stones over his heart, Aaron would carry the Author's people into His presence. Everything was exactly as the Author described it on the mountain. Everything looked, smelled, and shone beautifully just as it should.

"Friends, you did it!" Moses praised. "We have taken what the Author has given us and made something beautiful together—a place where He will meet with us!"

Just then, like a King entering His palace, the cloud of the Author's presence descended and settled over the Tent, filling it completely! So thick, so tangible, it was hard to see anything but His presence. Finally, the Author would always live among them, meeting with them in this Tent where heaven and earth overlapped.

Moses longed to enter the Tent, but the Author's thick cloud blocked him out. Like Adam and Eve kept from the Garden, it seemed that there still was no way to enter and be with Him.

"Oh, what good is this Tent if we're still unable to enter and be with You?" cried Moses in disappointment.

But the Author wasn't finished. He would show them the way into His presence.

Chapter 13

A Priest & A Tent
Leviticus

Aaron stood in front of the Tent, somber and pensive, deeply aware of the importance of this day. The Author's people were fasting from food; no one was working—no one except Aaron, the High Priest. The Author had shown His people how they could enter the Tent to meet with Him: through the blood of an innocent sacrifice. And Aaron's role was vital. The descendants of Jacob's son Levi had been chosen to care for the Tent and some, like Aaron, were appointed as priests. So for Aaron, this was perhaps the most important day of the year. Through his work today, the Author would cleanse and forgive the Israelites' sins.

For the past week, Aaron had been in solitude, rigorously preparing himself for this day, keeping himself from anything that could contaminate him and make him unclean. Even if he were to become unclean accidentally, it would disqualify him from carrying out the essential sacrifices of the day. Last night, he spent the whole night in prayer, preparing his heart for the day ahead of him. Earlier today Aaron had bathed, put on his clean priestly garments of beautiful embroidery, costly jewels, and the stones engraved with the names of the twelve tribes of Israel. Today, he would carry those names, representing these millions of people standing before him, into the very presence of the Author. The people stood before him, watching, waiting. Aaron was their representative, so they watched closely to be sure their representative dealt fully and completely with their sin.

Reader, do you remember back to the Garden where sin first entered the Story? Sin distorted and twisted Adam and Eve, seeping into their identity as image-bearers. Sin wasn't just something they *did*. Deeper than that, it was a deadly disease coursing through their veins and shaping all their actions and interactions. It permeated their families and communities, making it impossible for them to mirror the Author's image in the whole and beautiful way He intended at the beginning. Sin drove them from the Garden that had housed the Author's presence. Sin meant Moses couldn't enter the Tent that now housed Author's presence among them. But now the Author had made a way to enter His presence and taught Aaron how to do it.

For the whole year that Israel had been camped at the foot of Mount Sinai, Aaron had presided over the countless daily offerings and sacrifices given to the Author. Each of these offerings and sacrifices and the time spent in the Author's presence taught the Israelites how to be the Author's people, how to keep the Binding Promise and live in His Always Love, how to give that same love to others while displaying it to the nations around them. Through it all, He was training their eyes to see sin not just as wrong behavior but as a wrong heart, to realize they were not just dirtied by wrongdoing but deeply stained within. Despite their best efforts, they could not live rightly nor remove their stain. But the Author could. He would cleanse them so they could dwell with Him.

Aaron now stood at the entrance to the Tent, watching, heavy-hearted, as men led a bull and two goats toward him. He hoped he would remember all the specific ways to perform the sacrifices of this sacred day, the Day of Atonement. The bull was given to Aaron first. Before entering the Author's presence to cleanse the people of their sin, this bull's blood must cleanse Aaron of his own sin. He took the bull to the altar and with his own hands spilled its blood. Because the innocent died for the guilty, Aaron could enter the Author's presence.

But Aaron wasn't just learning about sin. He was learning about the supreme holiness of the Author, holiness like fire that is both good and dangerous. It can restore life to the shivering, but can also burn impurities from even the most unyielding metal or consume the person who comes too close.

"Be holy just like Me!" the Author had invited them. But it was evident they were powerless to become holy on their own. Dirty and stained by sin, their very being offended holiness. Aaron thought of his sons, Nadab and Abihu. The Author had killed them instantly after they waltzed fearlessly in His presence, treating His holiness as if it were common and meaningless. For an instant, fear gripped Aaron's heart as he realized that in a moment, he would be entering the Author's presence. What would happen to him?

Having sacrificed the bull on the altar, Aaron took the bull's blood in his right hand and sweet-smelling incense in his left and walked toward the heart of the Tent. There, before the innermost curtain of the Most Holy Place, he hesitated a moment, looking down at the blood he held. He was about to step into the presence of the Author of All Life, and it would only be this blood in his hands that would keep him alive.

Only the right person, with the right sacrifice, on the right day, could pass through the thick curtain and into the very heart of the Author's presence and live. Aaron took a deep breath, clung tightly to the blood, and walked through the curtain. He sighed, relieved to be alive. He stepped toward the Chest of the Binding Promise and sprinkled the bull's blood on it seven times. His own sin now cleansed, he turned to cleanse the people of their sin.

Back at the front altar, he took one of the two goats. This goat's blood would also spill out, this time to wash away the sins of the people. By now the whole place had gotten very bloody. Streams of red blood trickled across the slippery, stinky floor. Dealing with sin was a messy business. By the end of the day there would be blood everywhere…but that was fitting, was it not? For sin and its effects were everywhere also.

He retraced the steps he had followed, taking the goat's blood into the Most Holy Place. With hands full of faith, he sprinkled it on the Chest of the Binding Promise, believing deeply that it would wash his people just as the Author said it would.

Aaron left the Holy Place and walked back to the second goat. He sighed a heavy sigh as he placed both of his blood-stained hands on the goat's head. The goat bleated and ducked, trying to get away. Aaron steadied the goat, gently placing his hands on it once again, then stood there, minute after long minute, naming sin after sin after horrible sin that they as a community had committed, placing each one onto the goat as if the goat were the guilty one. He spoke things many people preferred to have forgotten. A year's worth of shame, fear, and anger welled up in the hearts of those gathered to watch, as tears welled up in their eyes. Could the Author's people—His image-bearers—be *that* evil?

When at last Aaron had finished, the goat, dirtied by both the blood on Aaron's hands and the peoples' sins he now carried, was led away from the Tent, away from the people, exiled into the wilderness, and left there.

Minutes turned into hours, as Aaron stood at the entrance to the Tent. "Is that him returning?" he asked another priest standing nearby. Aaron squinted his eyes to see better. Yes, it was the man who had led the goat away into the wilderness returning from the outskirts of the camp. Aaron sighed with relief. Fighting sin would be a constant battle, and this same day next year, all of this would be repeated. But at least for now, things were made right.

Aaron turned to walk back into the Tent, peeling off his high priestly garments, stained blood-red, and laid them aside. He washed off the dried blood that clung to his skin, and as he did, gratitude, like the sun, began to dawn in his heart. He hated that the innocent had to give its life for the guilty, but he was so very thankful that the Author had made a way to be right with Him. Everything they were experiencing at the foot of this mountain taught them that the Author would *never* be content with sin or its effects. Sin is filthy, and always causes decay and disease and death—in image-bearers, in their relationships, and in creation itself. But the Author would not let sin write the Story. One day His Always Wrath against sin would put it to death for good, and His Always Love would restore all things until decay, disease, and death were nothing more than a distant memory.

Somehow Aaron knew that one day better blood would have to be shed to make that happen. If year after year they must repeat the events of today, then animal blood wasn't powerful enough to free them from sin for good. These sacrifices could only cleanse them until they got dirty again. Their heart-stains were deep. What could wash away such deep, deep stains?

For now, Aaron couldn't think of better blood; so today he and the people of Israel rested in the Author's provision, grateful He wrote into the Story a temporary way for them to be cleansed, to enter His presence, and learn holiness. Aaron had arrived at the Tent today with a heavy heart, but as he left, he was full of joy!

Surely now, after learning to live together with the Author in the wilderness, the Israelites were ready to live with Him in the Promised Land where they'd become a nation ready to show other nations the Author's Always Love.

Chapter 14

Rebellion & Wandering
Numbers 13-14; 21:4-9
Deuteronomy 1

"We've never seen anything like it!" the twelve scouts exclaimed as they returned from surveying the Promised Land. "Tremendously rich and fertile, it flows with milk and honey. Look at these grapes we brought back! Have you ever seen bigger, juicier grapes? It took *two* men to carry back one cluster!"

The Israelites cheered in response to the excellent report the scouts brought back, in awe of the Author's generosity to give them such an incredible land.

But ten of the scouts weren't finished with their report. With fear in their eyes and in their words, they continued, "But there's no way we can take this land. What were we thinking? The land is incredible, but so are the people in it! They outnumber us, and they're *huge*—literal giants! We don't stand a chance!"

A buzz spread throughout the crowd. The size of the grapes now seemed irrelevant after hearing the size of the people. The buzz grew to a rumble as fear squeezed people's hearts. For a whole year, the Israelites had camped at the foot of Mount Sinai, learning to trust the Author. But now, camped at the edge of the Promised Land that the Author wanted to give them as their inheritance and their home, their hearts were wavering, backpedaling, doubting.

As the murmuring grew louder, two scouts, Caleb and Joshua, stood up to silence the people. "Friends, listen!" Caleb implored. "For forty days we saw with our own eyes the inheritance promised to us—promised to our father Abraham centuries ago! Yes, the people are strong and mighty, but so were the Egyptians! Have we forgotten how that chapter of the Story ended? Would the Author write such a powerful rescue Story for us yet be unable to give us this land? Remember, we are His, and He is ours! Let's trust Him!"

But the other scouts shook their heads, "No, we can't do it! We're like grasshoppers compared to them. They'll squash us like bugs!"

The crowd shuddered as fear slithered and snaked its way through the community. The people began to weep, "Why do we even follow this Author? He just brought us here to die! We should go back to Egypt before letting those giants kill our children!"

Moses, Aaron, Caleb, and Joshua tore their robes mirroring the brokenness of their hearts. They tried to calm the people, "Brothers and sisters! We're the Author's *treasure*! He's writing a good Story and offering us the Good Life in His Promised Land. His Always Love will fight for us. Don't be afraid!"

But feeling threatened, the Israelites picked up stones to silence Moses, Aaron, Caleb and Joshua, resolving to pack their bags to return to Egypt!

But suddenly the Author's presence appeared in the Tent, and their hands dropped all stones, their mouths shut in reverence.

"Moses," began the Author, "I've chosen My people, lavished My Always Love on them, but in spite of My tenderness, this slave-generation's knees knock with fear preferring My enemy's voice instead of Mine. Because they reject My Always Love, they cannot enter the Promised Land. Tomorrow, I'll lead My rebellious people back out into the wilderness to wander one year for every day the scouts were in the Promised Land. The giants won't kill the children; fear will kill the parents. Every last one of them will die in the wilderness, and then their children will take the land with great faith."

As night fell, the camp was still, everyone distraught from the news. But when morning dawned, there was movement in the camp. People rallied together excitedly, grabbing their weapons, readying themselves to go to war.

"Brothers, what are you doing?" Moses cried. "Why are you taking weapons? We should be packing for the wilderness!"

"Moses, we thought about it all night," the men replied. "We were wrong to forsake the Author's Always Love. We've decided to take the Promised Land after all. We are going up against our enemies today. Anyone who wants to fight may join us!"

The fighting men, who yesterday were withering from fear, now boldly cheered and waved their weapons in the air.

"Why do you persist in disobeying?" Moses reprimanded them. "Yesterday you wondered how you'd take the Promised Land, thinking the Author wouldn't be with you. He will not be with you today! How will you take the land without Him?"

But they shrugged off his warning and went to battle, for their hard hearts craved the Good Life and couldn't believe they'd find it while learning to trust the Author in the wilderness. They wanted the Promised Land.

Alone without the Author, their enemies proved too strong for them. Those who survived fled back to Moses like whipped dogs running with their tails between their legs, because Reader, this chapter of the Story was never about *land;* it was always about *hearts.* Before the Promised Land could become their home, the promise of His Always Love needed to find a home in their hearts.

So year after year they wandered in the wilderness, the fearful generation dying to make room for faith. At every turn, they struggled in the hostile wilderness with little food, sometimes no water, and enemies attacking from all sides. In every hardship, the Author invited His people to trust His Always Love; and in every hardship, the Author's enemy whispered fear into their hearts.

"The Author's Story is so painful for you," the enemy crooned, slithering through the camp spreading his lies from one heart to another, "but it shouldn't be this way. He promised you the Good Life, yet He's holding out on you. He seems to enjoy watching you struggle and go without while you wander in circles."

"Help! Moses, heal my little girl!" a mother suddenly screamed, running with her child in her arms. Before Moses could do anything, he heard another cry and turned to see a father running toward him, "Moses, save my son! He's dying!" Then another, "Moses, come quickly to my tent, a poisonous snake bit my father. He's on the verge of death! Do something!"

Cries rose up among the people as venomous snakes slithered throughout the camp. Through physical snakes, the Author opened His people's eyes to see what His enemy was doing in their hearts. The snake in the Garden was now the snake in their camp spreading fear and lies to destroy them. In desperation, they cried out for a Rescuer.

"Moses, pray for us! Beg the Author to rescue us from the snakes!" they cried out.

Moses went before the Author, calling on His Always Love, and the Author responded, "Moses, today I've shown My people that listening to the snake's voice instead of Mine will always lead to death. But I Always Love My people; I am theirs, and they are Mine. Here is My rescue plan: fashion a bronze snake and put it on a pole, lifted high for all to see. Anyone doomed to death by the snake's poison may come to the pole, look at it, and live."

One by one image-bearers came, each bitten and hurting, poison burning inside of them, zapping them of life, ushering them closer to death with each gasping breath they took. But as they looked with eyes of faith at the snake lifted high, the Author healed them.

Sweet winds of hope blew through the camp, reminding His people that the sin poisoning His image-bearers wouldn't write the ending to this Story. The Author would *never* rest until He had utterly defeated His enemy and reversed sin's effects, no matter the cost.

The enemy was still on the loose and many years of wilderness wandering would follow. But the same hope would keep blowing through the Story until one day, the long-awaited Rescuer would come. He, too, would be lifted high on a pole so that all image-bearers could look to Him for healing from the enemy's poisonous lies—and all who looked on Him would live.

Chapter 15

A Story & A Song
Deuteronomy

"Dear friends," Moses began, "my chapter in this Story is ending, but for you, the new generation, it is just beginning!" His eyes glistened, and his heart felt squeezed by the emotion of these parting words. The people reminded him of the sheep he'd tended in Midian a lifetime ago—needing so much, often so fearful and stubborn, yet so very precious to his heart. The oldest Israelites among them had been mere teenagers when they left Egypt and entered into their Binding Promise with the Author in the wilderness. Now they would enter the Promised Land without him, and he wanted to give them one final word.

"For forty years I walked with you and your parents before you. I've written our Story on scrolls for you to read generation after generation." Moses held up these scrolls for all to see. "Remember the Ten Words? Remember how the Author taught us to Always Love Him and our fellow image-bearers? Remember how the Author washes us, making us clean enough for His presence? This is our Binding Promise with the Author! We can never forget these words. They are the key to the Good Life!"

Moses handed the scrolls to Joshua, his assistant, and turned back to the Israelites with love in his heart and tears in his eyes. "My friends, in the Promised Land there are two mountains: Gerizim and Ebal. I want to tell you their story so you'll remember to choose the Author's Always Love.

Once there were two slave women in Egypt, Gerizim and Ebal. The Author saw them and Always Loved them, so He set them free. In a barren wasteland, He spoke tenderly to them, taking responsibility for their every need and inviting them into a Binding Promise of Always Love with Him. Their only requirement in the Binding Promise was to Always Love Him in return and look for the Good Life in Him alone.

"Fully convinced she could only find the Good Life in the Author's Always Love, Gerizim treasured the Binding Promise; and when she married and had children, she taught her family to do the same. Generation after generation, they Always Loved the Author and other image-bearers and never deprived another image-bearer of peace or justice. Before long Gerizim's family became a nation firmly established in the Author's Always Love, living abundantly in the Promised Land. In this nation the poor found hope, widows found protection, foreigners found a family, and the weak among them were their treasured possessions. Because Gerizim's family sought the Good Life only in the Author, their minds and souls were whole. They walked with heads held high. Deep peace permeated their bodies, giving them health and zest for life. Even creation itself flourished in Gerizim's faithfulness—animals were at peace with image-bearers, rain fell in its season, and plants grew up from seed, lifting high their fruit-filled branches as a joyful offering to their Creator and their cultivators. Their faithfulness gave them life!

"Meanwhile, Ebal grew suspicious of the Author's Always Love, thinking the Binding Promise only kept her from the Good Life. She found its terms too rigorous, its limitations wearisome. For a while, she pretended to keep the Binding Promise, but Ebal's heart wandered, convinced the Good Life was just beyond her reach. Eventually she left the Author's Always Love and set out to make the Good Life happen for herself. As Ebal began a family of her own, her heart was happy at first, for she believed they could help her get the Good Life. But her children grew up to live like their mother, each frantically striving to grab the Good Life for themselves. Ebal found herself competing with her own family—for resources, for power, for love. Filled with suspicion, they wore smiles on their faces while plotting against each other in their hearts. Ebal grabbed for power, forcing other image-bearers to give her the life she craved, filling her land with tyranny and violence. Ebal's family breathed in desperation and breathed out a poison that seeped into all their relationships and into creation around them. The more they demanded life from their land, crops, and animals, the more they choked out life. Famine ravaged the land. Ebal's descendants rose up to fight each other for power, filled with terror. They limped along and wasted away, ravaged by disease, minds fogged by confusion, souls consumed with fear. Before long the land they hoped would make their dreams come true became a walled city that trapped them. Besieged by enemies, depleted of resources, the only food left to eat was the fruit of their disobedience. They began devouring each other simply to survive. The only mercy left on the horizon for Ebal's family came as their enemies took them into exile, stripping the people of their power and ridding the land of their tyranny.

"Yet even in Ebal's exile, a breeze of hope began to blow, breathing life into broken image-bearers and pointing them to their Rescuer. Ebal's children cried to the Author to make something beautiful of their mess, and He rode on wings of hope to lift from the ashes His broken image-bearers, torn and tattered, battered and barely breathing. Breathing on them anew, He reminded them that they are His, and He is theirs, cracking their stone hearts to reveal beautiful new hearts, soft and supple, kept beating by Always Love.

"My friends," Moses implored, "choose today which example you will follow. Will you find your life in Always Love like Gerizim? Or reject Always Love like Ebal? There is no other option. I desperately wish I could live on to remind you to be faithful, but one day the Author will send the Rescuer to teach you the Binding Promise better than I ever could. Until then, sing this song of our Story over and over, so you'll remember the Author's Always Love and Always Love Him in return."

I am your Creator, making day and making night,
I have Always Loved you with all of My might.

I am your Maker. In Egypt, I shaped your family,
In everything I have done, I've drawn you close to Me.

I am Yours, and You are Mine!

I am your Rescuer. I walked you through the sea,
So nothing more would harm you, and you'd always stay close to Me.

I am your good Father. If ever you should doubt it, then
Just listen to My voice saying you are My children.

I am Yours, and You are Mine!

I am your Provider. My heart for you is good,
I led you in the wilderness giving you clothes and food.

I am your Deliverer. I protect you from all fear.
The enemy comes against you but cannot harm you for I am near.

I am Yours, and You are Mine!

I am your Sustainer. It is I who give you life,
The idols of this world will only ever give you strife.

I am the light of the world. My heart longs to set nations free.
Shine My light in darkness that all nations may find their way to Me!

I am Yours, and You are Mine!

So trust Me deeply, children. I'll Always Love you all your days,
Stay close to Me forever, and you'll never forget My ways.

I am Yours, and You are Mine!

Then Moses, who had climbed up and down mountains so many times in his 120 years of life, climbed up a mountain...but didn't come down again. The people spent the final month of their forty years in the wilderness mourning the death of their leader, their rescuer, their messenger. Many more chapters would pass before Israel would have a Leader, Rescuer, or Messenger greater than Moses.

A Canaanite Woman & Israelite Spies
Joshua 2

"Hurry! Go up to the roof! I'll hide you there!" Rahab urged her two guests. Men were banging loudly on her door, demanding she open it; so the three of them ran up to the roof. Rahab hid her guests under the stalks of flax she was drying then hurried down to answer the door.

"Where are they?" the men growled as they questioned Rahab. They were large men, towering over her, weapons in hand trying to intimidate her. "We know those Israelite spies are in here! They were last seen entering your house, so tell us where they are so we can take them to the king!"

"Oh, you just missed them!" Rahab said, feigning disappointment. "Yes, they came here asking all sorts of questions and trying to get information out of me and the others in the house. But they left, wanting to leave Jericho before the city gates shut for the night. I bet you could catch them if you go right away!" Rahab urged convincingly.

The men turned in a hurry, leaving without a thank you, racing down the road to pursue the spies who were hiding on her roof. Rahab stood in the doorway watching until they disappeared in the distance.

Men. They kept coming to her for something. She hated it. But what could she do? She was a woman in a city full of idols. The gods her people worshiped used girls for things that were degrading, dehumanizing, deadly. Baby girls were thrown into fire as offerings to their gods. Little girls were sold into a life of slavery to pay off their parents' debts. Young girls were hired by priests to work in the temple providing immoral services to men—services supposedly necessary for their gods. It was a mess, and she felt caught in the darkness and brokenness that permeated her people.

Earlier that day two men had come to her house, but these men were different. Not just different in the way they talked or dressed, though that was different too; these men handled themselves differently. She knew they were the future of her land. The questions they asked her indicated these men weren't here to take advantage of her. Instead, they could be her ticket out of this darkness. They could rescue her!

When she knew the coast was clear, she turned and slipped back into her house again and walked to the foot of the stairs that led to her roof. She hesitated a moment. She had hidden enemies, lied, and had risked her life for these men. Why? What was it about these men that made her treat them with kindness? Why had her heart stirred so deeply when they were talking earlier in the day? Deep within her heart, she knew why: it was their God, the one they called the Author. From the very first mention of His name, hearing His Story of Always Love for His people, her heart stirred deep within. How good life could be with the Author as her God!

Darkness was falling, so she knew they were safe. She climbed the stairs and slowly uncovered the men. They sat talking in the shadows on the roof. "Men of Israel, I know why you are here. We all know. Your reputation precedes you; the Author's reputation precedes you. We heard how He rescued you from the powerful Egyptians forty years ago, how He led you through the Red Sea and swallowed up your enemies! Everyone is terrified that you and your God will come and do the same to us. How will we stand against the Author and the people of His Always Love?

"Our walls deserve to fall!" Rahab continued. "We are desperately wicked. I feel the weight of that wickedness every day! Long ago we walked away from the Author and since then have only written stories of death for ourselves. But your God is the one true God! He is the Author of your Story, and I want Him to write mine too! He rescued you; I beg you, let Him rescue me too! I have heard His name, I have heard of His fame, and I want to belong to Him. I know it's just a matter of time before you overtake my land and my people. But if the Author's Love is Always, maybe He will love my family and me too? I have shown you kindness today. Will you show me kindness by rescuing us when you come to take Jericho?"

The spies smiled. From a young age they had learned they would be a blessing to the nations, and now this woman sitting before them was begging to be blessed. "Yes, Rahab," they replied, "because you have shown us kindness today, when we destroy your city, you will be rescued. Only do this one thing." One of the spies turned toward a pile of red rope in the corner of the roof, grabbed it, placed it in her hands, and said, "When we come to take the land, make sure this red rope is hung from the window, and make sure your whole family is in your house. If they leave the house, we are not responsible for their deaths. But if they stay with you, in the house with the red cord, they will be rescued."

"I will do as you say. Thank you," said Rahab, her heart filled with a sense of peace and anticipation she'd never known before. "The gates are shut now because it is dark, but I doubt they will open again for fear of you. But if we use this red rope, you can escape through the window downstairs."

The men thanked Rahab and climbed down. She stood at the window watching them walk into the darkness, the red cord still in her hands. When she could see them no longer, she tied the red cord to the window. She'd made her decision. It would now be just a matter of time before her life would be made new, and her rescue would be complete.

Though it was now completely dark outside, still a tiny light shone. In the darkness of a land heaving with the wickedness of its inhabitants, ready to vomit them out because it could take their wickedness no longer, a tiny light flickered in Rahab's heart and refused to go out.

The men of Israel had come and gone, taking nothing from her but the kindness she chose to give freely. As a result, daring faith sprang forth within her—faith greater than any of her people had—faith greater than the generation of Israelites who died in the wilderness because they doubted the Author would give them the land—faith so great it would declare, "If the Author can do it for them, He can do it for me!" And as the days unfolded, she let that faith grow in her heart as the red rope hung from her window, a constant reminder that her rescue was imminent.

Chapter 17

A City of Walls & A Family that Falls
Joshua 3-24

"Here they come!" the watchmen on Jericho's walls shouted as Joshua's army approached. "Every man to his station!" Jericho's fighting men positioned themselves for battle. They'd known this day would come. They had heard how the Author miraculously parted the flooded Jordan River to bring His people into this land—just like He'd done for their parents at the Red Sea. Hour after hour, their priests had stood in the river holding the Chest of the Binding Promise while millions of Hebrews walked across the river on dry land, into their inheritance. How would Jericho stand against a God like that?

"There are so many of them!" cried Jericho's watchmen, their hearts wilted from fear. Desperately they begged their gods for rescue, hoping their high, thick walls and bolted city gates would keep them safe.

Forty-thousand strong, the Israelite army drew near, priests carrying the Chest of the Binding Promise to remind them the Author was leading their army. But as they approached the city, they simply turned and, following the wall, marched around the city.

"They're heading back to camp!" a watchman shouted in amazement as the Israelites marched away from Jericho. No attacking, no shouting, no invitation to surrender. Simply the march, march, march of soldiers' feet as they circled the strong and strategic city of Jericho. "They're too afraid to fight!" laughed the watchmen, relieving their nerves by taunting the Israelite army as it faded into the distance.

The next morning, the Israelite army did the same thing. And the third day, and the fourth day, and with each passing day, the people of Jericho went from mocking to nervous confusion to silent dread as the ominous marching continued day after day.

Joshua rose early on the seventh day to gather his army. "A week ago, a Soldier approached me," he began, "Not knowing who He was, I called out, 'Are you for our enemies or for us?' He told me I asked the wrong question because this isn't a battle of Israelites versus Canaanites. He told me, 'I, the Commander of the Author's armies, am for Myself. My Always Wrath is against sin, but I offer My Always Love to all people. Over 400 years ago, I could've given Abraham this land. Canaan's wickedness was already great, but My Always Wrath against sin was patient for centuries, giving Canaanites the opportunity to turn to My Always Love. I waited until their wickedness grew to the point of no return. Their idolatry blinds them. They'd rather die than return to Me. Now the land heaves with urges to vomit them out and be free of their wickedness.' Then He gave me His battle plan for Jericho, and today is the day we see both the severity of His Always Wrath against sin and the power of His Always Love! Remember, save Rahab and her family, but destroy the rest of the city. Take nothing for yourselves!"

Joshua raised his arms in the air, shouting to celebrate their imminent victory. The priests took up trumpets and the Chest of the Binding Promise, each soldier grabbed his weapon, and together they marched one last time for Jericho.

"Oh, not again," the watchmen's hearts sank as they heard marching in the distance.

But today, after one lap, the Israelite army didn't turn back to camp but began a second lap around the city. The watchmen were less sure of themselves than ever. The city stirred, its inhabitants unnerved by the constant marching. Three laps, then four, the marching went on for hours. Five laps then six, for hours they marched. How long would this go on? What was the point of all this marching?

As they began their seventh lap, a thunderous roar rang out as each Israelite shouted and blew his trumpet! The watchmen on the walls covered their ears, crying out in pain. The deafening sound shook the people of Jericho's hearts with fear. But it wasn't just hearts that shook. A fierce rattle and deep groan came up from under the walls, shaking their very hope of protection. Watchmen lost their balance as the walls shuddered and then crumbled beneath them, burying their hopes with them.

Dust and rubble danced around them as Joshua yelled, "Jericho belongs to the Author!" and Israelite soldiers rushed to take the city.

But all was not lost in the rubble. Up rose a woman, a red cord laying at her feet. She reached out to take hold of her family members in the same way she'd grabbed hold of the faith offered by the spies. They stood there shaking the dust from their robes, coughing dust from their lungs. Jericho's destruction was judgment for their neighbors, yet rescue for their family. They squeezed each other's hands, tears welling up in their eyes as the two spies approached to escort Rahab and her family to safety, welcoming them into life in the Israelite community.

The soldiers brought piles of gold, silver, bronze, and iron, laying them at Joshua's feet, who gave it all to the Author and then burned Jericho to the ground, liberating the land of its wickedness.

Victory fueling them on, Joshua was eager to continue conquering the Promised Land. The Author was giving them this land, just as He promised! They set their sights on the strategic town of Ai, so small a mere 3,000 soldiers could conquer it, and marched into the distance to do just that.

But the Israelite soldiers, thrown into confusion and chased by their enemy, ran back in fear. Uncertainty set over them like a cloud, their confidence in the Author shaken.

"Author of All Life," cried Joshua in desperation, "why didn't you give us the city as you gave us Jericho? You said You'd be with me, just as You were with Moses. You told me to Always Love You and watch You give this land to us! I've obeyed! What went wrong?"

Then a voice rolled in low and commanding, "Disobedience has covered My people with filth, Joshua. How can I honor them with victory? Ready yourselves, for tomorrow all disobedience will be made known."

All the joy of victory crumbled to rubble around the Israelites. They'd committed themselves to faithfulness; who had disobeyed?

Standing among them in the rubble was a family. This family stood up, shook the dust from their robes, and held hands to keep the dark secret they'd hidden in their tent. Learning nothing from the Author's Always Wrath against Jericho's wickedness, Achan couldn't resist the temptation to snatch up a bit of the plunder after the walls fell. From beneath the rubble of Jericho, a lie slithered into his heart telling him he could have the Good Life if he just took a bit for himself. Secretly, he slipped gold and silver into his pockets, tucked a beautiful robe under his own, and slid away to his tent where he hid his plunder. Achan disobeyed, choosing death.

Early the next morning, Joshua gathered the people calling each tribe and family before the presence of the Author, asking, "Have these been disobedient?"

Achan's family clung to their secret with the twisted hope that just maybe they wouldn't be found out...but they were.

"What is it you've done?" Joshua demanded as he stood before Achan, the man whose folly had cost them precious lives at Ai and shook their precious faith as a community.

Achan took a deep breath and confessed.

Soldiers ran off to Achan's tent to find out if it was true, then returned to lay a box and its contents before Joshua, whose heart was broken. Believing the lie that the Good Life could be found by disobedience once again brought death into the Story.

Down under the stony rubble went Achan's family, their plunder buried with them. Disobedience had tricked them to death. The stone pile covering their bodies stood as a reminder of Achan's disobedience just as Jericho's crumbled walls were a reminder of Israel's obedience.

A fresh day dawned, and once again Israel's army prepared themselves for battle. They would go against Ai once more; but if they were honest, they had to admit that their faith wavered. Could they trust the Author as they went against Ai a second time? Could they trust each other? With fear and trembling, they attacked Ai, and this time took the city! The Author turned their recent defeat into total victory. Jericho and Ai taught the Israelites that obedience to the Author was the key to the Good Life.

After five years of conquering the land, Joshua gave each of the tribes of Israel their inheritance in the Promised Land.

Every mountain, valley, and river, every forest, sea, and plain was theirs to call home, to fill with the Author's Always Love as a light to the nations around them.

After many years had passed, Joshua's life and leadership were coming to an end; so he gathered Israel's leaders together in Shechem under a tree between two mountains.

"We've lived our chapter of the Story well!" Joshua affirmed. "Now, Mount Gerizim to the right calls us to be faithful, while Mount Ebal to the left warns us that disobedience always leads to death. And this oak tree we stand beneath reminds us of the promises the Author made to Abraham in this same place. The Author always fulfills His promises. The faithfulness in question will only ever be our own."

Then they stood together at the altar, in the same place where Abraham had stood five centuries before, and renewed their commitment to the Author's Binding Promise.

Though Joshua's life ended soon after, his influence rippled on through the years, pointing his people to a greater Joshua who would come into the Story. This Joshua would lead His people courageously into a better Promised Land, bringing about the fulfillment of even better promises, showing His people a greater faithfulness than Israel had ever known.

Chapter 18

A Leader & A Housewife
Judges 2:6-3:6; 4-5

"Army of King Jabin!" Commander Sisera yelled, standing before his 900 chariots and charioteers. "Barak is headed to Mount Tabor daring to rebel against us. So today, we will destroy him!"

The men rattled their spears on their iron chariots, yelling their war cries, as their war-trained horses snorted and stomped.

"Bring the sacrifices!" yelled Sisera, and the priests of their god, Baal, came forward. Sisera prayed, "Oh god, Baal, you are the one who gives us power. You, the storm-god, hold lightning in your hand and use it to show your power. You send rain to give life when the earth needs it, but today, we need victory! You've given us clear skies, a good omen! We give this sacrifice to you to ensure our victory today and to keep these worthless Israelites under our feet!"

A deafening cry rose up as the sacrifice was made. The men were ready for victory and raced to the river valley, eager to show their might.

Barak and the 10,000 Israelite men with him were waiting on Mount Tabor when they heard the sound of horses' hooves and saw dust clouds roll in. The dry season gave the advantage of this battle to the chariots in the dry, flat river valley below; but Barak took heart. Deborah, their leader and judge, stood confidently by his side. She wouldn't have led him here unless she were sure the Author would give them victory.

Joshua's faithful generation had passed away long ago, leaving in its wake a young nation with many enemies still in the land. Some tribes faithfully drove out their enemies; others didn't even try, befriending their evil neighbors instead. Comfortable with enemies living among them, their hearts moved closer to the false gods their enemies worshiped and farther from the Author. But the Author's Always Love was relentless. Over and over, He stirred up enemies to oppress His people, drawing their hearts back to Himself. Then over and over, He raised up a judge, like Deborah, to rescue them and call them back to His Always Love.

For twenty years King Jabin of Hazor, Israel's enemy, had held them tightly in his grip, letting Sisera intimidate them with his powerful army. But on this oppressively hot and dusty day, with not a cloud in the sky, somehow the Author would rescue His people.

"Go, Barak!" urged Deborah. "For the Author is on His way to the battlefield!"

So Barak raised his sword to give the signal, and his army cascaded down the mountain into the river valley below.

Unexpectedly, dark, ominous clouds, heavy with rain, rolled into the valley with the Israelite army. In an instant, clouds gushed forth their contents. The river swelled, unable to contain so much water at once, creating a flash flood. What once was a wide, dry plain, giving the chariots the advantage in battle, now served as a muddy trap for hooves and wheels. Charioteers abandoned their chariots, fleeing on foot, outnumbered by the 10,000 Israelite soldiers chasing them. The Author was fighting for Israel!

"Storm-god, Baal! You betray us!" Sisera shook his fist in the air, fleeing for his life.

Now it just so happened that the Kenites, descendants of Moses' brother-in-law, had formed an alliance with Sisera. When they caught wind of Barak's plan to attack, they leaked the plan to Sisera to give him the advantage. So when Sisera's god had failed him, he ran straight toward his allies' tents, wide-eyed, heart pounding, seeking the refuge they were obligated to give.

Jael, a beautiful young Kenite who knew of the battle and of her family's alliance, called out as he approached, "Come, my lord! Find what you're looking for in my tent. Don't be afraid; remember, we are your allies."

Sisera frantically entered the tent, drawn in by her warm welcome. "They're chasing me! Don't let them get me! If they come for me, tell them you haven't seen me!"

Jael led him into the tent's dark interior and pulled back the covers of a pallet on the floor. "My lord, you are tired. Why don't you lie down?" she soothed.

Sisera nestled himself in the comfort of the soft blankets, lowering his guard in the safety of his allies. "Bring me a drink of water before I sleep. I'm thirsty!" he commanded Jael.

Jael slowly turned to fulfill his request, her heart conceiving a plan. She had within her tent one of the most evil men alive. She had heard gruesome stories of what he'd done to women he'd conquered. She had seen first-hand his oppression of her people. And she had sat silently while her husband made a friendly alliance with this monster. She would stay silent, but she would do something about the evil. It would stop today in her tent.

She reached for a flask, not of water, but of milk, knowing it would calm Sisera and make him sleepy. She handed it to him, and he drank from it in draughts, then laid down to rest.

When she was sure he was asleep, Jael carried out her plan. She reached for a tent peg and a hammer, two tools she frequently wielded to establish her house, and with them she crushed the head of the enemy who threatened to tear down the home her people were trying to make in this land. With great courage she broke her family's alliance with the enemy and rescued the people of Israel.

Soon after, Barak came by, hunting Sisera from the battlefield. Jael heard him passing and slipped outside, calling, "Come, my lord! Come find what you're looking for in my tent." She led Barak inside, and he found his enemy was no more.

Great was the victory that day when Deborah and Jael rescued their people. Deborah, an influential leader, did her part to inspire Barak to battle. Jael, an average but courageous woman, became an unlikely heroine in the Story, taking the life of her violent enemy. Through their leadership, these women rescued their people from twenty years of oppression, showing them what was to come. Though their people had forgotten, the Author would never forget: one day He would send another unlikely Rescuer into battle against the enemy. He'd break the evil alliance His people had made with him…and crush his head for good!

Chapter 19

A Strong Man & the Philistines
Judges 13-16

"Go on, Samson! Perform for us!" the crowd jeered as Samson walked bound and blind to the center of the Philistine temple. Those gathered on the roof above and on the main floor below were enjoying their intoxicating drinks as well their victory over Samson, and now they were ready to see a show.

How could things have gotten so bad that the one the Author had intended to rescue His people was instead bound and blinded by the enemy and brought in for their entertainment?

For centuries now, the people of Israel had spiraled downward. Rather than turning the Promised Land into a place where heaven met earth and the nations saw Always Love on display, the people of Israel had progressively become more immoral, more violent, and more like their Canaanite neighbors around them. They had forsaken the Author's Always Love so much that if they even remembered to worship the Author at all, it looked an awful lot like the disgusting ways their enemies worshiped their gods. It was a mess.

Years before, the Author had given the Israelites over to the Philistines because of Israel's unfaithfulness. Usually when He did that, His people cried out for rescue. But this time they had become so complacent with oppression they didn't even bother crying out to the Author.

Although no one cried for rescue, the Author, Always Loving His people, prepared a rescuer anyway, appearing to Samson's barren mother. "I am going to give you a son. He will become a judge for My people and begin rescuing them from the Philistines," he told the woman. "From the womb, I'll call your son, and his whole life should reflect this calling. He is never to touch anything unclean, never to drink wine, and never to cut his hair."

But though he had only three simple instructions to follow, Samson's heart despised the Author's calling, and he lived as he pleased. Samson embodied everything that was wrong with Israel during the Story's chapter of Israel's judges.

Rather than rescuing Israel from the Philistines, Samson became friends with them. One day he returned home from Philistia to announce, "Father, mother, I have found the Philistine woman who is the girl of my dreams! Now, go make the arrangements for my marriage."

His parents rolled their eyes. "Oh son, why can't you marry an Israelite girl rather than a daughter of our enemies?"

"There's no harm in it at all," Samson asserted. "She's beautiful, and I love her. What else matters?"

Soon Israel's should-be-rescuer was off to the Philistines' land to arrange a wedding rather than to start a war. Along the way, a young lion came bounding powerfully out of the forest and onto the path toward Samson. But the Author's Spirit came even more powerfully onto Samson, filling him with supernatural strength to rip the lion to shreds. What an incredible gift—super-human strength to save lives in the face of danger! Surely this was how the Author would use Samson to rescue His people!

Days later, on his way to marry his Philistine bride, Samson walked down the same road where he had killed the lion. Smiling as he remembered his incredible strength, he went to find the lion carcass, chest swelling with pride as he walked.

"Ah, what is this?" he exclaimed. "The lion I killed is now home to honeybees!" Samson stooped over to dip his fingers into the decaying body of the lion. Disregarding the Author's instructions not to touch anything unclean, he scooped up a handful of honey and ate it.

Samson's wedding with the enemy took place, and wine flowed freely. Samson disregarded the instruction of the Author to drink no wine and in his foolishness he made enemies of his thirty Philistine groomsmen, getting his bride and her family killed by their own people.

Samson enjoyed flirting with both foreign women and disaster, stirring up trouble wherever he went. The Philistines were determined to destroy him and watched for an opportunity to do so. So when Samson struck up yet another relationship with a Philistine girl, the Philistine rulers devised a plan.

"Oh, Samson," said Delilah, his most recent Philistine crush. "You're such a strong man! Tell me, what is the secret of your strength?" Delilah batted her eyes and smiled to make him think he was the only man for her. Samson didn't know that the rulers of the Philistines had come secretly to Delilah, offering her great wealth in exchange for the secret of his strength.

Faking the need to stretch, Samson flexed his muscles, yawning to downplay how much this conversation boosted his pride. "Oh Delilah, it's nothing really. If you just tie me with seven fresh bowstrings, I'll be just like any other man."

Giggling inside, Delilah took the first opportunity to send word to the Philistine leaders to come that night with fresh bowstrings. As Samson slept, they wrapped him up, and Delilah called out in fake desperation, "Samson! Oh, Samson! Evil men have broken in to get you!" But with a mere flex of his muscles, the bowstrings popped off, and his strength remained a secret.

Over and over, Delilah begged Samson to reveal the secret of his strength. Over and over, Samson fabricated ridiculous stories of how his strength could be overcome. Over and over, the Philistines came to take him, but over and over Samson fooled them, showing off his strength instead. Flirting with disaster, he came closer and closer to the edge, seeing how far he could get without falling off, until one day his arrogance and self-sufficiency caught up to him.

"Oh, Samson, you say you love me, but you don't! You yank me around with your lies, refusing to tell me the truth about your strength!" Delilah burst into tears, using all her feminine powers to drive him to the edge, until finally, he tumbled over it.

"Fine!" Samson sighed. "You're making my life miserable with all your whining! Before I was born, the Author, the God of Israel, called Me to Himself, and I was supposed to follow three instructions. I have fully kept only one, so therein must lie my strength: I've never cut my hair. If my hair were to be cut, I would completely lose my strength."

Something within Delilah knew he was telling the truth. So that night as darkness fell, Delilah got him comfy and cozy, his head in her lap. She stroked his long, dark braids, lulling him to sleep. He slept deeply until Delilah screamed to wake him, "Samson! The Philistines have come for you again! Save yourself!"

Samson jumped to his feet but immediately felt something missing. His hair! It was gone! But even more unsettling, the Author's Spirit was now gone from Samson too.

In an instant Israel's judge, endowed with supernatural strength to rescue his people, was brought very low. Arrogant, self-sufficient Samson was now powerless; the angry Philistines easily overpowered him and gouged out his eyes. Bald, blind, and bound, he was dragged away and subjected to a life of slavery, looking very much like the Israelite nation he had been called to rescue.

Like Samson, Israel had been set apart from the beginning to live in the Author's Always Love and display His love to the nations. But they both despised His Always Love— Samson trading it for the love of foreign women, Israel trading it for foreign gods. They both wavered in their commitment to the Author, arrogantly picking and choosing when—or if—to obey. Until finally, both Samson and Israel found themselves blind and captive because of their disobedience.

"Go on, Samson, perform for us!" the intoxicated Philistine crowd cheered in the temple of their god. They led Samson into the middle of the temple to put on a show. Disgusted by their laughter and humiliated by their jeering, he turned to the man by his side and mumbled, "Can you guide my hands to the pillars so I can lean on them?"

Samson felt the solid pillars beneath his palms. Sighing deeply, he prayed his only prayer recorded in this Story, "Author of All Life, if you even remember me…my hair has grown back, but in my blindness I see that my hair never gave me my strength. You did. Now, I beg You, give me Your strength one last time to take revenge on these filthy Philistines for making me blind!"

With the crowd distracted in revelry, Samson braced himself between the two central pillars of the temple, and with all his might he pushed and yelled, "Let me die with the Philistines!"

The temple collapsed with a thunderous roar, swallowing up more Philistines in Samson's death than he ever killed in his life and hastening the chapter of Israel's judges toward its end.

The judges had gone from good to bad to pure evil. The Author's people had created new idols and almost wiped out the tribe of Benjamin in civil war. Enemies attacked from all sides, famine ravaged the land, and no leader was able to rescue and unite them as Moses and Joshua had. Could anything break this vicious cycle and lead Israel to faithfulness again?

A Jealous King & A Shepherd-Warrior
1 Samuel 15–2 Samuel 1

"Oh Israelites, you send a small boy to fight me? You underestimate me, shaking a stick at me like I'm a dog!" mocked the Philistine giant, roaring with laughter.

"Laugh while you can, you monster!" the young man challenged. "For I will silence that ugly mouth of yours when I cut off your head! How dare you threaten to enslave the Author's people and insult His Always Love? Now you'll know His Always Wrath against evil!"

Cowering in fear behind the brave young man was a king with an army full of Israelite soldiers. Israel believed a king could rescue them in ways the judges never could. A king could unite them and lead them into battle against enemies like Goliath, rescuing them from the vicious cycle of unfaithfulness they'd been in for centuries. But instead, they ended up with tall, handsome, and smooth-talking King Saul, who tolerated the daily taunts of his enemy, hid behind his crown, and bribed others to fight in his place. All hope was lost until a courageous youth from Bethlehem arrived on the scene.

"King Saul," the young man began confidently, "I'll put an end to this Philistine terror."

"You! You're just a teenage boy," replied Saul, entertained but hardly impressed.

"No, my king," the boy contradicted, "I am a shepherd who knows how to protect my sheep. I've killed every beast that ever attacked my flock, and that's all this worthless Philistine is—a beast!"

Surprisingly, Saul let him fight the giant. This unexpected rescuer prepared himself for battle in unconventional ways, shedding royal armor for a sling and smooth stones, and taking his place on the battlefield between the enemy and the family of Abraham.

"I'll finish you off with one sweep of my sword!" Goliath roared. Then the evil giant, sword in hand, began to advance.

But the boy was not afraid. He was swift and sleek moving toward the giant. Sling in one hand, he fit a stone into it with the other, swung it twice, and released. Before the giant even knew what hit him, he fell, the stone firmly implanted between his eyes. But the boy wasn't finished! He ran straight to the enemy, drew the giant's sword, and cut Goliath's head from his body.

Saul, watching the battle from afar, stood up quickly from shock. "Abner!" he yelled to his army commander, "Find out who that young man is!"

Moments later Abner returned with the young man following behind him.

"Who are you, boy?" King Saul asked.

Still grasping the giant's head by its hair, he answered, "I'm David, the youngest son of Jesse of Bethlehem."

Saul drafted David into his army, and quickly the young man earned the admiration of all Israel. David's heart was good, his courage unfailing, his trust in the Author's Always Love was steadfast. Women sang songs of his greatness; generals promoted him with good reason.

So successful was young David that before long a lie slithered into King Saul's heart, planting a seed of jealousy. "He'll be the one to tear my kingdom away from me!" Saul feared, for he'd been so unfaithful to the Author during his reign that the only promise left was that the Author would indeed tear his kingdom from him.

David, who had the heart of a king, loved Israel by destroying any enemy who defied the Author's Always Love. Saul, who had the position of king, hated David, turning him into an enemy, seeking to destroy him, jealous of the Author's Always Love for him. Mad with suspicion, he threw spears at David when he played the harp to soothe him. He sent him on impossible missions with the odds stacked against him so his enemies would take his life. He spread the word among his family and servants to kill David any chance they had, and when none dared, he screamed, "Then bring him to me, and I'll kill him!"

King Saul quit running the kingdom to put David on the run. And soon David found himself hiding in caves, forests, and deserts—even chased out of Israel—to flee this paranoid king.

Yet David was not alone. One by one, men disillusioned by Saul's kingdom, discontent with life as they knew it, came to David until he was leading an army of valiant men. But even with an army David was powerless when one day Saul and his army of thousands trapped David and his men in a cave. Outside, Saul and his men jeered, "David says he trusts the Author; well, let's see the Author save him now!"

Deep in the cave, the damp darkness reflected David's soul. "Author of All Life!" his heart cried, his mind racing, wondering what to do. "Why have you forsaken me? We're stuck! Day and night I cry to You, yet things have only gotten worse! Is this really how it's going to end?"

David let his mind wander back to the lush green fields of Bethlehem, his boyhood home. His father's servant had come to call him home because Samuel, Israel's last great judge had arrived and wanted to see him. Curiosity accompanied the young boy home, and before the night was over, things became more curious still as his head dripped with Samuel's oil, and he heard the promise that he'd one day be Israel's king. Yet the path to the throne had been a strange one, full of learning that the road of suffering is the path to honor.

"David, this is it!" his men whispered, awakening David from his reverie. "The Author is writing the Story to your advantage!"

David heard footsteps in the distance. Saul had entered the cave—alone! He must not have known David and his men were inside!

David's men urged him, "Here's your chance, David! Today the Author's promise to give you the throne will come true by giving you the chance to kill Saul!"

Silently David crept toward the mouth of the cave while drawing his knife. Saul was alone and vulnerable, relieving himself in a corner. David inched closer to his king, so close he could hear Saul's breathing. David hesitated and then carefully grasped the hem of Saul's robe, cut off a small piece, and retreated into the darkness. But his heart was torn by remorse. He hadn't taken Saul's life, but he *had* taken something. He ran to the mouth of the cave to confess. "My king!" David yelled, bowing before his king. "Why do you treat me like an enemy? Today the Author of your story and mine gave you into my hands! I could have taken your life but I didn't!" He held up a piece of Saul's robe for all to see.

Horrified, Saul searched among the folds of his robe, the weight of what could have happened sinking into the pit of his stomach.

"King Saul, you reward my faithfulness to you by trying to kill me! I leave it in the Author's hands to write the ending to our chapter in His Story. The Author will avenge the wrong you've done to me, Saul, but I will not. The pen is in His hand." David tossed the piece of Saul's robe to the ground and stood there, noble and strong compared to his dumbstruck pursuer.

"David, you've shown me goodness, and I've rewarded you with evil. I know you will be king in my place." Saul burst into bitter tears. But whether his tears were a sign of remorse or a sign he'd come to terms with his kingdom nearing its end, we don't know. For the tears he shed that day did not change him. He kept pursuing David to the bitter end.

With each passing day, like sand in an hourglass, the kingdom slipped from Saul's hands, until eventually, while on another wild hunt for David, Saul got word that the Philistines had attacked Israel. He'd become so distracted hunting his personal enemy that he'd left his people vulnerable to the real enemy. Saul changed course, leading his army to meet the Philistines in battle on Mount Gilboa. But arriving late to the battle, he was too late for victory; and the final grains of sand slipped through the hourglass. Saul breathed his last, unable to rescue his own life or the life of his people, unable to keep his kingdom in his hands. Everything Israel had longed for in a king proved only to bring heartache to the nation, and in the wake of Saul's death, his people were swallowed up by the Philistines, crying out for a rescue King Saul could never give them.

Saul had shown his people how dangerous it is for a king to dismiss the Author's Always Love. Through David, the Author would give them glimpses of the Rescuer, until one day, another unexpected Rescuer would come from Bethlehem to gather a band of image-bearers discontent with life as they knew it, desirous of a new kingdom. He'd show them what it looks like to wait patiently for the Author to give Him the Kingdom, and to walk the downward path of suffering to the very battlefield where He'd go toe-to-toe with the world's greatest giant. He'd slay that giant, rescue His people, and then take His place on the throne

.

Chapter 21

A King's Loyalty & Disloyalty
2 Samuel 2-24
1 Chronicles 11-22
Psalm 51

King David strolled along the roof of his palace in Jerusalem. It was a cool and peaceful night, light slipping away, trading places with darkness, and all his kingdom was at peace. He reflected on the Good Life the Author was giving him, "From shepherding sheep, the Author called me to shepherd Israel. Without a fight, He put an end to Saul and gave me his kingdom. Now my kingdom is united and growing strong. We've driven out the remaining enemies from our land and taken the Jebusite capital, Jerusalem, to be our own. My power increases because the Author of All Life Always Loves us!"

But suddenly David realized, "My family is flourishing and has a home. But what of the Author? I'm strolling along the roof of my impressive cedar palace, my family nestled inside while the Author of All Life lives in a *Tent*. This isn't right!"

He called for the Author's messenger to come at once. When he arrived, David shared his heart, "Nathan, I—a simple shepherd—dwell in this large and comfortable home, while the Author of All Life, lives in a mere Tent!"

"My good king," Nathan replied, "do what your heart desires. The Author is with you!" The two men embraced, grateful for the ways the Author loved His people through their leadership. Then they parted, David to fulfill his dream of building a permanent house for the Author, and Nathan to his home, where he unexpectedly had a dream as well.

"Nathan," began the Author in his dream, "the whole world is Mine, yet I've chosen to dwell among Israel. Since Israel left Egypt until now, I've gone here and there, living among them in a Tent, and I've never demanded a house of stone. My people don't live to give Me the Good Life. I live to give it to them. So tell David that instead of building Me a permanent house, I'm going to build a permanent house for him. Though David's chapter in this Story will end, I will always leave a lamp burning in his house. I will raise up his Son to sit on the throne and make His kingdom great! David's Son will build a house for Me, and His Kingdom will last forever."

The following morning Nathan went straight to King David sparing no detail. "Don't you see, David, the Rescuer will come from *your* family!"

David's heart welled up with praise! He went straight to the Author, knees bowed, joyful tears streaming down his face, letting all the words pour out of his heart as an offering, "Author of All Life, who am I, that You lavish me with Always Love? No one else is like You! You picked a small, broken family and have chosen to explode that family into millions like the stars! And like the stars, we shine Your Story to the world around us! Now You're promising to bring the Rescuer to the world through my family! By Your Always Love, You will do it, for we are Yours, and You are ours—*forever!*"

Having poured out all his praise, King David stood up, wiped the tears from his face, and went forward full of faith, doing whatever he could to serve this promised Son, setting him up well to build the Author's house.

But another night came when David was strolling along the roof of his palace. Once again it was a cool and peaceful night, light slipping away, trading places with the darkness; but David's heart was not at peace. It was restless and idle, and he couldn't sleep.

Feeling lazy, David had sent his general to lead his army to war while he stayed home. As he walked, something caught his eye—or rather, someone. On a nearby rooftop was a beautiful young woman, minding her own business, completely unaware the king was watching her.

The king called to a servant, "Who is that woman? Find out!"

The servant ran off, unsure why it would matter to the king. Obediently, he returned and reported, "King David, the woman is Bathsheba, the wife of Uriah who is away fighting in your army."

"Yes, yes," David waved his hand shooing away the servant's words as if they were flies buzzing in his ear. "Bring her to me."

The servant cocked his head, unsure if he had heard correctly, but left to obey his king. He returned momentarily leading Bathsheba, for what choice did she have but to come? She had no power. David had it all, and he planned to use it to his advantage.

Dear Reader, what David proceeded to do with Bathsheba reflected not the Author's heart of Always Love, but his own twisted heart; and he hurt Bathsheba and Uriah deeply. In a grave misuse of his power, he used his pen to write a story for himself that he was convinced would give him the Good Life; yet it proved to have awful consequences for himself and others.

When the night had passed, Bathsheba returned home, and David returned to his idle living, comfortable in the palace, while his men were faithful at war. That sleepless night had all but faded from David's mind until the day a servant arrived with a word for the king.

The servant bowed, "King David, Bathsheba—Uriah's wife—wishes you to know that she is pregnant."

Outwardly, David stayed calm, but inwardly, he was scrambling for a plan. He had vilely mistreated another man's wife, and if he didn't act quickly he would be found out. Like Adam in the Garden grabbing leaves to cover his sin, he called to a servant, "Bring Uriah back from battle!"

Uriah arrived in armor and smelling of the battlefield, while David played it cool. "Uriah, my friend," David said, "I thought you might enjoy a visit with your family. You've been away so long! Wash up and spend a night at your house!" Heartily David patted him on the back, sent him off with a charismatic smile and reassured himself everything would be alright.

But the next morning, King David learned that Uriah hadn't gone home; he had slept on the palace stairs all night. David had to work a bit harder now to keep his cool. "Well, a minor kink in my plan, but I can fix this," David muttered under his breath. He sent for Uriah once more.

"Uriah, I heard you slept on the uncomfortable palace stairs! Why didn't you go home to enjoy the comfort of your bed, to greet your wife and see how she's doing?" David plastered on a smile to hide the irritation he felt inside.

"My king," bowed Uriah, "The Chest of the Binding Promise dwells in a mere tent. Israel's army sleeps in tents on a battlefield. How could I go home to enjoy my wife and sleep with a roof over my head? No, sir—on my honor I could do no such thing!"

But Uriah's honor was no match for David's desperation. Soon Uriah was riding back to war, unknowingly carrying his death sentence in hand, authored by King David himself.

Uriah was conveniently killed in battle, and David breathed a sigh of relief. No one knew of his sin.

Except for the Author.

With overwhelming grief, Nathan, the Author's messenger, stood before David, "My king, the Author took you from shepherding sheep to shepherding image-bearers! He rejected Saul, putting you on the throne, and lavishing you with Always Love. If you needed more, you had only to ask! Instead, you stole from another image-bearer and killed him in battle to cover it up! Now because of your unfaithfulness to the Binding Promise, your whole family will suffer."

David's heart welled up with remorse. He went straight to the Author, knees bowed, sorrowful tears streaming down his face, letting all the words pour from his heart:

Only Your Always Love can wash away my sin.
Wash me, O God!
To cleanse me deep within.

My grievous sin is laid out in plain sight.
I've offended you, O God!
A twisted, sinful nature is obviously my plight.

Even from my mother's womb, my heart was bent and broken,
Only You can heal me, O God!
Through Your forgiveness, my heart You will awaken.
No animal sacrifice can cover up my wrong.

A repentant heart I give You, O God!
My eyes look to You,
I've nothing else to do,
Than believe Your Always Love for me is strong.

Having poured out his repentance, King David stood up, wiped the tears from his face, and went forward full of faith in the Author's forgiveness.

Though forgiven he was, the consequences of David's failure sent shockwaves throughout his kingdom. His family unraveled as Bathsheba's baby suddenly became ill and died. Incest, murder, and conspiracy all beat down on David's house. One of his sons usurped him as king and drove David out of his palace in Jerusalem for a season. Then a worthless rebel revolted and for a moment it looked as if the kingdom would split in two. Later the Author sent a horrible plague, and seventy thousand Israelites died in three days. The sheep paid a high price for their shepherd's sins.

For all the ways King David's heart was like the Author's, his heart was still tragically twisted. As his chapter in the Story ends, we can celebrate what the Author did through him but we're still left clinging—along with David—to the hope of a coming King who will only give *life* to His sheep, never death, who will sit on a throne never to be chased away, and whose heart will unwaveringly reflect the Author's Always Love.

Chapter 22

A Wise King & His Foolish Temples
1 Kings 1-11
2 Chronicles 1-9

King Solomon's calling to fulfill his father David's dream of building a home for the Author became a reality. The Temple in Jerusalem now towered behind him, majestic, awe-inspiring, finished. Solomon took his place before the Israelites gathered to dedicate the new Temple. He lifted his arms to the Author and prayed, "Author of All Life, you astound us! It seems silly to think the Creator of all things would live in anything our hands have made. We've given You our best, though it falls short of what You deserve. But by choosing to dwell here in this Temple, You reveal something beautiful about Yourself: You love to be with us! You lived among us in the Garden and then in the Tent, always desiring to turn the whole world into a place where image-bearers could enjoy You! Now we have made You a permanent home, that we might find our home in You!"

The Temple stood before them in all of its splendor, similar to the Tent of His presence that had traveled with Israel through the wilderness long ago, but bigger and more extravagant in every way! The altar alone could hold hundreds of sacrifices. The washbasin was like a huge sea carried on the backs of carved bulls. The Holy Place was tall and golden, embellished with pomegranate carvings. Inside, golden tables held the bread of His presence. On the golden altar burned fragrant incense, and ornate golden lampstands lit the way to the Most Holy Place where two huge golden angels sat, shading the Chest of the Binding Promise with their wings. A thick curtain of blue, purple, and crimson hung before the Most Holy Place. No expense had been spared to make this Temple the most impressive place in Israel. And after seven years of pouring their efforts into this massive project, it now stood finished before the people.

Solomon knew this Temple would be a place where heaven met earth, so as priests offered hundreds of sacrifices, he prayed, "When image-bearers from all over our nation and the world hear of Your Always Love, they will come to this place and pray to You. Hear our prayers! For You are a God who enters into our broken relationships, our broken hearts, our broken world. Heal us in Your Temple. You see how fickle our hearts are, how prone we are to wandering. When we forget You and the Story You're writing, draw us back to Yourself and to this Temple; for we are Yours, and You are ours!"

Solomon's prayer did not fall on deaf ears. Suddenly, fire fell from heaven consuming the sacrifices, and the Author's presence, like a thick cloud, filled the whole Temple like a King coming to sit on His throne, chasing the priests out and halting their work. The people fell to the ground bowing before their God, shouting their heartfelt praise, *"The Author is so good! His Always Love never, ever ends!"*

For two full weeks, the people celebrated together in Jerusalem, extravagantly feasting and enjoying the Author's presence among them. Was there ever a people so happy with their king or their God?

The Author's presence among His people made Israel so great that kings and queens of other nations streamed into Jerusalem. They heard Solomon's unrivaled wisdom, beheld his vast wealth, and learned of his worship of the Author. Solomon explained, "The Author's Always Love makes my kingdom great. Israel's borders now stretch farther than they ever have—finally encompassing all the land the Author promised our father Abraham. The Author has so richly blessed us with gold and silver they're as common as pebbles!"

"King Solomon," marveled an Arabian queen while on a tour of Solomon's kingdom, "while in my own country, the rumors of your greatness only told half the story! I am overwhelmed by what my eyes have seen and my ears have heard, what my mouth has tasted and my heart has felt! There is no problem too complex for your matchless wisdom. All of your people are at peace and full of joy. There truly is no other king like you and no other nation like Israel. This must mean there is no other God like the Author!"

Numerous times, the Author came to Solomon, cutting through the extravagance, the feasting and riches, and royal guests to speak to him in the quietness of his heart. "Solomon, remember when you dedicated the Temple to Me? You said it was not big enough to hold Me, and you were right. The whole universe cannot contain Me! But I've chosen this place—this people—to be Mine so the whole world will live in My Always Love. But Solomon, listen closely: it's not about a *building*, it is about your *heart*. If your heart keeps My Binding Promise, your throne will last forever. But if you refuse My Always Love and chase after other gods, then no building can rescue you! If you forget Me, your Temple will fall to rubble, and all of this honor and fame, all the wealth and extravagance you are enjoying now will become ridicule and shame."

But dear Reader, wouldn't Solomon want to Always Love the Author who had Always Loved him? Well, with all the extravagance of Solomon's life—his unparalleled wealth, wisdom, and worship—he added yet another extravagance also unparalleled by others: *wives*. And here is where his chapter of the Story unravels.

"Solomon, my husband, my love, you've done an outstanding job on the Temple to your God! But honey, we both know I don't worship your God. And sometimes, being in this foreign land, I long for my home in Egypt, for the temples to my own gods and for the ways we worship them. Since you're so good at building places of worship, will you build me one, too? Please?" Solomon's Egyptian wife batted her eyes and smiled, asking for what seemed like an innocent favor. She was a foreigner, after all. Wouldn't this make her feel more at home in Solomon's country? Of course, he wouldn't make it as big and beautiful as the Temple he built for the Author.

"Oh, I love it!" his Egyptian bride exclaimed when she saw the finished product. "Now come with me. Watch me worship! You will learn more about my culture this way; come on!"

Now Solomon's heart was torn. It was one thing to build a temple to a foreign god, but quite another to join in worship. "Well, I'll go but only to observe, my dear. You know I worship the Author in His Temple," Solomon replied. A fresh sense of self-confidence reassured his heart as he resolved only to watch, not participate.

However, Solomon had stepped onto a slippery slope, because he didn't marry only an Egyptian princess. He also married a woman from Sidon; and of course, she needed a place to worship her goddess, Ashtoreth. Then Solomon married an Ammonite woman; and of course, she also needed a place to worship her god, Molek. Later he married a Moabite woman who wanted a place to worship her god, Chemosh. He married foreign women one by one, and one by one he built shrines and temples to all their foreign gods.

With each of them he may have only taken a small step away from the Author, but after taking one thousand women for himself, loving them and the gods and goddesses they brought to Israel with them, that meant one thousand steps away from the Author and one thousand ways he forsook His Always Love.

"Solomon, you've broken our Binding Promise," the Author said sadly. "Over and over, I have come to remind you that extravagance in what you give Me doesn't matter if your heart rejects My Always Love. I have made you greater than any king in Israel has been or will be, and you've traded it all to follow other gods. Your unfaithfulness to our Binding Promise has led others to follow your footsteps. Solomon, your unfaithfulness will cost you the kingdom. When your son sits on the throne, your kingdom will tear in two."

Solomon's great kingdom began to fray around the edges. Adversaries attacked here and there, and he handed his son, Rehoboam, a kingdom on the verge of civil war. Neither wisdom, nor wealth, nor an immaculate Temple could take the place of faithfulness in Solomon's heart.

In the forty years Solomon reigned, he led the people of Israel to the most celebrated time in their history…and then set Israel on the path toward the greatest shame and sadness they would ever know. Perhaps at the height of Solomon's greatness, we might have wondered if Solomon, the wise king of kings, would be the long-awaited Rescuer. Yet we see that his heart, like so many potential rescuers, was unfaithful; and we are left waiting once again. But if we keep reading, we will find that a greater King of all kings from the house of David will indeed come. He will amaze the crowds with greater wisdom than Solomon. He will establish a Temple more awe-inspiring and glorious than Solomon's. He will draw all nations to the Author and give greater peace, prosperity, and joy to His people than Solomon's people ever knew. But dear Reader, this King will have only *one* Bride, and the King's Always Love will influence His Bride to Always Love the Author. But we must turn many, many more pages and follow Israel down a path from the height of her splendor to the lowest of lows before we meet Him.

Chapter 23

The Stubborn South & The New North
1 Kings 11:26–12:33; 14, 21

"Don't think for one minute I will go easy on you! You think life under my father King Solomon was harsh? Well, get ready for what I've got planned!" King Rehoboam laughed haughtily as he flexed his political muscles and put Jeroboam and the people he represented in their place.

Jeroboam had come three days earlier to ask that newly-crowned King Rehoboam lighten the labor and financial burdens throughout Israel. The kingdom Solomon had built was awe-inspiring, but the final years had gotten out of hand. The people were languishing under a heavy load of taxation and forced labor. Rehoboam took three days to consider their request, and now Jeroboam had his answer.

Jeroboam's blood boiled. David's family was getting out of hand! Rehoboam was stubborn, and years ago Solomon had tried to kill Jeroboam, running him out of Israel and into Egypt. But more surprising than Solomon trying to kill him was the fact that before Jeroboam left Israel, a messenger took hold of him and declared, "One day the Author will write an unexpected twist into the Story, a twist that tears away ten tribes from David's unfaithful family and gives them to you. Jeroboam, you will become king!"

The messenger's words surprised Jeroboam that day, but now as he stood before the king, they made sense. Fed up with David's sons, Jeroboam made history with his next words and tore the nation of Israel in two, "Is this how you take care of family, David? Then you can just take care of yourself! We want no more to do with you!"

In the blink of an eye, Rehoboam's kingdom split in two, and he was left ruling two tribes, Judah and Benjamin, a grace given him merely because the Author promised to always leave a lamp burning in David's house. Jacob's family, chosen and Always Loved by the Author, now split and spiraled down from the height of its glory into what would be the saddest and most destructive time in their history.

"People of Israel!" declared newly-anointed King Jeroboam to the ten northern tribes gathered for this momentous occasion. "Behold your gods who brought you out of Egypt!" He pulled back a sheet to reveal two shiny, golden calves.

"My people," Jeroboam continued, "do not feel burdened in your worship of the Author by making the long trek to the Temple in Judah. The Author is now here in the north among us!" Jeroboam presumed. "I will set up one of these in the north of our new kingdom and another in the south. Worship at whichever is most convenient for you!"

That day Jeroboam proved how thoroughly his people had forgotten the Story; for this was not the first time someone fresh out of Egypt had crafted an idol to provide a place of worship for his people. This time, though, there was no Moses to reduce the idols to dust. In fact, no one gave it a second thought. The people had long become used to strange idols mingled with their worship of the Author. So it made sense that they should worship the Author in their own Northern Kingdom, rather than going to His Temple in the Southern Kingdom.

Like a whirlwind, Jeroboam swept in, changing the landscape of the kingdom, and writing a story for Israel no one had anticipated. As he ruled Israel, a term now referring only to the ten northern tribes, he began to build up and reinforce his kingdom in a way that cut them off from ever returning to Judah, politically or spiritually.

For centuries, man after man grabbed at the power of the throne, killing anyone who got in the way. With no Binding Promise to keep, no Author to heed, and no Always Love to remember, king after king after nineteen evil kings came and went, dragging the Northern Kingdom down into the muck and mire of disobedience. The worst of them all was King Ahab, the seventh king of Israel. Compared to Ahab, Jeroboam looked like a saint. No king was more desperately wicked than Ahab, as this one brief snapshot will prove.

One day Ahab was walking near his palace in Samaria, the capital of the Northern Kingdom, when he passed a lush vineyard owned by a man named Naboth.

"Naboth, I'd like to offer you a deal," Ahab smiled, feigning friendship with him. "The land your vineyard is on would make a great vegetable garden for my palace next door. And I bet you I could get you a better vineyard elsewhere—or I could pay you more money for it than this measly vineyard is even worth! So what do you think? How about you sell me your vineyard?"

But Naboth's heart had stayed more faithful to the Author and clung more deeply to the Story than Ahab's had. Naboth knew the Binding Promise well enough to know that even making such a request violated the Binding Promise. Naboth replied, "Oh my king, I could never do that. This vineyard has been in my family for generations. It is the inheritance we received from the Author when Joshua led us into this land. They worked very hard to take possession of it; I could never give it away!"

King Ahab scowled at Naboth, clenched his fists, and stormed off to his bedroom in the palace where he sulked for the rest of the day, throwing a tantrum like a small child denied a piece of candy.

"Ahab, why are you moping?" asked his wife Jezebel, princess of Sidon and Baal-worshiper extraordinaire. Jezebel knew how to turn the heart of the king. She had influenced him to build a great temple in Samaria to the god Baal, fed hundreds of Baal's priests and messengers at her dinner table each day, and had drawn Ahab's heart—as well as the hearts of the people—to worship her Sidonian gods.

Muttering and mumbling, the king replied, "Well, I want Naboth's vineyard, but he won't give it to me!" He turned away to keep pouting.

"Ahab, look at me!" Jezebel responded fiercely. "Are you not the king? You have *power*, Ahab! You can use it to get whatever you want!" She sighed dramatically, drew near to her gloomy husband, and put her arm around him smiling slyly as she continued, "I'll cheer you up, Ahab. I'll get you that vineyard. Just sit back and watch how it's done." Then with a few strokes of a pen, Jezebel wrote letters in Ahab's name, authoring a plan to have Naboth killed.

When the news of Naboth's death reached Jezebel, she went to her husband. "There! Now that's how a king gets what he wants. Go take possession of the land I got for you." And that's exactly what Ahab did.

The Northern Kingdom's nineteen kings reduced themselves to tyrants and reduced the value of the image-bearers they ruled to less than that of vegetable gardens. Convenience and autonomy redefined worship of the Author, creating a kingdom of violence, mistreatment of the poor, and eventually even to sacrificing their children, the very image-bearers they had borne, to the evil gods they worshiped. Gone were the days of good kings and cherished citizens, because gone were the days of loving the Author most of all.

Chapter 24

A Victory & A Defeat
1 Kings 18
2 Kings 17

"When will you make a decision?" Elijah passionately shouted. "How long will you waver back and forth?"

People from all over Israel, King Ahab himself, and 450 messengers of their false gods gathered with Elijah on Mount Carmel. Mount Carmel, "God's Vineyard," was a fitting place for this showdown because Naboth's vineyard was not the only inheritance at risk of being stolen by an enemy. Though the Northern Kingdom had forgotten the Author, He had not forgotten them. They were His inheritance, and He would not quickly let them go. He had sent His messenger, Elijah, to call His people back to Himself.

"As I see it," Elijah continued, "you have two options: either Baal is the true god, and you should follow him wholeheartedly, or the Author is the true God, and you should follow Him wholeheartedly. But no more of this mixing the two as if they're equal! Today, Israel, *you must choose!*" The tension was thick on the mountain, and no one said a word.

"I am the only messenger of the Author left in Israel," Elijah boldly continued. "But look at all these messengers of Baal! They have their huge temple in the capital city, and they're all kept fat and happy at Queen Jezebel's dinner table. So today let's see who the real God is! And Israel, when you see which one is the real God, worship Him and Him alone!"

The terms of the showdown were as follows: Baal's messengers would sacrifice a bull and arrange it on the wood of their altar and then call to their god. Elijah would then do the same, but neither of them would light their sacrifice. The god who answered by fire would prove himself to be the true God.

Baal's messengers prepared their bull sacrifice for their bull-man god, Baal. Then they began to call out for him to send fire. Hundreds of them danced around the altar, shouting, "Oh Baal! The great one! Answer us with fire!" Around and around they went, dancing and shouting. But minutes turned into hours, and soon their confidence turned into desperation. Baal still had not sent fire.

Around lunchtime, Elijah began poking fun, calling loudly above their desperate shouts. "What do you think happened? Is Baal on vacation?" he laughed. "Isn't it odd that a powerful god like Baal, who holds lightning bolts in his hands, is having such a hard time lighting your sacrifice? Maybe it isn't that he's not powerful enough—I bet it's just that he's too busy!" Elijah snickered. "He's probably tending to some other sacrifice right now, too distracted to show up. Or—I know! I bet he was up late partying last night and overslept! Just call louder! Try to wake him!" Elijah couldn't hold back his laughter from the ridiculousness of it all. If their god were real and powerful and needed to prove it, why didn't he?

Urged on by Elijah's taunting, the priests more fervently danced and shouted around their sacrifice. Knowing Baal preferred blood, they shed their own to get his attention.

But no one heard their cries. No one responded to their pleas. Exhausted, bloody, bodies racked with pain, their exuberance died down to mere whimpering.

Then Elijah stepped forward as the false messengers faded into the background. Long ago an altar to the Author had stood on this mountain; now the altar stood in disrepair. Stone by stone, Elijah rebuilt the altar. He took twelve large stones, one for each tribe of Israel to represent the family Always Loved by the Author, now broken in two, limping along unfaithfully.

But Elijah didn't stop there. After he placed the sacrifice on the altar, he dug a large moat around it and commanded, "Pour water on it!" as his chest heaved from the labor of building and digging. Men moved forward with four large jars to do as they were told, pouring water all over the sacrifice and the altar.

"Now, do it again!" Elijah commanded, completely saturating the sacrifice with water. People turned to each other, shrugging their shoulders, wondering what Elijah was thinking, and then watched as four large jars of water drenched the sacrifice and the altar.

"One last time!" Elijah shouted with confidence.

Twelve full jars of water soaked the sacrifice, ran down the twelve stones of the altar, and filled the moat around it. The people drew near, astonished! Baal hadn't even responded with one flicker of hope. And now the Author was going to burn up a drenched offering?

Elijah lifted his arms and his voice, "Author of All Life, You have Always Loved us since the days of Abraham, Isaac, and Jacob. But our hearts have not Always Loved You. Answer me now, so that everyone will know that You alone are God and that You are drawing their hearts back to Yourself! Remind them that You are theirs, and they are Yours!"

Then quick as lightning, fire fell from heaven and gulped down not just the sacrifice, but the wood, the stones, and the dirt beneath, and even licked up all the water! Thousands of people gasped—some with amazement...some, like Baal's messengers, with horror. The people had made their choice, and began chanting, "The Author is the true God! The Author is the true God!"

"Then destroy the messengers of Baal!" Elijah commanded; and he and thousands with him chased them down into the valley to do away with them.

Though Elijah witnessed that day what seemed like a significant victory, the victory was short-lived. He could call the people to clean house, but they didn't want to clean their hearts. The people could be wowed by the Author's fire but refused to be wooed by His Always Love.

If on the day of this great victory Elijah could have looked into the future one hundred twenty years, he would have seen a kingdom still divided because so were the people's hearts. He'd see a Binding Promise completely forgotten, exchanged for gods they had imported and created themselves. He would have seen Israel and Judah constantly at war, recruiting outside nations to help fight each other— sons of Jacob fighting and oppressing sons of Jacob bitterly, relentlessly, violently. While in the past we wondered who would rescue Israel from their enemies, we now have to wonder, "Who will rescue them from themselves?" Is there any hope for Abraham's family?

The Northern Kingdom so brazenly rejected the Author that He had no choice but to write line after line of attacks from Assyria, the superpower of the day, until the Israelites were written out of their land, taken away as captives to Assyria, and the Northern Kingdom was no more.

But He left a small flicker of hope: the Israelites left in Samaria mingled with the foreigners imported by the Assyrians, and soon the Author moved the heart of the Assyrian king to send a few of the Author's faithful Israelite priests back to Samaria to teach them the Binding Promise. From this, the Author birthed the Samaritans. Now, dear Reader, tuck away the name "Samaritan" for the future, because while the Northern Kingdom's story is now over, the story of the Samaritans is just beginning. The Author will write them into the Story in a beautiful way.

One day, the Author will also write into the Story a Messenger far greater than Elijah, and with the tenderness of a shepherd looking for lost sheep, He will search out lost Samaritans and draw them back to the Author. To show them the extent of His Always Love, He too will climb a mountain to participate in an even greater showdown than the one Elijah experienced. And the victory He will win on that mountain will bring incredible joy to the Samaritans— and to all the lost sheep of Israel—leading them to shout and sing, "The Author is the true God!"

Chapter 25

An Angry Messenger & A Repentant City
Jonah

"Get up, Jonah! How can you sleep in this storm?!" the sailors yelled above the sound of the whirling wind and the water crashing onto the deck. The sailors were used to rough waters, but these were not just rough waters. This storm was the hand of some fierce god coming against them. "Call on your God, Jonah! Beg Him to save us!"

Jonah sat dejectedly in the belly of the boat. He lived in a time when the Northern Kingdom was still intact, though the Northern Kingdom's faith was not. Jonah was a messenger of hope to the people of Israel. But the Author had asked him to take that same hope outside the borders of Israel, and Jonah refused.

"I don't need to pray," Jonah sighed with indifference. "I'm the reason for this storm. I belong to the Author of All Life. I'm His messenger of hope to the people of Israel. The Author wanted me to carry a message of hope to Nineveh, the capital of the Assyrian empire, but I would not. The Assyrians are our worst enemy; I would rather die than see them repent and share in the Author's Always Love. So I boarded your boat in the city of Joppa to go as far from Nineveh as I could. Just throw me into the water, and the storm will stop."

"What?!" the sailors asked incredulously. They were salt-sprayed and soaked to the bone, scared for their lives, and desperate for rescue; but surely tossing a man into the sea wasn't the only way to get out of this storm.

"Everyone to the oars!" the captain shouted, and they tried desperately to row back to shore. But the more they rowed the worse the storm got, bringing the sailors to their knees. "Author of All Life, rescue us! We're out of options! We beg You, don't punish us for killing an innocent man!"

Reluctantly and with great fear, they threw Jonah overboard. Immediately the storm subsided—the storm in the sea and the storm in each sailor's heart—and they all began to worship the Author. Even in disobedience, Jonah the Israelite was a light to the nations.

However, the storm continued to rage in Jonah's heart as waves swept over him, and he gasped for breath. Water swirled around him, jerking his body this way and that. Down, down, down he descended into the depths of the sea, until the turbulent water became calm, and Jonah simply sank. Darkness surrounded him, threatening to swallow him whole until suddenly he realized this wasn't how he wanted it to end. But how could there still be hope? "Author of All Life, rescue me!" his heart cried out. Then he surrendered to the darkness.

Suddenly, a rushing current twirled and flipped Jonah around. Fear gripped him tightly, and so did strands of seaweed which began wrapping around his head and his limbs. What was happening? Then as fast as it started, the swirling subsided and so did the water, gently placing Jonah on a surface. Jonah's thoughts swirled inside his head as he gasped for air, "Is this the sea floor? What is that awful stench? How can I *breathe*?! *Where am I?*"

For three full days Jonah lingered, neither fully dead nor fully alive, trapped in the belly of a great fish. In his desperate attempt to outrun the Author, he found his plans foiled. Now he was in the depths of the sea, at the end of his rope, and all he could do was pray, "Author of All Life, my disobedience swept me into such recklessness, yet that's where Your Always Love recklessly met me. You hurled me into depths so deep I couldn't imagine You there with me! But here in this fish I can say with confidence that there will be life for me beyond this watery grave! Grasping for the Good Life in all the wrong places forfeits the Always Love You give us! You are the Rescuer!"

Jonah lived to walk on dry ground again, this time choosing to go to Nineveh. But gratitude for his own rescue still would not move his hard heart to desire the rescue of his enemies. As Nineveh came into view on the horizon, the messenger's resolve to obey was the only thing that made him put one foot in front of the other. The people of the massive city looming before him were despicable to Jonah.

It would take him three full days to walk through Nineveh from end to end. It was a city filled with violence, decorated with images of brutality toward those they conquered. Jonah shuddered as he walked through the large, ominous gates of the city, then muttered under his breath, "Let's just get this over with."

"Forty days until your judgment!" was the message Jonah forced out his lungs because it wasn't in his heart. Five vague words were the best message this messenger of the Author could muster. For one full day, he walked the streets shouting his message over and over, and that was all it took. He was barely a third of the way through the city when the people were already on their knees, begging the Author to show them mercy, crying, "Author of All Life, rescue us!"

How did those five words do that? Had Jonah's reputation preceded him? Did they whisper as he passed by, "Is that the Israelite messenger everyone's talking about? The one who spent three days in the belly of a great fish and lived to tell about it? Look at his bleached skin and hairless head! If his God rescued him from the depths of his disobedience, maybe He will rescue us from the depths of ours!" Even in reluctance, Jonah the Israelite was a light to the nations.

Disappointed by their repentance, Jonah left the city, planning to watch their judgment from a distance. But nothing happened. The scorching heat beating down on him was nothing compared to the seething anger inside his heart. "I knew this would happen!" Jonah yelled out in frustration as he raised an angry fist at the Author. "This is *not* how it should be!"

But the Author spoke calmly to Jonah's turbulent soul, "Tell me why you think your anger is right, Jonah."

Jonah's words rushed madly from his heart and out his mouth, "Because You know what they do to us! They are *brutal*, and I *hate* them! I want You to wipe them off the face of the earth; but look at what You've done instead! You've given Your Always Love to my *enemies*! I would rather die than witness this! You've always been this way! You're compassionate and give grace when it's undeserved. Your Always Wrath against sin is patient when You have every right to be angry and judge. Well, I have every right to be angry, too! *We* are Your people! Yet, You show mercy to *evil people!* I just can't take it anymore. Write me out of Your Story, because I don't want to live in a world of such extravagant mercy!"

Jonah had sunk to the depths of another turbulent sea, a storm raging inside him that threatened to swallow him whole. But there was nowhere to hide—no belly of a boat, no belly of a fish—just the makeshift shelter of a fast-growing vine meagerly shading him from the sun. While

Ninevah's citizens were afraid the Author wouldn't be merciful, Jonah was afraid that He would be.

Jonah turned and noticed a little green worm eating the leafy green vine that had woven its way through the lattices of his shelter. In moments, the shady vine began to wither, and Jonah began to wither from the heat. He sat dejectedly; everything was miserable.

Once again the Author met him in his storm. "Jonah, you care more about getting a sunburn than you do about 120,000 people burning from My Always Wrath against sin. You care more about a little green vine that grew up in a day and then withered because of a worm than you do about 120,000 people made in My image who have spent generations withering because of the age-old lie of the snake. You were grateful when My Always Love rescued you from the depths of your disobedience. Can you not be at least a little grateful when My Always Love rescues a whole city from the depths of theirs?

Dear Reader, it may be hard to believe that Jonah, the Author's messenger, could be so hard-hearted, so disobedient, so very much in need of rescue himself; but such is the state of all image-bearers. Often it is through such broken messengers that we see the Author's Always Love so clearly. Yet one day, His Always Love will shine clearly through another Messenger who, unlike Jonah, will be consumed with fervent love for His enemies, preferring to be swallowed whole by the Author's rescue plan than see them consumed by His Always Wrath.

Chapter 26

A Bloodthirsty Queen & A Boy King
2 Kings 8:16-12:21
2 Chronicles 22-24

"Queen mother, your son, King Ahaziah, is dead!" A servant ran into the palace, bowing before Athaliah to give her the news. Expecting the king's mother to be grieved, the servant was shocked when her eyes lit up, and she exclaimed, "Then kill them *all,* and we will wipe out the line of David!" She laughed wickedly, sending the guards on a violent rampage through the palace, and then muttered under her breath, "Then I will be queen!"

The palace erupted in chaos. Guards who once kept the peace now turned on King David's descendants, taking their lives with no warning. Men, women, and children ran here and there, trying to make sense of what was happening. Who knew King Ahaziah's death, evil as he was, would jeopardize the line of David, to which he belonged?

King Ahaziah's sister, Jehosheba, ran into a bedroom yet unfound by the palace guards. "Quick! Nurse! Grab baby Joash! There's no time to explain!" Frantically, she grabbed a blanket here, a change of clothing there. The nurse, trying to stay calm, scooped up King Ahaziah's infant son and followed the princess. They ran through dark corridors amid screaming and crying, exited the palace, and ran as fast as they could for the Temple. "If there's one place this baby will be safe, it's the Temple! The queen never goes there!" Jehosheba thought as she urged her weary legs to run faster, begging the Author to let them escape.

Safe in Solomon's Temple, Jehosheba led the baby's nurse to a small back bedroom used only for storage. Both women sat down, breathing heavily. Baby Joash, completely unaware of the danger he was in, quietly cooed and babbled, bringing a much-needed sense of peace to the situation.

Once she caught her breath, Jehosheba explained, "My brother, King Ahaziah, died in battle. As soon as the Queen Mother found out, she unleashed her fury on the house of David. All of the princes have been killed—except for Prince Joash."

"Why would she do that?" Joash's nurse whispered.

Jehosheba frowned. "You know how much Athaliah is like her mother, Queen Jezebel. Her marriage to my father was simply a political alliance between the Northern and Southern Kingdoms. But now, if she succeeds in wiping out the line of David, she will be Queen!"

But Reader, we know it was more serious than that. If Athaliah were to wipe out the family of David, she would wipe out all the Author's promises to his family. The lamp left burning in Judah would be completely snuffed out, and the promised Rescuer would never come.

Later that day, Athaliah, believing she'd successfully destroyed all heirs to the throne, proclaimed herself Queen of Judah even though not one drop of David's blood flowed through her veins. Wickedly she ruled, never once suspecting that hidden in the Author's Temple was the rightful heir to the throne growing older and stronger every day.

Six years later

"Now is the time. Gather the commanders who are still faithful to the Author and bring them here to the Temple," Jehoiada whispered to his servant, who left quickly to do his bidding. In less time than expected, he returned with the commanders to stand before Jehoiada the priest.

"Listen closely," began the priest. "What I am about to share with you will endanger our lives, not to mention the future of our kingdom! Before I tell you anything, you must all swear to me by the Author Himself that you will protect what I am about to show you and be willing to die for the plan I have made!"

Jehoiada was firm and strong, not an ounce of nervousness within him. Wise and advanced in years, he easily won the commanders' trust. The priest continued, "For six years, Queen Athaliah has run our nation into the ground, and most people think all hope is lost. But for six years the Author's promise has been safe here in the Temple—a place Athaliah never bothers to come." He signaled to a servant girl in the corner, who stood behind a boy about the age of seven. She gently pushed the young boy toward the priest as he continued, "My friends, this is Prince Joash, the rightful heir to King Ahaziah's throne!"

The commanders gasped! Their lungs filled with breath, their hearts filled with hope, and immediately they knew what this meant. It was time to take Queen Athaliah from her throne. And they were ready.

The commanders dispersed, having heard Jehoiada's plan, taking King David's spears and shields stored in the Temple. Each of them went to rally the temple guards under their command. Today would be a great day for the people of Judah! They scattered to their positions and waited for the signal.

Jehoiada led Prince Joash to the Temple courtyard and put a crown upon his head. "Joash, rule by this Book," the priest said as he placed the heavy scroll of the Binding Promise on the small boy's outstretched arms. His little arms struggled to hold it up as many a king before him had struggled to hold fast to its words. Judah's faithfulness to the Author had been spotty since Rehoboam. Some kings were good while some were so bad that they filled the land with unfaithfulness to the Author. But if the priest knew anything about this Binding Promise, he knew it meant the Author would be faithful, and Joash's very life was proof of that. Together the priest, the boy king, and the people renewed their Binding Promise with the Author.

"Long live King Joash!" Jehoiada cheered, and all the people and the palace guards joined in the celebration, shouting, "Long live King Joash!"

"What is the meaning of this?!" interrupted the shrill voice of Queen Athaliah moments later. Their joy had been so great that she could hear them from the palace and came to investigate. Upon seeing her grandson, so small and yet wearing a crown, her blood began to boil. Someone had escaped! "Treason!" she shrieked, "Guards! Kill them all!" She signaled to the commanders to do her bidding.

But they would not, for they were sworn to protect King Joash. Outnumbered, Athaliah ran for her life. But trapped in the Temple courtyard, the guards swiftly brought an end to her reign as well as her life.

That day was a great day for the people of Judah. Once again, a son of David sat on the throne, and the country was free from King Ahab's wicked family. They tore down the temple to Baal and smashed all the idols and altars to pieces. The people were full of joy, and the city was at peace.

One day many years later, King Joash, now thirty years old and much wiser, came to the old priest. "Jehoiada," he said, "I am forever indebted to you. You welcomed me as an infant into the Temple with open arms. You raised me as your grandson. You taught me the Author's ways, teaching me to keep the Binding Promise. Your faithfulness to the Author has brought life to our kingdom once again! But Jehoiada, the Author's Temple is not as it used to be. You told me stories of its greatness…but look at it now. Well over one hundred years old, it is showing its age. The priests of Baal ransacked it; the people have neglected it. It's just not right! It saved my life after all." Joash's eyes sparkled with excitement as he shared his plan with the priest. "Let's repair it! Let's restore the Temple to the greatness it had when Solomon first built it!"

Before long, gold and silver were streaming into the Temple as people gave generously to see it repaired. Finally, the Temple stood majestically before them once again.

Jehoiada lived his part of the Story faithfully; but eventually his chapter came to an end, and he was no longer there to guide Joash. The king's heart began to wander without the priest's constant influence. Soon idols and altars to false gods littered Jerusalem once again.

One day, long after Jehoiada had passed, his son Zedekiah came to the king. "Joash, you know the Binding Promise: if you hold onto your wickedness, forsaking the Author's Always Love, you'll be swept away by His Always Wrath against sin. Why would you want that?" Zedekiah's heart was filled with pain. He loved the king like a brother, but his heart broke from the compromises Joash was making. Surely because of their friendship, surely because of Joash's fondness for Zedekiah's father, his words would not fall on deaf ears and the king would humbly turn back to the Author. But nothing could have prepared Zedekiah for what Joash did in response.

"Stone him," the king whispered to the commander by his side. "Follow him out of the palace and be sure he doesn't make it home."

Rescued by Jehoiada—only to kill Jehoiada's son; his life preserved by the Temple—just to fill the land with its rivals, King Joash epitomized everything that was wrong with the Southern Kingdom. The Author had been so good to Judah, sending messengers to woo them back to Himself, giving them faithful priests like Jehoiada to call the people to keep the Binding Promise, and preserving the line of David so all His promises to David's family could be realized. Some kings who came after Joash clung to the Binding Promise, knowing it was their only hope as a nation. But the nation's short bursts of faithfulness lasted only as long as the life of their faithful king. Steadily over the years, Judah's faithfulness faltered and declined to such a low place that they even made the Northern Kingdom look faithful.

After 400 years of the Author's faithfulness to keep a son of David on the throne of Judah, the lamp of David barely flickered, leaving us to wonder: in spite of all the Author had done to keep it burning, would the lamp go out?

Chapter 27

Jerusalem's Fall & A Promise of Hope
Jeremiah
Lamentations
2 Kings 24-25
2 Chronicles 36

"Jerusalem will fall! There is no more hope! If you stay in the city to fight the Babylonians, you will die; if you surrender to them, you will live!" Jeremiah shouted in the streets. What a heavy message from the Author to relay to the people of Judah!

"There he is!" a man shouted as he rounded a corner and saw Jeremiah. "Grab him! Don't let him get away!" he yelled as his men ran toward Jeremiah. Taking hold of him, the king's officials bound Jeremiah with ropes, led him to the courtyard of the king's guard, and lowered him into a well. Jeremiah sank into the thick mud.

"There!" his captors shouted, the echo reverberating down the well and into Jeremiah's ears. "That's what you get for discouraging the few soldiers left in this city and telling the people to surrender to our enemies!" They laughed as they walked away, leaving Jeremiah helpless.

Jeremiah fought against the sticky mud, his legs and the folds of his robe trapped in the ooze. The smooth walls of the well were impossible to climb. Trapped with no possible way to get out, he faced death from either starvation or suffocation. "So this is what becomes of the Author's messengers in Judah," Jeremiah groaned, sinking into the mud but trying not to sink into despair.

Just as Judah was caught in the crossfire between Egypt and Babylon's struggle for supremacy in the region, Jeremiah was now caught between the Author's messages to His people and their violent response to His voice. But when the Author had called Jeremiah to be a messenger rather than a priest like his father, the Author had whispered a message of hope to Jeremiah's heart saying, "Even while in your mother's womb, you were Mine, and I was yours. I am with you and will rescue you. Don't fear!" That promise gave hope to Jeremiah's heart in the depths of despair as he sunk deeper and deeper, hour after hour.

"Jeremiah!" a voice called from above. "We've come to rescue you!" The end of a rope dangled into the well, flooding Jeremiah's heart with gratitude. It was a rough rescue, taking the strength of thirty men to pull Jeremiah free from the mud that held him fast. Once freed from the well, he stood before the king.

"Why?!" the enraged King Zedekiah yelled. "Why can't you prophesy something nice for a change?"

Jeremiah stood sad but unafraid before his king.

Zedekiah mocked Jeremiah in a high, squeaky voice, "'Nebuchadnezzar will capture Jerusalem, Zedekiah! You won't escape; you'll be taken to Babylon, Zedekiah! Just give in to the Babylonians, Zedekiah!'" He glared at Jeremiah, "Do you have *nothing* good to say? For years you've only stirred up trouble in this land! I am trying to *protect* Jerusalem, but you seek its downfall!"

It was true, Jeremiah didn't have much good to say these days. Century after century, the kings of the Southern Kingdom exploited the Author's Always Love to fuel their idolatry and exploited image-bearers to build luxurious palaces for themselves. The streets of Jerusalem flowed with innocent blood. The land of Judah had as many false gods as it had towns. Social injustice was rampant in the land, and dishonest gain was the order of the day. Leaders took advantage of the fatherless and the foreigner and celebrated wickedness and deceit. And all the while they believed that because the Author's Temple still stood in their midst like a good luck charm, they were safe.

For decades, the lonely messenger Jeremiah struggled under the weight of his calling. The message that the Author would judge His people, destroy the precious city of Jerusalem, and let the Temple be burned with fire was a message that made him many enemies. People hurled curses on him as he passed by, others plotted to take his life. A priest even beat him and put him in stocks. False messengers proclaimed attractive messages of peace and safety from the Babylonians, making Jeremiah look like an enemy.

"No more roaming the streets spreading these disheartening messages, Jeremiah!" the king raged. "You're confined to the courtyard of the guards. We will break the yoke of Babylon. You will see!"

As Jeremiah returned to the courtyard, hope whispered a message to him. He *did* have something good to say! He knew Nebuchadnezzar would return to finish what he started, and Jerusalem would fall; but those already in exile could still be encouraged. He began to write:

To all my dear brothers and sisters in exile,
The Author says, "You went into captivity because you rejected My Always Love. Jerusalem will fall, but I will not forsake you forever. I will Always Love you! I am writing a good Story for you, and after seventy years of exile, I will scoop you up into My arms and carry you home again. So embrace your captivity: build houses, marry, start families, and pray for the cities where you live. Shine brightly as you

trust Me in dark places. Return to Me with all your heart! Evil will not have the final word in My Story."

Jeremiah sent the letter to the exiles already in Babylon, hoping to encourage them with the Always Love of the Author. Meanwhile, he stayed confined in the courtyard of the guards, which is where he was the day the siege began.

It was a cold, wintry day in January when a low hum rumbled through the city. Hearts stopped from fear, wondering if the sound was what they thought it was. It grew louder and louder as the most powerful army in the world drew nearer to Jerusalem.

"Surround the city!" growled King Nebuchadnezzar, the most powerful man in the world. "It's time to show this impertinent King Zedekiah and his ridiculous nation a lesson they'll never forget!" An evil smile spread over his face as the Babylonian army marched to surround the city.

Years ago, Babylon had swept through the region, conquering and taking its place as the supreme world power. Nebuchadnezzar had put Zedekiah on Judah's throne, and for years Zedekiah paid tribute to Babylon. But being the stubborn man that he was, Zedekiah had recently allied himself with Egypt, rebelled against Nebuchadnezzar, and now he and his people would pay dearly for it.

Jerusalem tried to weather the siege, but days turned into months and years, and King Zedekiah's refusal to surrender brought the people of Jerusalem very low. Trapped inside the city by their arrogant king and surrounded by Babylon's army, the people of Jerusalem cried out in despair. Mothers wept as their children withered from hunger and thirst. Men and women, once clothed in riches, now sat shriveled to skin and bones, begging on street corners. Streets filled with tears and fallen bodies, and heavy darkness hung over the

152

city as they realized not even the Author would come to their rescue. Centuries of unfaithfulness had caught up with Jerusalem. The city that was once the glory of the Author and a light to the world now lay barely breathing, humiliated and abhorred by all nations.

With great swiftness, the Babylonian army breached Jerusalem's walls and burned its gates with fire. Without mercy they killed all of Zedekiah's sons and left him, the last of David's sons to sit on the throne in Jerusalem, blind and alone. They led him to Babylon, bound hand and foot, just as Jeremiah had prophesied.

"Set the place on fire!" yelled Nebuzaradan, commander of the Babylonian army, and the city went up in flames. The royal palace that had housed David's family dissolved into ashes. Solomon's great Temple, where fire had fallen and the Author's presence had filled the place like a cloud, was now blackened by enemy fire and choked by clouds of smoke. The Author had done the unthinkable. He let His house, His city, His people fall to ruins.

"Gather up the people!" commanded Nebuzaradan. Soldiers scurried here and there to obey. "Leave the poorest people to work the fields. Put the rest in shackles and take them to Babylon—except for Jeremiah! Where is Jeremiah the Author's messenger?"

Jeremiah, withered from the siege and bound for the trip to Babylon, stood before the brutal warlord. Nebuzaradan removed his shackles and looked the messenger in the eye. "Everything you said would happen to Judah has happened. So I have strict orders from King Nebuchadnezzar not to harm you. You are free, Jeremiah. Go with us to Babylon; or if you prefer to stay, here is a gift from King Nebuchadnezzar and enough food to get you healthy and feed you for many days. Go now; you are free!"

"Free?" thought Jeremiah looking down at his wrists and his feet and then at his people—the Author's people—bound hand and foot. "No, we are not free," Jeremiah said to himself. "But one day we will be."

Jeremiah's thoughts wandered with him as he walked away from the cloud of smoke that was now Jerusalem. His heart ached for what could have been and longed for what one day would be.

Quietly, the Author's voice met him in the ruins like a beautiful song of hope speaking courage to Jeremiah's heart. "Jeremiah, one day I will make a new Binding Promise with My people. But this time, I won't write it on stone tablets but on each person's heart! I will raise up a new Israel to keep this new Binding Promise, and like My Always Love, it will never end. One day, I will rebuild Jerusalem—never to be broken down again! I will bring My people back from captivity. I will heal them and give them a King—the promised Son of David—to sit on the throne forever! All nations will see My Always Love for My people for I am theirs, and they are Mine."

Jeremiah clung to hope amid the ashes. He knew this chapter was over for his people, but the Story would still go on.

Chapter 28

A Refugee & His Visions
Ezekiel

"Fallen! Fallen! Jerusalem has fallen!" a man ran into the camp shouting, clothes tattered and torn, hair disheveled, a wild look in his eyes. "Our great city has fallen!" And then, his strength leaving him, the man fell as well.

Refugees from Judah gathered around the man to revive him, anxious to hear more details. They had been warned Jerusalem would fall but never wanted to believe it would. Many false messengers had assured them they'd soon return to the land of Judah.

Already this community, 10,000 strong, had spent years living by the Kebar River, which was much more like a drainage ditch than a river. The city of Babylon swelled with the people of Judah—people like Daniel and his friends. The rest were forced to live in this refugee camp south of the city of Babylon. As they had been waiting on the banks of the Kebar for the political storm to blow over, back home in Jerusalem King Zedekiah had been rebelling against Nebuchadnezzar, sealing Jerusalem's fate, ensuring its fall.

And now it had fallen, according to this nameless fugitive who had escaped from Jerusalem, somehow surviving the 900-mile journey to the refugee camp. His strength slowly returning, he continued, "We couldn't endure any longer. The Babylonian army surrounded us; no one went in or out of the city. People began eating their own children to survive!" He cringed at the memory. "Jerusalem's wall is a pile of stones. The Temple, the palace, the houses...they all went up in flames!"

Everyone gasped. Even if they could return, now there was nothing to return to! They all sat down and wept.

Ezekiel wandered off quietly. He knew this day would come and had warned the people not to get their hopes up. Jeremiah had sent a letter saying Jerusalem would indeed fall and that their captivity would last seventy years. But no one wanted to believe it.

Ezekiel thought back to his arrival at the refugee camp. He had just turned thirty. Being of the priestly line, that would have been the year he began serving in the Author's Temple in Jerusalem. Oh how he longed to be doing just that: greeting the people as they led their offerings to the altar, daily placing the bread of the Author's presence in the Temple, remembering that the Author is more essential to life than food itself, lighting the candles to shine the way to the Author's presence! But what of the Author's presence now?

Meandering through the camp, Ezekiel remembered the first time the Author gave him a vision, shortly after the Babylonians captured his family and brought them here from Jerusalem. It was a vision of the Author's presence—alive, active, moving, on the go! It challenged how he understood the Author. Wasn't the Author's home in Jerusalem? Isn't that where He stayed? He remembered the voice, like a beautiful Word, spoken into Ezekiel's soul as he saw something he could barely describe, let alone understand. He saw the Author and heard the Word! He knew the Author wanted to teach him something about His presence.

As he walked, he remembered another vision. Six years after arriving at the refugee camp, when Jerusalem was still bustling with life, the Author's Spirit carried Ezekiel in a vision to Jerusalem—to the Temple itself! Ezekiel's heart filled with joy—until he began to see the Temple as the Author saw it.

"Ezekiel," the Author began solemnly, "do you see what I see? There are altars and shrines to false gods in My House. See those women crying? They've come to My House to cry in My presence to their favorite god to save them!" His heart seemed ready to burst. "Dig through the Temple wall, Ezekiel, and see what you find. The people think they can hide from Me by a mere wall, but I see what they are doing. Dig, Ezekiel; see for yourself." Ezekiel dug through the wall, thick incense and grotesque images overwhelming him on the other side. More than seventy Israelite leaders had gathered for a secret ritual to their false gods in the inner rooms of the Temple! Ezekiel was speechless.

"I am no longer welcome in My own House," the Author continued, His voice resolute yet betraying sadness and grief. "My heart aches within Me. I want to live among My people, to be their one and only, giving them life in My Always Love!" Love and wrath mingled together, splashing tears around Ezekiel. "For all the strength and ferocity of My Always Love, it has one vulnerability. I cannot force it on anyone. Otherwise, it would cease to be Always Love. So I let My people decide. I gave them two trees in the Garden, then two mountains, Gerizim and Ebal, in the Promised Land. I gave them a choice between life and death, and once again, they have chosen death."

Ezekiel shuddered as he kept walking, recalling what happened next in the vision. The Author gave Jerusalem over to destruction and then did the one thing the people of Judah *never* thought He would do. He left. The Author's presence, beautiful and awesome, simply lifted and headed east.

"East! Why that's where we are—east of Jerusalem, in Babylon," Ezekiel realized, quickening his pace. "The Author's words to me in that vision now make sense! His presence departed from the Temple, but then He said to me, 'Even though My people have filled My home with filth, I will go to them in the filth of their captivity and be their home. Even though My people's evil has carried them off into exile, I will go into exile with them.' But that wasn't all He said. He promised to restore us to our land! One day He will gather us from the nations, scoop us up into His arms, and carry us back to Jerusalem!" Ezekiel's steps lightened as he walked, his heart swelling with joy. "He promised to take our wicked, idol-loving hearts of stone and replace them with new, soft hearts that Always Love to keep the Binding Promise—but not the old Binding Promise! *A new Binding Promise!*"

Night was falling, but Ezekiel kept walking. There was no Temple among them, yet he knew that someway, somehow, the Author was here with them—even here in a camp as they paid miserably for their disobedience.

Suddenly, the Author's Spirit whisked Ezekiel up to the top of a mountain in Judah. Ezekiel struggled to comprehend what he saw. A lush green garden sprawled out before him, but it wasn't just a garden. A Temple, bigger and more extravagant than Solomon's stood, imposing and majestic, in the midst of the garden; but it wasn't just a Temple in a garden. It was miles and miles of a fresh new Jerusalem that bustled with life and joy. Then something caught Ezekiel's eye. He looked to the east. Could it be? As it came closer, it was unmistakable! The presence of the Author was returning to this City-Temple-Garden! Ezekiel's eyes welled up with tears as the Author's presence returned through the eastern gate of the Temple, and His Spirit drew Ezekiel closer, into the Temple courtyard.

"Ezekiel," the thunderous yet gentle voice of the Author began, "this is My home, and this will be My people's home forever! Forever and ever we will live together in My Always Love!"

Just then, tiny streams of water began to tickle Ezekiel's toes. "Where is the water coming from?" Ezekiel wondered, looking around. A Man appeared beside Ezekiel inviting him to wade into the water. But the farther Ezekiel followed Him, the deeper the water got. The trickle at his toes rose to his ankles, then to his knees, finally turning into a river so deep and wide Ezekiel couldn't see the other side. He grabbed hold of the Man, who helped him out of the water.

Back on shore, the Man asked Ezekiel, "Do you know what this means?"

Dripping wet and overwhelmed, Ezekiel could only shake his head.

"Ezekiel," replied the Man, "this is the river of the Author's Always Love. It begins at His throne and flows throughout the world, turning it into a place where image-bearers live with the Author forever! Wherever this water flows, it brings life! And the leaves and fruit on these trees, finding life along its banks, give life and healing to all!"

Ezekiel was stunned. Jerusalem had fallen, ravaged by famine and war, its Temple and wall reduced to rubble. Yet the Author was promising restoration—a lush, life-giving Garden, a bigger and better Temple, a City where the Author sits as King on His throne, image-bearers finding healing and life forever in His Always Love.

"Do you know the name of this new world, Ezekiel?" the Man asked with a smile, eyes shining, revealing His excitement.

Ezekiel shook his head.

"The Author is Always with Us!" the Man smiled.

With that, the vision was over. Night had fallen, its darkness matching the darkness of his people's grief. But Ezekiel couldn't run back to the camp fast enough to share this vision with his people. With renewed hope he ran, believing that just as light would dawn tomorrow, everything the Author said would come to pass. The Author was with them—even in their exile.

Chapter 29

Faithfulness & Exile
Daniel

Daniel's heart skipped a beat. Did he really just read that his people's exile would last only seventy years? He reread Jeremiah's letter to be sure, *"To all my dear brothers and sisters in exile the Author says, 'You went into captivity because you rejected My Always Love. Jerusalem will fall, but I will not forsake you forever. I will Always Love you! I am writing a good Story for you, and after seventy years of exile, I will scoop you up into My arms and carry you home again…'"*

There it was—a promise of restoration and hope! Jeremiah's words sank deep into Daniel's heart, while questions rose to the surface. Decades had passed; the seventy years were almost over. What would this mean for Daniel and his friends who had been among the first carried away from Jerusalem? Would they perhaps live to see the restoration of Jerusalem? The thought filled him with joy. Oh, but what about his people? Suddenly, the joy was gone. Unfaithfulness in Judah had led to their exile, yet exile hadn't changed his people's hearts. Many were as unfaithful now as they had been in Judah.

Daniel gazed out his window toward Jerusalem, letting his mind wander back half a century. His body was showing age now, but when he first arrived in Babylon, he and his friends were teenagers. Physically, they were in their prime, groomed for positions of power and prestige in Jerusalem. He winced as he remembered the horror of the most powerful and evil kingdom in the world invading their country and carrying them off. For three straight years, they were steeped in Babylonian language, immersed in Babylonian culture, and inundated with Babylonian myths, history, and religion. Nebuchadnezzar planned to take Judah's elite and transform them into the elite of Babylon. Daniel sighed as he remembered how, early on, he and his friends committed themselves to living faithfully in exile. They knew it could cost them their lives but agreed they would rather die than deny the Author's Always Love. Multiple times, Nebuchadnezzar almost put them to death, but each time the Author rescued them.

Once, Nebuchadnezzar threatened to kill all of his wise men—including Daniel and his friends—if they couldn't tell him both the dream he'd had and its interpretation. The Author rescued Daniel by revealing both to him. The next morning Daniel stood before the bewildered king and shared both the dream and its interpretation. But Daniel had more to say, "Although you are powerful, your power is nothing compared to the Author's. Any power you have, He loans to you. On top of that, King Nebuchadnezzar," Daniel continued calmly and tactfully, "Babylon will fall, and many kingdoms after you will rise and fall, but the Author's Kingdom will always remain. One day it will crush all other kingdoms and stand victorious forever!"

The Author had rescued their lives that day; but He did more than that, for Daniel needed to hear that message just as much as Nebuchadnezzar did. Daniel encouraged his friends after he stood before the king, "Even though we're in exile, even though an evil kingdom reigns on this earth, it will not always be this way. Kingdoms will rise and fall, but the Author is the true King, and His Kingdom will never be shaken. Let's continue to be faithful in exile!"

Nebuchadnezzar spared the lives of Daniel and his friends, promoting them to higher positions in the government and even praising the Author's greatness. But Nebuchadnezzar loved power. He wouldn't give up that power and let his kingdom fall if it were up to him. Instead, he would show the world his greatness and command the worship and allegiance of his whole kingdom. Unwilling to bow to the Author, Nebuchadnezzar made everyone bow to himself— or die.

"Bow to my golden image or be thrown into the fire!" Nebuchadnezzar shouted at Daniel's friends, giving them one more chance to obey. But they knew that if they bowed, it wouldn't just be to a golden statue; it would be to a kingdom that had exalted itself against the Author's Kingdom. Epitomizing what the Tower of Babel attempted thousands of years before, Babylon existed only to make a name for itself and boast of its fame.

"King Nebuchadnezzar," Daniel's friends told the king, "we belong to a different Kingdom and serve a King greater than you. He will either rescue us from the fire or He won't; but either way, we belong to Him—not to you or your kingdom."

Insane fury filled Nebuchadnezzar, and he threw Daniel's three friends into the flames. But rather than fire consuming them, awe consumed King Nebuchadnezzar as he saw with his own eyes how intimately the Author walks with His people in exile. There in the fire were not just three people, but *four*, as the Author Himself entered the flames of an evil kingdom to rescue Daniel's friends.

Daniel now walked to his window and leaned upon its sill. Decades had passed since that fiery rescue, but Daniel's own great test of faithfulness was fresh on his mind. He had found the Author's presence not in a fiery furnace but in a den of lions. He looked down at his hands which could still remember the feel of the lions' soft fur. He would not soon forget that night with the lions.

"Daniel?" King Darius called down into the pit at the first light of dawn. "Did the Author rescue you?" The king, tricked into throwing Daniel to the lions, was hopeful the Author had intervened.

"Yes," Daniel laughed in reply, "the Author rescued me!" Daniel came out of the pit to the tune of King Darius singing the Author's praises. "The Author is the living God! His kingdom will last forever, and He is intimately involved in life on earth—rescuing those in need!"

Babylon had fallen to Persia, but still the Author, the true King, walked intimately with His people in exile. He quenched fiery flames, gave dreams and visions to His people, and shut the mouths of lions, reminding his image-bearers that even when they behave like violent beasts, they are still no match for the Author's power.

Daniel looked intently toward Jerusalem. He longed to be back in Judah and for the exile to be over. Yet he couldn't deny that here in Persia, and years ago in Babylon, the Author's presence had never left him. And now Jeremiah's recently-found letter, written long ago, promised the exile would soon be over!

Daniel sank to his knees to beg the Author for mercy, "Author of All Life, You offered us Your Always Love, but we rejected it, preferring to seek the Good Life without You. You were right to exile us and judge our wickedness. We are covered with shame."

Daniel hung his head and wept as his people's sin weighed heavy on him. But confidence in the Author's promises to

His people urged Daniel to keep praying, "We do not deserve Your Always Love, yet it keeps pursuing us. So I beg You, look at Jerusalem in ruins and remember Your promise. Look on Your people, whom You have Always Loved, and forgive us. Be true to who You've always been. Be faithful to us in our exile."

Suddenly, an angel appeared before Daniel.

"Gabriel!" Daniel exclaimed, recognizing him from a previous vision.

"Yes, Daniel," said Gabriel smiling warmly. "The Author sent me to you because you are His, and He is yours. His Love for you is Always, and He wants you to understand something very important." Gabriel drew closer and continued, "Daniel, it will take much more than an exile of seventy years to restore your people thoroughly. The Author's Story for His people is bigger than giving them a certain piece of land or their own earthly kingdom. He is waging a war against sin and His enemy and will not stop until He is victorious over both!"

Daniel thought deeply. This rang true in his heart; but like many visions he'd had, this was hard to understand. The angel continued, "Jerusalem will indeed be restored and rebuilt, but your people will still need a Rescuer, Daniel, because all people are captives in a worse exile. You see, the Rescuer will come, but not as anyone expects. To set captives free, He will take their place. Evil kingdoms will rise and fall, so will Jerusalem, and it will look like evil will reign forever. But Daniel, don't believe it for one minute!"

With that, Gabriel departed, leaving Daniel dumbfounded, struggling to make sense of what he just heard. All people captive in a worse exile? The Rescuer taking our place? For a long while, Daniel sat there silently until it made sense. He looked out his window toward Jerusalem once more, and said, "Jeremiah was right. Our physical exile will only last seventy years, but it all seems to point to a more serious captivity—a spiritual exile caused by sin in our hearts. But just as the Author will restore us from our physical exile, He will restore us from our spiritual one too! And when He does, we will see the extent of His power and the immense greatness of His Kingdom!"

Throughout Daniel's long life, he learned that the secret of living faithfully in exile was remembering that no matter how circumstances played out on earth, the Author is always on His throne. The Author's Always Love would have the final say, and one day the Rescuer would prove that to the world.

A Broken-Down Wall & Broken-Down Hearts
Ezra
Nehemiah

The moon shone brightly on the ruins of the city as Nehemiah rode his donkey to survey the broken-down wall. Not even the darkness could hide the truth: Jerusalem was in shambles. Where once the wall around the city stood tall and strong, protecting its inhabitants and identifying them as the Author's people, both protection and identity were now missing. Their identity as a people was now as weak as these burned-down city gates, their protection as worthless as this broken-down wall overgrown with weeds. Nehemiah's heart stirred within him; something had to be done.

As he inspected the rubble, Nehemiah remembered the Author's faithfulness to His people. Just as the Author had promised through Jeremiah, the exile lasted seventy years. Then He judged wicked Babylon and through Cyrus, a Persian King, He returned His people to their land. Sadly though, when given the chance, few Israelites chose to return. Many had gotten comfortable in exile, and few had the courage to uproot themselves and rebuild their people and their city.

"But the Author is not finished with us yet," Nehemiah heard himself say, as if the winds of hope that had blown through time since Adam and Eve left the Garden were whispering hope to him in these Jerusalem ruins.

Nehemiah had first heard of Jerusalem's sad condition while back in the citadel of Susa where he served as cupbearer to King Artaxerxes. Nehemiah then spent four long months praying and fasting, begging the Author to do something to restore the honor of His people and the city they called home. "Author of All Life," Nehemiah had prayed, "we are Yours, and You are ours, but we have broken the Binding Promise and experienced everything Moses said we would if we followed Ebal's example. But remember Your promise! You said that even if You had to exile Ebal's children to the furthest parts of the world, hope would stir their hearts to pray and beg You to make something beautiful of their mess. That is what I am doing! Remember us and give me favor with the king." Before long, he was ready to be the answer to his own prayer.

The next day, while serving King Artaxerxes, Nehemiah dared to let his sadness for his people show, and the king noticed.

"Nehemiah," began the king, "I've never seen you look like this. You are not sick. Are you sad?"

Courageously, Nehemiah shared both the grief in his heart and the plight of his people. By the end of the conversation the king had commissioned Nehemiah to go to Jerusalem with his blessing and all the authority and resources he would need to rebuild the city and its walls.

But now, standing amid Jerusalem's rubble, Nehemiah was starting to think this project wouldn't be as simple as replacing a stone wall and re-hanging gates. Not all of the Author's people had been faithful in exile. Some that stayed in Jerusalem married foreign women and worshiped their gods, heading down the same evil road that had led them into exile. Decades ago, Zerubbabel bravely led the first wave of people back to Jerusalem to rebuild the Temple, but his Temple was small and simple compared to Solomon's. Fire hadn't fallen, nor had the Author's presence filled it. Ezra, the teacher, had been faithful to teach the Binding Promise, but so few were faithful to keep it. The city wasn't the only thing in shambles; the people were, too.

But Nehemiah remembered the Author's Always Love; and the following morning he called the people together, inspiring them all to rebuild Jerusalem, no matter the cost. Leaders, priests, merchants, goldsmiths, women and men, young and old all rose to the challenge, working together, remembering that the Author was theirs, and they were His!

The opposition was great, for outside the city Tobiah and Sanballat, enemies of Israel, snickered and sneered, stirring up trouble trying to halt the work and take Nehemiah's life. But worse than that, Nehemiah's own people stirred up trouble.

"Friends! What is this I hear of one Israelite enslaving another?" Nehemiah demanded. "How will we rebuild the walls of Jerusalem unless we first tear down the walls in our hearts? You deny the Author's Always Love for you by squeezing the life out of each other, looking for ways to profit at the expense of other image-bearers. Such injustice cannot stay inside these walls! What does it matter if we have a Temple, offer sacrifices, and rebuild Jerusalem's wall if we forget that the reason we exist as a people is because of the Author's Always Love? A stone wall will only protect us from the enemies outside but not from the enemy inside our own hearts!"

While the wall around the city was rebuilt in a miraculous fifty-two days, the harder work of rebuilding the people took much longer.

"Once before there was time, there was an Author whose heart was Always Love," began Ezra, who had gathered the people together to rebuild the people's hearts by teaching them the Author's Story. For hours on end he told them of a beautiful Garden where the Author lived in a friendship of Always Love with His image-bearers and of a snake bringing a lie into the Story. He spoke of the separation between the Author and His image-bearers, the innocent dying for the guilty, and the age-old promise that a Rescuer would come. He called Abraham's family back to life and to the Author's Always Love as they gathered before him, reminding them of their special calling to make this whole world a place where the Author and His people would live together!

But the further Ezra got into the Story, the more the crowd buzzed with questions. "A talking snake?" asked one. "Well, has the Rescuer come yet?" asked another. "Why did our people end up in Egypt? Oh, it's so hard to understand Ezra since I don't speak Hebrew!"

The Author's people were in shambles indeed. Their own Story confused them; whole chunks of it were missing like a broken-down wall, and to top it all off, because the Israelites had mixed so long with the people around them, many of them had never learned the language of their own people.

Levites, serving as interpreters, wove their way through the crowd answering questions and clarifying details until suddenly someone in the crowd began to cry. Then another. Then another, until everyone was weeping. Hearing their Story from the beginning, in order, had touched a deep part of their souls. They began to see who they were created to be and saw how far they had fallen. The Story of the Author's faithfulness revealed how unfaithful they were to Him.

They stood to their feet crying and confessing their brokenness and disobedience as a people. "Author of All Life, on every page of Your Story, You have Always Loved us. But over and over we have rejected Your Always Love, seeking the Good Life apart from You. You promised that a Son of David will be our King and rescue us from everything that is evil in this Story. But although we have returned to our land, a foreign king rules over us and owns us. Set us free! Send the Rescuer-King!"

To prove to the Author they would be faithful to Him once again, they drafted a binding promise and signed it in His presence. "We will obey every word You have ever given us!" they declared boldly. "Our ancestors before us failed to keep Your Binding Promise, but this time, we will not fail!"

A cheer went up through the crowd as their prayer ended and a grand celebration began. With choirs singing, they dedicated their new wall and gave sacrifices to the Author. All the people feasted with joy. Everything seemed right in Jerusalem once more, so Nehemiah returned to his post as cupbearer to the king.

Dear Reader, I wish this chapter could end here with joyful celebration. But the passing of ten years proved that signing a binding promise with their hands wasn't the same as signing it with their hearts.

"What is this?!" Nehemiah shouted angrily, having returned to Jerusalem to see how things had gone the last ten years. "Tobiah, the foreign god-worshiper who had tried to stop the wall from being built, now lives in the *Temple*? Get him out of here! And why is no one attending to the Temple? Why are there no daily sacrifices? What is this I hear about people buying and selling on the Sabbath? Has *no one* been faithful to the Author these past ten years?"

"Well, you see," Nehemiah's attendant hesitated, hanging his head in shame, "the Levites have to work in the fields to provide for themselves because no one gives to the Temple to care for them anymore. And since it's not the custom of foreigners to rest on the Sabbath, and so many Israelites have married foreigners, I guess we haven't kept that part of the Binding Promise either."

Nehemiah flew into a rage, cleansing the Temple of its filth, yelling at the people, pulling hair from the beards of men who ten years before had sworn to keep the Binding Promise better than their ancestors but had proved to be just as unfaithful. Exhausted and discouraged, Nehemiah flung his arms in the air, giving up the fight. "Oh, Author of All Life," he cried, "this is a mess! We can rebuild temples and walls from the ruins but are powerless to rebuild the ruins of our own hearts!" Nehemiah's eyes filled with tears. He lowered his arms, shoulders sagging, head hanging low. "Zerubbabel's Temple cannot make the people worship You. Ezra's teaching cannot make them want to keep the Binding Promise. And the wall we built cannot keep unfaithfulness out of the city, because unfaithfulness is in our hearts! I tried as hard as I could to rebuild Your people, but it didn't work. What will it take for us to be made new?"

Chapter 31

Messengers & Their Song

What will it take for us to be made new?

For the next four centuries, while the Author quietly sets the stage to reveal the answer to that question, the Author's people will pour over the words of His messengers, searching for hope when all seems lost.

Though their messages and lives spanned different centuries and regions, if the Author's messengers had ever gathered together at one time and place, their message, like a song of hope, would've sounded something like this:

"Listen! I hear a voice!" Isaiah shouts, "It's hope calling out from a barren wilderness, 'The King is coming! Make way for the King!' Hope demolishes mountains that stand in the way, fills in chasms that divide people from the King. A light dawns in darkness, shines the way back to His Kingdom, smooth, straight, and unmistakable. The road to this Kingdom runs past a young girl whose heart remembers the song of hope the Author began singing long ago. 'One day a young girl will bear a Child to reveal My presence among you,' He sang, and now she sings it too." (Isaiah 7:14; 9:1-2; 40:3–4)

"And the road winds back through Bethlehem," Micah the messenger sings. "Like King David of old, another King comes from this seemingly insignificant village in Judah, yet His power and reign began before this Story began!" (Micah 5:2)

"Yet what is this I hear?" interjects Jeremiah, tears welling up in his eyes, "Weeping! Bitter cries from other mothers who have had sons. An evil king is on a wild rampage because the true King has been born! Rachel, Jacob's wife, weeps uncontrollably, her children snatched from her arms!" (Jeremiah 31:15)

But Hosea brings a glimmer of hope. "Don't despair," he sings. "The Rescuer escapes the evil king and hides away in Egypt—not unlike our people at one point in the Story. At just the right time, when it's safe, the Author will call His Son, our Rescuer, out of Egypt—alive and well and full of peace!" (Hosea 11:1)

"Peace! Yes, our Rescuer will be our peace," Micah exclaims. (Micah 5:5)

"His whole Kingdom will be peace—because He is peace!" Isaiah smiles as he sings, "His peace will permeate all corners of the world, His justice making everything right once again." (Isaiah 9:7)

"I see it, too!" Daniel jumps in, "All kings and their kingdoms will fade from view. The Author of All Life will wrap up this beautiful Story by setting the Rescuer on His throne! He will have no rival and will bring all other kingdoms to nothingness. Forever and ever He will reign." (Daniel 2:44)

Jeremiah moves to center stage, singing of what he sees, "Like a branch growing out of a fallen tree, our Rescuer-King is starting a new family, calling all nations to Himself. Image-bearers from around the world stream into the magnificent house He built for them to share with the Author." (Isaiah 11:10, Jeremiah 23:5)

"Yes," Amos chimes in, "the walls of David's house are broken down. We tore up the Author's promises with our own hands, and they lay in shreds at our feet. But the Rescuer is picking up each piece, putting the house back together, making a new house with room enough for image-bearers from all corners of the world!" (Amos 9:11-12)

"See how gently He does it!" Isaiah sings tenderly. "He comes gently to the hurting; they stream to Him! Bodies are broken, racked with the disease of sin, eyes blind, legs lame, tongues mute. He heals them, saying, 'Come to Me! For I am yours, and you are Mine!' Filled with the Author's Spirit like His Temple, He stoops to bind up broken bodies, whispering hope to the downcast, gazing deeply into the eyes of those who have known more tragedy than an image-bearer ever should. With the sound of His voice, He's breaking off chains, prison doors swing open. Everyone cries tears of joy, dancing, and singing, and celebrating! This is what we've longed for!" Isaiah shouts his praise, unable to hold back his joy. (Isaiah 42:1–4; 35:5–6; 61:1-3)

"Here He comes to be crowned King!" joins Zechariah, heart overflowing with excitement. "Listen as the people rejoice! They're shouting and waving, welcoming their King into Jerusalem! Like the kings of old, He rides into the city on a young donkey, humble yet victorious!" But suddenly grief-stricken and shocked, he cries out, "What is this I see? The Rescuer's close friend sneaks away. He sells our Rescuer for a mere thirty pieces of silver?!" (Zechariah 9:9; 11:12-13)

King David, no stranger to betrayal, steps forward to sing, "This close friend has turned against our King. Before it's all over, His other close friends will flee, dreading the thought that what is about to happen to Him might happen to them, too. He welcomed them as brothers; now they pretend they never knew Him, and our King is all alone. We are about to see the extent of His Always Love!" (Psalm 31:11; 35:11; 41:9; 69:8; 109:4)

"I hardly even recognize Him," Isaiah mourns as the tune becomes slow and dismal. "Could this be the same King we welcomed into Jerusalem? Battered and bleeding, disfigured from beatings, is there even life left in Him? Why is such suffering in this song?" (Isaiah 52:13-15)

King David puts his arm around Isaiah, "I heard our Rescuer say, 'Here I am. I've come to do everything this Story said I would do, however brutal it may be, whatever sacrifice it may require.'" (Psalm 40:6–8)

Isaiah sings through his tears, "I see a Lamb—like a Passover lamb—perfect and trusting, taken in by our family, but going quietly to His death. But friends, *we* are the sheep! We wandered from our Shepherd, believing we could find the Good Life on our own. Now He takes our place. They yell at Him, accusing Him of things He never did. It's just an excuse to kill Him." Isaiah doubles over in grief, "How could the Author write a Story like this? Like a Temple sacrifice, He takes the sin of the world on Himself, as if all the evil ever done in this world were His own. Then He surrenders. With the last drops of His life dripping out of Him, He cries out His last words, 'My life is in Your hands.'" (Isaiah 50:6; 52:13-53:12)

"I see Him, too," Zechariah quietly joins the singing once again. "We all see Him, pierced, broken...gone." (Zechariah 12:10)

"Lifeless, they put Him in a grave," Isaiah can barely speak, "but I thought He was the King. I thought He was our Rescuer." (Isaiah 50:6; 53:9)

The music stops. Bitterness and grief beyond words holds the messengers captive as they sit mourning for three days. The Rescuer, who was to make everything in the Story right again, had died and buried their hope with Him.

But then, something like a ray of light—like the beginning of a new song—streams into the hearts of the messengers. A breeze brings hope into their despairing hearts, giving melody to their voices once again, for they see something even more surprising than a suffering Rescuer. A Rescuer brought back to life!

Infused with new strength, Isaiah sings again, "There on the hill, the Rescuer answered the question of what it would take to make us new! He destroyed death by death, and now the death sentence that hung over us all is gone, wiped away by His new life. He's the Rescuer after all!" (Isaiah 25:7–8)

"His death swallowed up sin, our greatest enemy, and all that remains is righteousness, newness, and the unending Good Life the Author always intended!" sings Daniel. (Daniel 9:24)

"Yes, it's Your heart of Always Love!" Malachi's voice explodes in praise to the Author. "You sweep away our sins into the deepest sea and pour out Always Love on us. As far back as Abraham, Isaac, and Jacob, You promised to be faithful, and You have been, oh Author, You have been!" (Malachi 7:19-20)

"But there's more!" Joel exclaims, and he and Isaiah begin to sing a beautiful duet, "The Author pours His Spirit out on image-bearers like water poured out on thirsty ground. Women and men, young and old, will house the Rescuer's Spirit!" (Joel 2:28-29, Isaiah 44:3)

"Yes! Image-bearers from every nation gather around His throne, each a Temple of the Author, worshiping the Rescuer in their own language!" Tears stream down Daniel's face as he sings with joy. (Daniel 7:13–14)

"The troubled and oppressed from all over the world stream to Him," David sings. "Crowds and crowds of image-bearers come to His throne, trusting Him, for they are His, and He is theirs, and He lives with them forever!" (Psalm 9:7–10; 68:18; 110:1)

"So keep singing," the Author whispers over His messengers. "Sing because My Story is not over yet. Sing because My people have wandered far from Me and need to hear the way back. Sing because I am faithful and Always Love, and the Rescuer will come, just as I promised!"

Chapter 32

400 Years & Changes
Intertestamental Period

"Author of All Life, thank you for writing me into Your Story as a man—not as a Gentile, a woman, or a slave," Jacob prayed as he did every morning, bowing toward Jerusalem. It was commonly believed that all three were decidedly lower in worth than a Jewish man, and Jacob wholeheartedly agreed. He finished his prayers and rose to leave for the synagogue.

Jacob was a Jew, a term now used for Israelites who survived the exile, since most were from the tribe of Judah. And being a devout Jew, he embodied many of the commonly-held opinions and beliefs of the people of his day.

"Joseph, come, my son! Let's go to the synagogue!" Jacob called. His eleven-year-old son appeared in the courtyard and ran to follow his father out of the house and into the street. "Father, do you think *you* would have become king if it weren't for the Romans?" he asked excitedly.

Jacob gave his son a sideways glance. "What have you been thinking about to ask such a question?" Then without waiting for an answer, he continued, "Well, my son, it's not for us to know what would have been. We are of the royal line of David, this much we know. We can trace our family history back to him—and back through Abraham to Adam himself!" Jacob's heart swelled with pride as he thought of his pure and noble blood. But then he sighed, "But it's not just the Romans who keep a son of David from being on the throne again."

"Really?" asked Joseph inquisitively.

"You know the Story, my son," Jacob replied. "Centuries ago the Author picked up His pen and wrote us out of this land because we were unfaithful to the Binding Promise, and it simply hasn't been the same since. After the Babylonians came the Persians."

"Which is when Zerubbabel rebuilt the Temple!" interjected Joseph.

"Yes, then the Greeks came along and conquered the Persians," Jacob continued.

"Alexander the Great!" Joseph interjected once again, trying to hide his boyhood fascination of the great leader. "By the time he was thirty he ruled the whole world!"

Jacob raised an eyebrow, hardly amused. "Well, yes, our lives are influenced by the Greeks. In fact, Jews all over the world read the Book of the Binding Promise in Greek since Ptolemy II translated every book ever written into Greek. That's helpful for Jews who have forgotten Hebrew. But we are not like that. Remember, we are pure Jews." Jacob emphasized the difference for his son.

"Anyway, Greek rule of Jerusalem wasn't always good," Jacob shook his head in disgust. "What Antiochus Epiphanes did to our people was detestable! He stopped Temple sacrifices, tortured our people in the Temple court, made us eat unclean things, and built altars to his gods around Jerusalem and turned Zerubbabel's Temple into a house for Zeus!" Jacob grew angrier as he spoke. "But the worst thing of all was when he sacrificed a *pig* on the altar of incense!"

"Was the Author mad at us again, father? Did we deserve to have our enemies come against us like that?" Joseph asked genuinely.

"No, my son," Jacob replied with a sigh. "Of course, we are by no means as faithful as we should be. Jews must strive to keep the Binding Promise better than we have; but if there is one thing our exile did, it purged us of idolatry! Since then, our people have worked hard to do the right thing."

"Then why did it happen, father? First, Babylonians destroyed Solomon's Temple, then Antiochus Epiphanes defiled Zerubbabel's Temple. Why?" Joseph searched his father's eyes for the answer.

Jacob could only shrug his shoulders and say, "My son, we do not know. At times, it seems the Author has forgotten us. He hasn't sent us a messenger now for almost 400 years! He hasn't been silent this long since our people were in Egypt. How are we to make sense of the Story now? That is why we must be faithful to the Binding Promise. Unfaithfulness got us into this mess; faithfulness will get us out of it. Sometimes I think the Pharisees may be right," Jacob wondered aloud. "Sometimes it seems they add more rules than necessary to the Binding Promise, turning the Ten Words and the Author's Always Love into a long list of rules. But perhaps it is better to be safe than sorry, as they say—better to make *extra* rules to follow than to accidentally break the Binding Promise." Jacob shrugged, "Well, at least we have the synagogue! We only need ten Jewish men to start one, and there we can memorize the Book of the Binding Promise, hear the Story explained, and pray to the Author together."

"Sacrifices aren't made in synagogues, though; but at least King Herod is building us a new Temple in Jerusalem," offered Joseph. "We can sacrifice there."

"Yes, they say it will be nice. Herod drew up the plans, put them on display, and things are well underway, but it will take decades to build. And of course, King Herod does it only to gain our favor. Never forget, Joseph, Herod is *not* the true king of the Jews! He's a worthless son of Esau put in power by the Romans!"

"Well, the Romans have done a *little* good for our people, right father? They got rid of the Greeks!" Joseph offered.

"We Jews have such mixed feelings about the Romans," sighed Jacob. "Yes, we welcomed their help to overthrow the Greeks, thinking Roman rule would be better; but it's just as bad—only in different ways."

"Yesterday, I heard a Roman centurion built a synagogue for his Jewish friends!" Joseph marveled.

"Not all Romans are bad, I suppose," Jacob conceded. "They've united the world with their roads and brought peace to their empire like the world has never known."

"I suppose," Joseph thought aloud, "the only thing to do is to keep hoping the Rescuer will come. He will come, won't He, father?"

"Of course! I don't know when, but surely if we're faithful enough the Author will send the Rescuer," Jacob hoped, lowering his voice, not wanting his patriotic sentiments to get him into trouble. "If He were to come now, He would overthrow the Romans, dethrone King Herod the imposter, sit on the throne in Jerusalem, and everyone would see that we are the Author's chosen people!"

"But what if we don't recognize the Rescuer when He comes? Suppose we don't support Him enough, and He can't overthrow the Romans?" the young boy grappled with questions that felt heavy on his mind and heart.

"Nonsense, my son. You know the Book of the Binding Promise," Jacob replied. "The messenger Malachi says Elijah will come right before the Rescuer. We won't miss the Rescuer with Elijah pointing Him out!"

"But will He rescue just the Jews—or the Samaritans, too? They're also waiting for the Rescuer, right?" Joseph asked inquisitively.

Jacob cringed, "Not the Samaritans! They're a bunch of filthy half-breeds! They only *wish* they were the Author's people. Half-Israelite, half-pagan Gentile, they claim to worship the Author but make sacrifices to Him outside Jerusalem! Can you believe it? But the Rescuer will make all things right. Just keep away from Samaritans in the meantime," he added emphatically. "A good Jew has nothing to do with Samaritans—or Gentiles."

"Why do we hate Gentiles?" Joseph inquired.

"Gentiles worship idols and eat things that are unclean. They don't care about the Author or His Binding Promise. We must stay pure and not mingle with them. Ah, well, here we are!" Jacob said with a sudden change of emotion as they arrived at the synagogue.

Jacob and Joseph washed outside before entering the synagogue, then found their seats as the rabbi, their teacher, stood up to begin. Young Joseph's mouth followed along reciting the verses and prayers, but his heart was too distracted to pay attention. His father's conversation with him stirred his heart in ways he didn't understand. Suddenly, his ears perked up. What was the rabbi saying about kingdoms coming and going? The rabbi continued reading from Daniel's book, "The Author's Kingdom will always remain. One day it will crush all other kingdoms and stand victorious forever!"

Daniel's words made Joseph's heart soar. If only the true King would come—or at least a messenger like Daniel! Surely it was time for the Rescuer to put an end to the long list of kingdoms that had ruled over his people. Joseph's thoughts wandered as he imagined what the Rescuer would be like. Would He be young and brave like Alexander the Great? Would He ride in on a majestic horse, setting His people free? Would Joseph get to fight in any battles? Would he live to see the Rescuer become King and sit on His throne?

Hope still whispered on the wind. And even though the Author seemed silent, dear Reader, we know too much of the Author's faithfulness to believe He has forgotten. For centuries, He had been working on a worldwide scale to ready not just the Jews—but the whole world!—for the next chapter of the Story.

Chapter 33

A Priest & A Maiden
Luke 1

"No!" cried Zechariah the priest, shaking with fear. "Please don't hurt me!" He shielded his eyes from the magnificent creature that had suddenly appeared before him.

"Zechariah," the angel replied, "don't be afraid. I'm not here to hurt you!" The creature stood still beside the altar of incense waiting for Zechariah to compose himself.

On that particular day, Zechariah was serving as priest in Herod's Temple in Jerusalem. It was an honor to enter alone into a place where few were allowed to go, to symbolically take the people of Israel into the Author's presence and worship Him in a way few were privileged to worship. Zechariah's heart was full of excitement when he walked in, but now his heart was gripped with fear.

"Zechariah, I'm bringing great news! After four hundred years of what may have seemed like silence, the Author is beginning a new chapter in the Story and inviting you to be a part of it. He has heard your prayer, Zechariah, and will give you and your wife, Elizabeth, a son and will fill him with His own Spirit even before he is born!" The angel could hardly contain his joy as he spoke. "The Author is about to send the Rescuer, Zechariah! Like Elijah, your son will be a messenger going before Him, preparing people's hearts to be faithful to a new Binding Promise. Oh, and Zechariah, when he's born, name your son John."

"But I am so old!" Zechariah doubted. "And so is my wife! Can you prove to me this is true?"

Zechariah and Elizabeth were indeed much older than first-time parents usually are. For so long they had been faithful to the Author and for so long they had wanted a child. Now the Author was going to give them a son who would play a crucial role in the Story, but Zechariah doubted it was possible.

"Zechariah," the angel admonished, "I, the angel Gabriel, am always in the Author's presence. He gave me this message, and I came straight here to relay it. Yet you don't believe me? The proof you will get is this: while the Story continues to unfold around you, your mouth will be unable to tell of its joy until the day my words come true." With that, the angel left him.

Zechariah was literally speechless. He quickly turned to leave the Temple after wrapping up his priestly duties and left Jerusalem to return home to his wife. Though his lips could not explain it, and his attempts to communicate it hardly felt sufficient, it was unmistakable that the Author was doing something incredible in the life of this faithful couple.

In the quiet town of Nazareth, a young girl was going about the ordinary business of any girl her age. Excited and hopeful, she was waiting for the day when her fiancé, Joseph, would take her as his bride to begin their new life together.

"Mary," called a voice behind her. She turned to see who it was. But her eyes grew wide, and she stood there, not knowing what to think or feel with this creature standing before her.

"Mary! The Author Always Loves you!" the angel said to her.

Mary's lower lip quivered. What could this mean? Who was this standing before her?

Once again, Gabriel appeared to relay another special message to another special person about another special Baby. "Mary, don't be afraid," the angel spoke soothingly to the trembling young girl. "Today the Author is writing you into the Story in a most incredible way! The Author has handpicked *you* to be the one to usher in the long-awaited Rescuer! You will give birth to Him!" The angel could hardly contain his joy. "Mary, He is the one the Story has pointed to from the beginning. Every promise the Author ever made will come true in Him! He, a son of David, will sit on the throne and rule as King, and His Kingdom will never end! And Mary, the Rescuer's name will be Jesus, which means 'The Author rescues!'"

A quizzical expression came over the young girl's face as she replied, "Yes, but…how? Because I'm not yet married…" and her voice trailed off in wonder.

"Remember how the Story began?" Gabriel replied. "Everything was dark, and the Author's presence hovered over the vast, empty canvas of creation and gently breathed the most beautiful words ever heard. Suddenly, a brilliant and beautiful light pierced the darkness, and on that day, creation was conceived and birthed! Well, Mary, the Author's presence will do something similar in you. His presence will come, and in this world held captive to darkness, in the hidden depths of your being, the Author's voice will speak the most beautiful Word. A light will dawn.

A new creation will be conceived in you and then birthed. The Author's rescue plan is already well underway. Six months ago I went to Zechariah with a similar message; and his wife, your cousin Elizabeth, is expecting the messenger who will prepare the way for your Son."

It was too much for Mary's human mind to comprehend, yet her human heart with all its might, grabbed hold of the Always Love being poured into the world and said, "Yes! I am the Author's, and He is mine! May He bring to pass everything you have said!" With that, the angel left her.

Mary was speechless. She was an ordinary girl. Her name was the most common name for girls in her day, and yet she was picked out of all the girls, out of all the Marys for something extraordinary. The Author invited her to be a new Eve. Where Eve gave in to unbelief and disobedience, Mary obeyed and believed. Where Eve had listened to the enemy, a fallen angel, Mary instead listened to an angel of light. Eve came from the first Adam while Mary would give birth to the new Adam! She would give birth to the Rescuer who would undo all the brokenness and death created by sin, just as the Author had promised in the Garden! Her heart felt like it could burst; yet how could she explain what she just experienced? The only one who would understand would be Elizabeth. She turned to gather a few belongings and left town to visit her cousin.

Elizabeth bent over to coax the hot coals into flame before they burned out completely. Even the simplest tasks now required more effort with her round and growing belly often getting in the way.

"Cousin Elizabeth?" called a voice from behind.

Suddenly, the baby inside Elizabeth startled her—wiggling with excitement! She dropped the stick she had been using to poke the fire, grabbed hold of her life-filled belly, turned, and exclaimed, "Mary! To what do I owe this honor, that my Rescuer's mother would come to visit?"

In reply, Mary's heart burst forth in song! What else could it do? What else would *you* do, Reader, if you were swept up into the Author's rescue plan in the way Mary had been?

Unfolding we see a wonderful Story, filled with all the Author's glory,
Oh, the great things He will do!

Everything within me wants to sing, to give praise to our King,
Oh, the great things He will do!

He entered our world, spoke of good news to a young girl,
Oh, the great things He will do!

He calls all to His name, because of me all will hear of His fame!
Oh, the great things He will do!

The rich become poor, those without food hunger no more,
Oh, the great things He will do!

Those who abuse power soon will cower,
Oh, the great things He will do!

When He puts on the throne, one of Israel's own,
Oh, the great things He will do!

He hasn't forgotten us. His mercy astounds us!
Oh, the great things He will do!

Then all hearts will be thrilled, all His promises fulfilled!
By all the great things He will do!

Young Mary stayed with her cousin for the rest of Elizabeth's pregnancy, watching her belly grow bigger every day with the same hope that was now growing in Mary. Then, just as the angel had said, Elizabeth gave birth to a baby boy who washed away the shame that had hovered over barren Elizabeth all her adult life, a boy who brought his parents unspeakable joy, a boy who would usher in a move of the Author that would astound all who heard of it. He was the new Elijah, and his name was John.

Mary sat at the feet of Elizabeth and Zechariah, awed by their faith, gazing at the baby messenger with her own eyes. She placed her hand on her belly as she listened to John's infant cries that would grow to be the cries of a man calling all people to the Author's Always Love.

When Zechariah, the old doubting priest, held his baby boy in his arms, his tongue, suddenly loosed, let out nine months of pent up praise:

All praise to the Author! We have nothing to fear!
The promised Son of David is now drawing near!
To bring us back to the Author of All Life!

What mercy He's showing,
All our enemies He's overthrowing!
He will show us the Author of All Life.

And you, my son, will prepare His way,
Showing through forgiveness, the dawn of a new day,
When all can be made right with the Author of All Life.

Fear, darkness, and death will be overcome,
By the great mercy of David's Son.
He'll guide us back to the Author of All Life.

Chapter 34

Courage & A Baby
Matthew 1
Luke 2:1-20

Mary swayed back and forth as the donkey took step after step toward Bethlehem. She sighed, trying to adjust her stiff and tired body. They would be there soon, which was good because she wasn't so sure her pregnant body could take much more of a trip like this. The timing of this journey was hardly convenient.

Mary let her mind wander back to the day Joseph came home and told her the news. "Mary, we have to leave town," he had said. He drew near and explained, "The Roman emperor is taking a census, and we all have to register. Because my family is from the line of David, I—we—have to go to Bethlehem."

"Bethlehem?" asked Mary, "but that's so far away…and the Baby?" She looked into her husband's eyes wondering how it would work out.

"I know," Joseph sighed. "You'll have to have the Baby there—far from home."

Courage had been key since the day the angel appeared to her. Courage to say "yes" to an invitation that would change her life and reputation forever. Courage to tell her community that she was pregnant, but that it was the Author's doing, not her own. Courage to tell Joseph and risk the awful ways he could have ended their relationship—or even her life. Now she was courageously leaving behind her community, her home, to have her Baby far away. She, a young woman of such great courage, looked down at the man beside her, leading the donkey, walking step by step to Bethlehem. The mystery of it all welled up inside her. Joseph, son of David, leading Mary, mother of the promised Son of David, back to Bethlehem, to the place where this royal line began. It seemed mysteriously fitting.

Joseph, sensing Mary's gaze on him as they traveled, turned to look up at her and smiled. Then it was Joseph's turn to get lost in his thoughts. His mind wandered back to the afternoon when he left his father's carpentry shop to wander along the outskirts of Nazareth to clear his mind and heart. Oh, the turmoil he had felt inside! Mary, his fiancée at the time, had just returned from visiting family, and had come back pregnant! He remembered wondering, "How could she do this? My whole family thought she was a woman of character and purity. Doesn't she know what this will do for her reputation—the shame it brings on her family?" He resolved that afternoon to break their engagement—but in a way that didn't ruin Mary's life. "I'll do it quietly," he determined. "Poor girl, her reputation— her very life—is in my hands! She deserves to be stoned! I could really hurt her, but I won't. She has hurt me dearly, but I won't do the same to her." There. That was his decision.

He returned to his father's carpentry shop in town to finish his day's work and then lay down early to sleep, tired from such an emotional day. But his sleep was fitful that night. He tossed and turned as if the emotions that had played tug-of-war with his heart all day were now playing tug-of-war with his body as he slept. Suddenly he stilled.

"Joseph," a voice called to him, but Joseph didn't wake up. He didn't need to for the voice was calling to him in his dream.

"Joseph, son of David," the voice continued; and as it did, the one speaking became more clear: it was an angel! One of the Author's angels now stood before him in a dream! "Joseph, don't let fear keep you from marrying Mary. Take her as your wife. She is pregnant, yes; but do you remember what the messenger Isaiah said long ago? He said a young girl who is not yet married will give birth to a Baby. Well, guess what—that's Mary. So marry her, and name the Baby 'Jesus,' because He is the one who will bring the Author's presence to live among His people!"

Joseph bolted upright, wide awake, sweating, and overwhelmed with what he'd just heard. The Rescuer? Growing inside Mary?! "Well," Joseph muttered to himself, "the mystery is no longer because of the actions of Mary. It's the Author's actions that are a mystery! And how courageous of Mary to say 'yes' to this! What reproach she will have to bear! But now, we will bear it together."

Joseph smiled as he looked up again at Mary as they journeyed closer to Bethlehem. "To think I almost said 'no' to this!" he reflected. He still was unsure of what it would mean but he knew they were in it together.

As Joseph led their donkey into Bethlehem, a sense of dread came over him. It seemed that all the world claimed to be a descendant of King David. Bethlehem was bursting at the seams. Where would all these people stay? Where would *they* stay?

A blinding light burst across the night sky. The sheep went berserk, bleating and darting here and there.

"Don't be afraid!" a glowing, other-worldly creature said to the poor shepherds cowering before him.

Once again, an angel had appeared. He smiled saying, "I'm bringing the greatest news in all the world!" trying to reassure the shepherds that he meant them no harm. The Author was inviting them to be among the first to meet the newly-born Rescuer. The angel continued, "Today, in Bethlehem, the Rescuer all Israel has been waiting for was born! You'll recognize Him when you see Him because you will find Him, snuggled tight in strips of cloth, sleeping in a feeding trough."

The shepherds blinked their eyes and turned to each other as if to ask, "Are you seeing what I'm seeing and hearing what I'm hearing?" But suddenly it was as if heaven couldn't contain itself. The sky lit up, filled with angels shouting, "The Author's Always Love is on display! May the world be filled with His peace!" While all the world lay still and quiet, thinking it just another night, heaven could not contain its joy—for the Story had just gotten so good!

What a spectacular birth announcement to the most unexpected audience! Of all the kings, religious leaders, and important people who could have received this honor and heard this incredible announcement, the Author chose a group of unimportant men, the working-class poor, and invited them to be among the first to meet the Rescuer. As so often has happened in the Story, once again, in an upside-down way, the Author wrote those at the bottom of society into a place of honor.

"Let's go!" each of the shepherds blurted out as they ran off together in the direction of Bethlehem, swept up into the mystery unfolding before their eyes.

They searched and searched until they found Him. "There He is! It's just like the angel said!" they whispered as they entered the room and stared at the Baby sleeping peacefully before them.

There He was, dear Reader. The long-awaited Rescuer had slipped quietly into this world, wrapped in simple cloths, and entrusted to two young parents who needed a Rescuer as much as anyone else. His tiny body housed a presence the universe could not contain. His powerless form held within it the power that flung the stars into the sky and put planets into motion. His tiny, pursed lips, yet unable to form one intelligible word, were the lips of the Word Himself who had brought the words of this Story to life. What a mystery that the Author Himself would come to us like this! What an unexpected way to keep the lamp in David's house burning! What a strange way to rescue the world!

Were it not for such a clear announcement that the Author was writing a new chapter in the Story, everyone would have missed it. And so many did; but a few did not. Seemingly insignificant shepherds watching sheep at night, a seemingly insignificant young married couple with an invitation to be a part of rescuing the world, all meeting in a seemingly insignificant town to witness the most significant part of the Story yet: the birth of our Rescuer. That night, in a room in a house in Bethlehem, Always Love came to live among us, and the Story would never be the same.

Faithful in the Water & in the Wilderness

Matthew 3-4:1-11
Mark 1:1-13
Luke 3-4:1-13
John 1:19-34
Deuteronomy 6:13-16; 8:2-3
Psalm 91:11-12

Grown-up John, son of Zechariah and Elizabeth, had created such a stir in Jerusalem and Judea that a crowd of Pharisees came to scowl and sneer. "Look at him!" they mocked, peering down their noses, "He's treating real Jews as if they were Gentiles! Only Gentiles wanting to become Jews should be baptized. What a disgrace!"

But John saw them coming and had his own words to share. "Serpent children, what brings you to the river today? Surely you haven't come to be baptized! You're too stuck in your ways, thinking you're the true Israel—as if being born into Jacob's family and keeping your list of rules makes the Author accept you. The Author is creating a new Israel, sealing it with a new Binding Promise! Your life shows which Israel you belong to. These river waters will rescue some, but for others, it will sweep them away to destruction."

The Pharisees' hard hearts kept them from seeing the Author at work among them, but in spite of their snickering, many people longed for a new Israel. Anticipation for the Rescuer was high, and John kept preaching his simple message to point people in the right direction: "The Author's Kingdom is here and now! So change the way you live!"

John's message stirred up such a longing in people's hearts that they came to the riverbank in droves to be baptized in water, anticipating the day when the Rescuer would baptize them with the Author's Spirit. One by one they followed John into the Jordan River to name their sins, openly expressing their need for the Rescuer. Under the water they went, to then be raised new and fresh, proving the Author's Kingdom was already breaking into their hearts.

The Jordan River was a significant river in Israel's history. More than a thousand years before, Joshua led his people across the Jordan to enter their new life in the Promised Land. Now John was inviting Israelites into that very same river to enter a new life in a new Promised Land—the Author's Kingdom.

Every day John preached his simple message, and every day people responded. But everyday John was doing something else: looking for the Rescuer. And one day He showed up!

"Here He is!" the new Elijah pointed out the Rescuer. "Like a sacrificial lamb, the innocent will give His life for the guilty!"

Jesus came to the riverbank asking John to baptize Him.

"Oh, but that isn't how it should be!" John replied, "What sort of an upside-down Kingdom would this be if I wash You? You should wash me!"

But Jesus insisted so that He could be faithful in all the ways Israel was not. As He waded into the water, He willingly identified with image-bearers, with our soul-deep need for the Author. Like a new Joshua, He went into the Jordan

River to lead His new Israel into their new life. Submerging Himself into a Story older than time, He rose from the water, hair sopping, beard dripping, clothes clinging to His wet skin, to be met by the Author's presence as heaven invaded earth once again. The Author hugged Him with His presence and, like a dad delighted with his child, the Author proclaimed, "Son, I am Yours, and You are Mine! You bring Me immeasurable joy!"

Through water, the Author's Spirit birthed a new Israel that day. And just as the first Israel was birthed through the Red Sea and immediately went into the desert, the new Israel experienced the same.

The desert sun beat down on Him, and the parched ground crunched beneath His feet. After forty days without food or drink, feeling the pain of hunger and the ache of thirst, the Rescuer was weak, just as the first Israel had been in the wilderness. In His weakness, He heard the voice of a creature slithering up behind Him. "I heard the Author call You His Son," it hissed.

It was the voice of the one who had snaked his way into the Garden to sow doubt and fear into image-bearers' hearts and bring the beautiful Garden relationship to ruins. He had slithered into the Israelite camp in the wilderness, sowing doubts that the Author would provide, sowing fear that He wanted them to suffer. The enemy knew the first image-bearers were meant to take the Garden relationship global, and he hated it. He knew the Israelites were meant to take the Promised Land relationship global, and he hated that. And he knew the Rescuer had come to take the Author's Always Love and make it global, and he hated that, too. Once again, he slithered into the Story to try to ruin it.

"Well," the voice hissed, "if You're really His Son, prove it. Provide bread for Yourself in this barren wilderness!"

In spite of His hunger, the Word drew a sharp sword and cut the enemy's temptation to shreds with His words, "When Israel wandered in the wilderness, the Author humbled them with hunger and thirst to see if they'd trust Him. He taught them that the Author's Word sustains them—not bread. I will trust the Author to provide the bread I need."

"Alright," hissed the enemy. "If You trust Him, prove it! The Author once said He would send angels to protect His people. Why don't You climb to the top of the Temple in Jerusalem and throw Yourself down!" The enemy smiled cleverly. "He'd surely send His angels to rescue *You*! How will You rescue the world if You die?" The enemy cackled, "When the Author rescues You then everyone will be in awe and follow You!"

Jesus glared at his enemy. "So, you want Me to grab the pen from the Author's hand and write a Story for Myself like Israel tried to do in the wilderness? Your schemes worked on them but won't work on Me."

But the enemy was quick on his feet and ready with another proposition, "Perhaps, but I know every image-bearer hungers and thirsts for power. I rule all the kingdoms of the world! I could give them to You with a snap of my fingers! All it would take is a simple bow," he paused. "Bow to me, and the world is Yours. Isn't that why You came after all— to rule the whole world?"

Oh Reader, isn't that what the Rescuer came to do? To take all nations and make them His own? To sit on the throne as the true King while all the earth's kings acknowledged His rule? With a simple bow, Jesus could bypass anything that might lie ahead in the rescue plan and become King *right now!*

But the enemy had gone too far.

"Enemy, you'd better run far and fast!" Jesus firmly replied. "There is *NO* way I'm bowing to you. Moses taught the Israel of old not to worship *any* other god, or the Author would destroy them. I see what you're up to and I'm not falling for it. I worship the Author alone. Now get out of here!"

The enemy slithered off for now, but as he did he muttered, "He may have won this battle, but the war is not over!" Determined to foil the Author's plan, he crept into the shadows to wait for another opportunity.

The Author kept His Word, sending angels to care for Him in danger and providing bread in the wilderness, for no sooner had the enemy departed than glorious angels arrived with sustenance for His faithful Son.

While faithfulness to the Author seemed to elude the Israel of the old Binding Promise, Jesus' heart beat with fidelity. Where Israel doubted the Author's provision, constantly putting Him to the test, Jesus didn't question it—waiting patiently, knowing both provision and power would come in the Author's time, in the Author's way. Pain and suffering revealed Israel's lack of trust in the Author, while pain and suffering caused the Rescuer's trust to flourish. While Israel bowed to the gods of this world to try to ensure the Good Life, Jesus refused, convinced it would only bring death. Rejecting immediate power and glory, Jesus trusted the Author to give both in His time and in His way. Israel had struggled to live like the Author's Always Loved children, but Jesus never doubted for a moment that Always Love was His, and the Author would be a good Daddy.

Confident in the Always Love of His Father, refreshed by the Author's bread in the wilderness, filled with power from the Author's presence, Jesus left the wilderness victorious. Faithful in all the ways the first Israel was not, He was ready to begin His rescue mission.

Chapter 36

Mundanity & Mystery

Matthew 2:2-18; 4:12-25
Luke 2:21-40; 4:14-5:1-11, 27-32; 6:12-16
Mark 3:13-19
John 1:35-51

"Jesus will read today from the Book of the Binding Promise," the synagogue attendant announced, handing Jesus a scroll.

The people in Nazareth's synagogue knew Jesus as Joseph's son, a carpenter by trade, firstborn in His family, born to Mary whose pregnancy was shrouded in scandal. Despite His questionable beginnings, Jesus had amazed His teachers with His wisdom; but despite His wisdom, He was very plain—an ordinary part of Nazareth's mundane, everyday life.

Standing before family and long-time friends, Jesus opened His mouth to read Isaiah's words, "The Author's Spirit has filled Me to send Me to the fringes of society—to the outcasts, poor and rejected, to tell them the Author's incredible Story. He sent Me to forgive debts, to release all captives from chains. He sent Me to open blind eyes, to free the oppressed, to tell them the Rescuer-King is here!"

Jesus rolled up the scroll, gave it back to the attendant, and took His seat.

All eyes fixed on Jesus as they waited for Him to explain the text He read, as any synagogue teacher would do after reading. But Jesus simply said, "Today, these words are no longer a distant hope. They've come true."

Immediately, the synagogue buzzed with chatter. "But this is Joseph's son? He's just a carpenter. What does He mean by saying these words are no longer a distant hope?"

Others, enraged by what Jesus implied, scowled, "Who does He think He is, calling Himself the Rescuer?"

As the synagogue hummed with questions, Jesus' mother sat listening and remembering old Simeon from thirty years ago. Standing in the Temple in Jerusalem, Simeon had scooped Jesus up into his arms exclaiming, "This Child of yours is the Rescuer! A gift to Israel, a light to all nations—right here in my arms!" But then, as he gently placed the newborn back in Mary's arms, a sadness came over him as he said, "This Child's role in the Story is hardly ordinary. Like a sword, He'll separate kingdoms and people, deposing rulers, setting up new ones. He'll cut through life, exposing what is deep and true and real; and Mary, my daughter," Simeon paused, "the sword will cut deeply through your own heart, too."

Mary hadn't known what to do with such declarations over her Baby. All day, all night He needed her for life, comfort, and care; and in the haze of sleepless nights and new motherhood, it was hard to see how it would lead anywhere. He was such a mystery! Yet now her grown Son spoke of the Rescuer—called Himself the Rescuer! She stared at her Son, who sat shrouded in both mystery and mundanity until suddenly her heart stopped with fright as she heard someone shout, "We should stone Him for claiming equality with the Author!"

In seconds, an angry mob of Jesus' friends and relatives forced Him out of the synagogue and toward a cliff where they would throw Him to His death. Who did He think He was, claiming to be more than just a guy from a small town in Israel?

Tears welled up in Mary's eyes, and fear gripped her heart as the mob carried away her Son. Frantically, she rose to follow, her mind flooded with another flashback from decades ago.

"Mary!" Joseph had exclaimed, bolting upright in bed in the middle of the night. "Mary, we have to leave Israel this instant! The same angel that told me to marry you just told me King Herod has heard of Jesus and is searching for Him—to kill Him! He thinks Jesus is a threat to his throne! We have to go to Egypt right away! This very minute!"

Darkness hid the young family as they sneaked out of Bethlehem, sneaked out of Israel, and sneaked into a nation that earlier in the Story had enslaved their people violently, yet would now shield them from the violent fury King Herod was about to unleash.

But now, what could rescue her grown Son? She couldn't whisk Jesus away to Egypt; no angel had warned them of His impending doom. What was it about her Son that had already endangered His life twice?

For all the joy Jesus' life brought into the world, it also rattled the chains of darkness, upsetting a long-uncontested reign of evil. For centuries it looked as if the Rescuer would never come. For millennia, the kingdom of darkness seeped into all corners of the world. Now feeling threatened, a dark force was at work, slithering into the Story to stomp out any trace of hope, to snuff out the light that began to pierce the darkness.

Suddenly, Mary gasped as she watched her firstborn calmly walk away from the mob, mysteriously unscathed! Gratitude overwhelmed her, even while her Son became more mysterious to her.

As Mary watched Him walk into the distance, leaving Nazareth behind, she thought of the days when He toddled about, exploring His world within the safety of her reach. What a shock the day she glanced outside the window to see a royal caravan stopped at her front door! Camels knelt to allow their riders to dismount, and the riders grabbed hold of rich treasures, carrying them to the young Child's house.

"We've come from far away," the foreigners explained, "where we heard of your Son, seeing His coming in the stars! We came to worship the Rescuer of the world!"

Grown men knelt before the Toddler who bashfully hid behind the folds of Mary's robe, overwhelmed by the flood of visitors and shiny things into His usually mundane surroundings.

"We've brought gifts for the King," they told Mary, handing the young mother a treasure trove of gold so pure she could see her reflection in it. "Gold, because He is King!"

"And frankincense," said another, placing the gift in Mary's arms, its rich smell reminding her of the incense used in Jerusalem's Temple. "Frankincense is the tears from a tree that grows tenaciously in unforgiving soil. May the life of our small King grow, even in unforgiving soil, even through many tears, as a fragrant offering to the Author."

"And myrrh," a third guest said, presenting a final gift. Young Mary's heart twinged with mystery, and she pulled tiny Jesus close to her. How odd to give a toddler something ordinarily used in burial!

Already in His life, Jesus had shepherds running from the fields to meet Him, men journeying from a foreign land to bow before Him, and hopeful old Simeon singing His praises in the Temple. But now their quiet community was in an uproar, running Jesus from His hometown. She watched her carpenter Son fade into the distance, shrouded in mundanity and mystery.

Jesus left Nazareth, rejected by His community but resolved to create a new community and carry out the rescue plan. One morning, after spending the whole night praying on a mountain, He began calling out names from a crowd, "Peter, Andrew, James, and John, come stand with Me," Jesus motioned for them to come to Him. "Philip and Bartholomew, come to Me, too," Jesus invited. "Matthew, Thomas, James and Simon, Thaddeus, and also Judas Iscariot—all of you come close."

Like Jacob standing with his twelve sons, Jesus stood with His twelve disciples. As the not-yet-crowned-King David gathered around himself a band of courageous but questionable men, Jesus gathered this group of fishermen, tradesmen, zealots, and a tax collector. As people on the fringes, they were rough around the edges, not very educated, with thick accents and from small towns. They were hardly the obvious choice as disciples; but in the upside-down Kingdom Jesus was bringing, they were the exact sort of people the Author would write into this chapter.

And like the Author inviting His first image-bearers to take up their pens and collaborate with Him in the Story He was writing, Jesus invited these men to something similar, "My friends, I'm inviting you to live closely with Me and watch how I live in the Author's Always Love. We'll live out our role in His Story together, sharing the news that the Author's Kingdom is here and the reign of the kingdom of darkness is over!"

Though He was rejected in His hometown, wherever else He went Jesus drew a crowd. Filled with the Author's presence, He did everything He declared in Nazareth that He would do and taught His disciples to do it, too. When He taught, the words of the Author came alive, and image-bearers hung on His every Word. With a mere touch of His hand or whisper of His mouth, He could heal the most debilitating sickness or drive away the most stubborn evil spirit. Word spread from town to town as people lined up to be healed, set free, or simply hear Him speak. Each time the crowd gathered, this Man from Nazareth, still shrouded in mystery, took the news of the Author's Kingdom into mundane, everyday life—causing many to whisper among themselves, "Do you think Jesus could be the Rescuer, the one we've all been waiting for?"

A Mountain & A New Binding Promise

Matthew 4:12-17; 5-7
Luke 6:17-49
Isaiah 2:1-5

"The Author's Kingdom is here and now, so change the way you live!" was the message John the Baptist declared. But like so many of the Author's messengers, John the Baptist suffered for his message when King Herod threw him into prison and later took his life.

So Jesus picked up where John left off, proclaiming, "The Author's Kingdom is here and now! So change the way you live!" But what exactly did He mean by that?

Reminiscent of Moses climbing a mountain to receive the old Binding Promise for the Israelites, Jesus gathered His followers on a grassy mountainside to explain what He meant and teach them the heart of the new Binding Promise.

"You were created for the Good Life, living forever in the Author's Always Love, and Always Loving each other," Jesus began. "In the Author's upside-down Kingdom, He makes this possible by radically changing His image-bearers from the inside out. Rather than thinking He just wants you to *do the right thing*—like obeying laws on tablets of stone— you'll see He's inviting you to *become the right person,* whose heart longs to obey because your heart mirrors His own.

"The Good Life is found when you recognize and admit how bankrupt your spirit actually is. In My upside-down

Kingdom, your poverty becomes overflowing abundance, for I am yours, and you are Mine!

"The Good Life is found when you allow pain and grief to move you toward the Man of Sorrows. One day the Man of Sorrows will wipe all tears from your eyes and fill you with joy!

"The Good Life is found when You realize the Author's Kingdom doesn't come by force, but by surrendering to the Author, embracing weakness, and trusting Him to bring His Kingdom His way.

"The Good Life is found when you live like this world can never satisfy. Your satisfaction in My upside-down Kingdom will be all the richer because you've gone without."

Jesus' disciples shifted on the grass as they listened. Was it the hard ground beneath them or the hard words they were hearing that was making them feel uncomfortable? They chose to follow Jesus thinking He would overthrow their political enemies and restore the greatness Israel once enjoyed under King Solomon. They looked forward to sharing in the greatness of that Kingdom. So what did Jesus mean about not using force and embracing weakness to bring the Kingdom? Poverty, sorrow, and going without weren't very attractive.

"But there's more," Jesus's eyes twinkled. "Because the Author Always Loves His image-bearers, they can Always Love each other.

"The Good Life is found when you show mercy to each other, because you know you can never show more mercy than the Author shows you.

"The Good Life is found by Always Loving from the heart, not taking advantage of other image-bearers or grabbing for power. You'll be so refined, so pure, the Author's reflection will show in your heart!

"The Good Life is found by pursuing peace, imitating the Author by spreading peace in the same way He does.

"But friends, the world around you will resent your upside-down pursuit of the Good Life. So choose to feel the sting of rejection and persecution rather than self-protect, even when it causes you pain and rejection from your community. You'll lose citizenship in the many mini-kingdoms of this world but will get the Good Life in the Author's Kingdom in return. You'll be so full of joy you can't help but dance, because you are the Author's, and He is yours!"

The disciples weren't sure they liked what they were hearing. Rather than inviting them to start a revolution, Jesus was inviting them to suffer, make peace, and show mercy. They hadn't signed up for that!

"Friends," Jesus continued, "the brokenness of the world began in image-bearers' hearts. So acknowledging that brokenness is how you get the Good Life—not acting like you have it all together or forcing others to keep it together."

"But what about all the rules in the Binding Promise?" one disciple whispered to another, unsure of whether he should ask his question to Jesus.

Jesus heard him and answered, "This new Binding Promise doesn't mean the old one didn't work. The old Binding Promise is beautiful and wonderful and did what it needed to do. I'm here to fulfill *every* word of it! But the old Binding

Promise was never about following rules. It's about living with a heart that surpasses the faithfulness of Pharisees' hearts."

"What?" His disciples' eyes grew wide. "The Pharisees are the keepers of the Binding Promise! We're just common people—fishermen, a tax collector, nobodies! How can we be more faithful than the Pharisees?" Jesus' disciples muttered to each other.

But Jesus went on, "Let Me draw out some differences between a faithful heart and the heart of a Pharisee. Long ago, Moses taught you through the Binding Promise that it's wrong to murder, correct?"

The disciples all nodded their heads.

"Many say you get a perfect score if you never take anyone's life," Jesus continued, and His disciples felt a little better. None of them had killed anyone, so they were happy to receive a good grade.

"But do you know what the first step toward murder is? Anger. Murder would never be a problem if anger did not exist. Anger sets you on the path to murdering another image-bearer. Outside the Author's Kingdom, people lightly value the lives of image-bearers and highly value following rules to receive praise. So while you may not ever kill a person and break a 'rule' in the sight of others, in your heart you have already broken this rule."

The disciples' eyes grew wide again, doubting anyone could ever measure up to that standard.

"Let me give you another example," Jesus continued. "Think of the common ways male image-bearers treat female image-bearers. The Binding Promise says not to be unfaithful to your wife. But unfaithfulness happens in your heart. With a mere look, you can be unfaithful to your binding promise with your wife. Sin is deeply rooted in hearts, and behavior tends to only mask filthy hearts. Be ruthless as you fight sin! Don't be so naive as to think that you can keep the Binding Promise with mere actions. Keeping it starts in the heart.

"Even our treatment of our enemies is upside-down in the Kingdom," Jesus continued. "I've heard people teach us to love our neighbor and hate our enemy. But how does the Author view His enemies? He gives them air to breathe and food to eat, good gifts and generosity. He invites us to follow His example."

The hillside was quiet as Jesus' words weighed heavy on the disciples' hearts, creating in them a hunger for this Good Life. He was painting a picture of the Author they'd never seen before. This was an upside-down Kingdom, indeed!

"Ultimately, the Good Life is found in trusting the Author, and He is a good Father! We don't have to create our own kingdoms here on this earth, frantically running around grabbing possessions and clothes and food because we are afraid He won't provide. We can live open-handedly, knowing He Always Loves us. We can invest in His Kingdom because He invests in us.

"With that confidence, you can pray to the Author like this:

Daddy, You're the true King, no one is like You! With all I am, I long for Your Kingdom to come to earth, for all that is true about You to be reflected in the world around us. We trust You for our daily bread. You will always provide! The Good Life is knowing You forgive us and forgiving others in response. When the enemy comes at us with lies, may we never doubt Your Always Love!"

213

Jesus' eyes danced with joy as He said, "I have shared so much with you today! Let me share just one thing more." He leaned forward to emphasize His final words. "There are only two kingdoms: the kingdom of this world and the Author's Kingdom. And they each are built on very different foundations. So take a look at what you're building your life on." He paused and let His words sink into His listeners' hearts.

"The world's kingdom is built on shifting sand, saying you must do the right things to be accepted. But the Author's Kingdom isn't about *behavior*; it's about *becoming*. Building that sort of life is like building a house on a rock-solid foundation. Storms will inevitably come against both kingdoms, and the storms will reveal what's at the foundation.

"So embrace the Good Life—upside-down living with the new Binding Promise written on your hearts! The Author is ours, and we are His! Let His Always Love root your hearts firmly in His unshakable Kingdom!"

Jesus was finished speaking, but no one moved, no one said a word. Everything He said had just turned their hearts, their relationships—their entire world—upside-down.

A Religious Leader & A Samaritan Woman
John 3:1-21; 4:1-42

Darkness, like a blanket, hid the man walking the streets. Maneuvering from one shadow to the next, Nicodemus was on a secret search for answers. As a religious teacher, he spent his life asking questions and pursuing truth. His family's wealth gave him an elite education and access to high social circles. But lately, Jesus' teachings had called into question everything he thought to be true. Nicodemus needed to talk to Him—but alone. He knocked quietly on a door. A moment later the door opened slightly.

"May I speak with Jesus?" Nicodemus asked hopefully.

The door opened all the way, and Jesus welcomed him, His eyes smiling at His guest.

"Teacher," Nicodemus sat down, "everyone knows the Author sent You to teach us. The incredible miracles You do are proof of that!"

Jesus leaned toward Nicodemus as if to share a secret, answering the question Nicodemus hadn't asked yet, "Nicodemus, only through re-birth will the Author's Kingdom make sense."

"What are you talking about?" Nicodemus asked, already confused. He came hoping for clarity, yet things were only getting more confusing! "Surely You don't mean that to enter this Kingdom I have to be birthed from my mother's womb again? That's impossible!" Nicodemus was truly shocked. He saw himself as the epitome of a faithful Jew, yet Jesus spoke like Nicodemus was an outsider needing a drastic change to enter the Author's Kingdom.

Jesus waded into the confusion with him, "The Author is establishing a new Kingdom where only His Always Love matters. Religious knowledge, good behavior, or Jewish ethnicity mean nothing. The Author's Spirit gives you a new heart and births you into the Kingdom."

Nicodemus' face was blank, his whole world crumbling around him. "I still don't understand. How does the Spirit give me a new heart?"

Jesus slipped to the floor next to the confused teacher, excited to connect a few dots and dispel some of the confusion. "Nicodemus, you're a respected teacher of the Story. Why the confusion? Everything in the Story points to this. One example is Moses and the bronze snake. The snake's poison spread through the camp, threatening them all with death. Likewise, sin spreads its poison, enveloping the whole world in the darkness of death. Just as Moses lifted up the bronze snake, giving new life to those who looked on it, so the Rescuer will be lifted up and give life to all who look to Him!"

Nicodemus hung on every word Jesus spoke, even if he didn't understand.

Jesus continued, "Do you know why the Author wrote the Story this way? Because of His Always Love. And the Rescuer is the most tangible expression of His Always Love! When all the world had turned its back on Him, choosing sin, the Author moved toward the world with Always Love. One day, His Always Wrath against sin will have its way with all evil, but because of the Rescuer, broken image-bearers can find unending life in His Always Love. Nicodemus, it's as simple as light and darkness. The Rescuer came into the world like light chasing away darkness. Will you choose to stay in darkness, which feels safe and familiar? Or will you come to the light?"

At this point in the Story, Reader, we don't know what Nicodemus chose. Nicodemus, who used the darkness of night to cover his tracks to Jesus, was now being asked to come into the light and embrace Always Love. This would take a lot of courage for an educated and influential leader like Nicodemus! Eventually we will see how he responded, but for now, let's turn to someone whose response was immediate.

Like Nicodemus, she too was trying to hide, but did so in the blazing noon-day sun rather than in darkness. She arrived at her local well with beads of sweat on her brow, looking like she was carrying a burden heavier than just her empty water jar. Every other Samaritan woman from her village drew water earlier, enjoying the coolness of the morning and each other's company. But here she was alone, in the heat of the day.

As she drew closer to the well, she saw a Man sitting beside it. "Oh great," she thought to herself. "Why is that Jewish man sitting there?" She determined to simply ignore Him, quickly draw water, and return home.

"Excuse me, ma'am, would you give Me a drink of water?" Jesus asked the woman when she arrived, foiling her plan.

"Sir," she began, not looking Him in the eye, "You are obviously a Jewish man, and I'm obviously a Samaritan woman. Why are you asking *me* to give you water?" she asked bluntly, feeling uncomfortable and unsure why she would have to remind him of the barriers between them. Jewish men looked down on women in general, but Samaritan women were the lowest of the low. An upstanding Jewish man would have considered it unclean and disgusting to drink from her cup.

Jesus gently brushed aside the barriers and the centuries of hostility between their people groups and said, "Do you know that the Author's Always Love is at work this very moment? If you knew it, *you* would be the one asking *Me* for water. And if you asked, He'd lavish living water on you like He does His Always Love!"

"Who does this guy think he is?" she thought to herself. Turning to draw water, she simply shrugged and said, "Jacob, our father, dug us a deep, reliable well, while you sit here empty-handed. You think you're better than Jacob?"

"You'll get thirsty again drinking Jacob's water," replied Jesus. "But the water I give is like the Author's Always Love flowing freely and unfailingly, satisfying forever!"

The woman threw up her hands, half-annoyed, half-curious, "Fine! Then give me this water. I'd *love* not having to come to this well every day!"

"Alright then," Jesus replied, "I'd like to meet your husband."

The woman's eyes narrowed; she felt uncomfortable again. Asking a woman for water at a well was a typical way a man flirted with a woman. Now He brings up her husband. What were this man's intentions?

"I don't have a husband," she sighed and turned to draw water from the well, giving up all hopes for both unfailing water and Always Love.

But Jesus continued to speak with the woman any other Jewish man would have disdained, wanting to draw out a deeper thirst in her soul that well water would never satisfy. "I know you don't have a husband. You've had five and now live with a man, not even bothering to get married."

Her heart stopped. "How does He know this about me? And if He knows, why does He keep talking to me?" she marveled.

Somehow Jesus knew her story included being either divorced or widowed five times, which turned her into a complete failure as a woman in the eyes of her village. No wonder she was at the well alone.

She laughed nervously, "I guess you're one of the Author's messengers. Well, I've had a lingering question; perhaps you can answer it. Samaritans worship there on Mount Gerizim," she pointed to the mountain nearby. "It's an important mountain in the Author's Story, yet Jews say we must worship in Jerusalem. Who's right?"

"Dear woman," Jesus smiled warmly, "the Author's Story is far bigger than geographical locations. It's about the heart—not holy places. *Everything* is leading to the day when image-bearers will worship the Author together in His Kingdom."

The woman's expression turned quizzical as she thought to herself, "He breaks religious and cultural barriers between us and reframes everything I know about the Author." But she waved her hand dismissively and with a lighthearted laugh said, "Well, one day the Rescuer will come and make sense of it all," and she turned to finish drawing water.

Jesus leaned toward her as if to tell her a secret and said, "I am the Rescuer."

The woman was speechless. But just then Jesus' disciples arrived and seeing Him leaning toward the woman—talking with her!—they were speechless, too. They awkwardly stood there, holding the lunches they had bought in the woman's village, not knowing what to say. The woman turned and ran home.

Meanwhile, the disciples spread lunch before their Teacher, trying to forget the awkward scene they had stumbled upon as they arrived at the well. But Jesus kept looking toward the woman's village. "Friends, I'm too excited to eat! The Author is up to something right now. Let's not miss it! Look up! A whole village is hungry for Always Love like a field ripe for harvest!"

The disciples turned toward the village to see a crowd of people coming toward them—including the very people from whom they'd just bought their lunch. But what sort of harvest could Jesus mean?

After two full days in the Samaritan village, watching Jesus demonstrate and declare the Author's Always Love, the disciples understood what Jesus meant by a harvest. They watched in amazement as a whole Samaritan village embraced Always Love more readily than many Jews did and entered the Author's Kingdom.

Whether in darkness or bright daylight, Jesus was finding thirsty image-bearers and drawing them into the Author's Kingdom with His Always Love. Wealthy Nicodemus with his high social status and coveted reputation longed for Always Love just as much as a poor, uneducated Samaritan woman with an immoral reputation, who was despised by her society. And they both found it in Jesus.

A Storm at Sea & A Storm in a Man
Matthew 8:23-34
Mark 4:35-5:20
Psalm 107:23-31

The wind whirled and swirled around them, tossing their fishing boat as if it were a toy. Waves rocked the boat, crashing onto its deck, drenching its passengers, and barraging their souls with a fear they'd never known before. Many of the disciples on board were fishermen, experienced with wind and waves. They were used to storms coming up quickly on the Sea of Galilee; but so far from shore, weathering a squall of this intensity—they were in over their heads! Their physical bodies were exhausted; their emotions ragged.

Amid the storm, Jesus, tired from a long day of teaching, slept soundly in the boat while the twelve disciples struggled for their lives.

"Why is Jesus still sleeping?" one of the disciples yelled above the sound of the storm, sea water spraying in his face. "Somebody wake Him up!"

The disciple closest to Him shook Him awake, "Teacher, how can you sleep in a storm like this? We're struggling to stay alive! Don't You care if we drown?"

There wasn't much they thought their Teacher could do, but He should at least wake up and show some concern, struggle with them, and lift a hand to scoop out the water filling the boat.

But Jesus didn't jump up in a frenzy to help His disciples in their frantic attempt to survive the storm. Instead, He rose to His feet with a peace and confidence that starkly contrasted the fear and desperation of His disciples. Then He opened His mouth, and with authority older than time, He spoke to the wind and waves saying, "That's enough! Be still!"

"We know that voice!" the wind and waves responded in surprise, their attention arrested by the same voice that spoke them into being long ago. The wind bowed in reverence to its Maker; the waves settled themselves calmly under their Master's feet. Where once there was a raging storm, now there was complete stillness. All was as it should be.

The disciples stood on the now steady deck of the boat, chests heaving, hair and beards dripping with water, clothes drenched and clinging to their skin, eyes glued to their Teacher. Suddenly, Jesus seemed more threatening and scary than the raging storm had felt.

"My friends," Jesus asked tenderly, seeking to comfort them in their fear, "why were you afraid? Has faith still not taken deep root in your hearts?"

But the disciples couldn't respond. They were now in a desperate struggle—like a storm inside their souls—to understand, "*Who is this Man?*" Jesus had stepped across any lines they'd drawn around their Teacher. He had mesmerized them with His healing miracles, captivated them by His great teaching. But if He could speak to creation and harness such power with mere words, *then He wasn't just a Teacher*!

The rest of the boat ride was quiet—not just because the storm had subsided but because the disciples hardly knew what to say. Some remembered a Psalm they'd memorized as children, telling of the Author rescuing His people from a storm by speaking to the wind and calming the sea, bringing His people to safe harbor. "Let those rescued praise the Author for His Always Love!" the Psalm encouraged them, but they were too shocked and in awe to know how to do that right now.

When they reached the other side of the sea, they slipped out of the boat and into Gentile territory. They smelled pigs and saw a graveyard up the hill. Few Jews lived here or even traveled here for that matter. The whole place reeked with an uncleanness abhorrent to decent Jews. What business could Jesus possibly have here?

Suddenly, a raging storm of an entirely different nature blew upon them! A man, half-naked, hair unkempt, fresh wounds all over his body and eyes wild with terror came running from the graveyard toward them screaming, "Jesus! We know who You are!" The man knelt before Jesus while the disciples gasped in horror and hid behind their Teacher. They had seen Jesus set people free from evil spirits, but this was an intensity of evil they'd never seen before.

"That's enough!" Jesus demanded. "Come out of him!"

But the evil spirit spoke back, "Why did You come here? Are You planning to torture us before the Story ends? We appeal to the Author; don't torture us yet!"

"What is your name?" Jesus asked the evil spirit.

"Legion!" snarled the voice, and the disciples gasped in horror, wondering if they'd heard clearly. A Roman legion was over five thousand soldiers! Did he mean that...?

"Yes," laughed the evil spirit haughtily, "there are many of us inside this man!" The man writhed as the spirits revolted and threw his body down at Jesus' feet. The disciples couldn't help but think of the storm they'd just been rescued from as the man's body, mind, and soul seemed caught in a storm too. "Don't send us away!" the demons cried. "Let us stay in this area! Jesus, look at those pigs over there. Send us into them if we have to leave this man!"

"Go!" commanded Jesus; and with one simple word, He calmed the raging storm inside the man, who now lay still and quiet at His feet.

Suddenly, shrill squeals of a whole herd of two thousand swine pierced the air. Filled with frightening chaos, they ran hysterically here and there and then straight off the steep hillside, throwing themselves to their deaths in the very sea Jesus had just calmed.

All the commotion drew a crowd. People came in droves to see with their own eyes the man that had always lived on the fringes of their community.

"Is this really the same guy?" they asked. "The same guy who broke himself free of every chain we ever tried to put on him? The one who wandered night and day wailing among the tombs?"

"It must be!" answered another. "But look at him now! He's sitting still, clothed, carrying on a normal conversation, and smiling! What in the world happened?"

"Well, I don't like it one bit!" one of the men in the crowd began to yell. "This Man just cost us a fortune!"

"Yeah!" yelled another. "Forget that lunatic; he was always a freak! But those were my pigs! I've lost an unbelievable amount of money because of this Jew!"

"That's right!" another voice piped up. "Our whole community will suffer because that herd is gone! Get Him out of here! We were better off without Him!"

Agreement rippled through the crowd as their hearts filled with fear. They didn't know who Jesus was and they didn't want to know! They just wanted Him to leave. An image-bearer was set free, yet they couldn't see past what it cost them personally.

Nature and evil spirits were two forces Jews and Gentiles felt helpless against; and yet with mere words Jesus disarmed them both, rescuing those held in their clutches. How interesting, dear Reader, that as Jesus calmed a storm at sea and a storm inside a man, His actions stirred up storms in the hearts of His disciples and in this Gentile community. Everyone had to decide what they'd do with Him.

Jesus returned to the boat, but the man set free ran after Him shouting, "You rescued me! Please, let me go with You!"

Jesus smiled at the man. Evil had ravaged him just a short time ago. Now precious faith filled him instead.

"No, My friend," Jesus refused, "go to the places where I'm not welcome. Your family won't receive Me, but they'll receive you. 'Let those rescued praise the Author for His Always Love'!"

The man did that very thing, telling countless Gentiles of the Always Love that calmed his storm.

A Bleeding Woman & A Dead Girl
Matthew 9:18-26
Mark 5:21-43
Malachi 4:2

"I shouldn't be touching all these people," the woman thought to herself, her conscience shaming her. "But I have to get closer to Him! Everything else has failed. Malachi, the Author's messenger from long ago, said the hem of the Rescuer's garment would be able to heal. If I can touch even just the blue and white tassel on His robe, I know I'll be healed!"

Her faith brushed aside Jewish law and pressed on. She was unclean and had been for twelve straight years. Touching all of these people made them unclean, too. Her face reddened with shame as she thought of what she was doing. "By touching Jesus' garment, I'll make Him unclean! But He's my only hope!" The struggle within her was agonizing.

A swarm of people had enveloped Jesus and swallowed the desperate woman. But suddenly the crowd parted to make way for their synagogue leader, Jairus, who rushed toward Jesus, falling at His feet, giving the woman a chance to get closer.

"Please, Jesus, I beg you," Jairus implored. "My precious daughter is on the verge of death. Come quickly and heal her! Please!"

While Jesus and Jairus spoke together, the woman in the crowd wriggled her way forward a bit more. Oh, but now

Jesus had turned to walk away with Jairus, and the crowd was moving once again. Desperately she forced her way through the crowd with all her might. There was urgency in Jairus' steps, leading Jesus quickly along, but there was also urgency in the woman who longed for healing. With great struggle and strain, she worked her way through the jostling crowd until she managed to get right behind Jesus. She took a deep breath and courageously reached out to touch the hem of His robe. There, she did it! She touched Him! And immediately she knew it worked; she was *healed*! The impurity that had made her life miserable vanished in an instant! Tears sprung to her eyes as she stood still, relief and joy washing over her, as the crowd moved on without her.

But suddenly, the crowd stopped…for Jesus had stopped. People bumped into each other unexpectedly. Jesus turned around and asked, "Who touched Me?"

The woman's heart stopped from fear.

Annoyed at the delay, Jesus' disciples questioned, "Everyone is bumping into everyone—many people have touched You. The little girl is about to die…shouldn't we hurry?"

"No, this is important," Jesus said, distracted and searching the crowd.

The woman's whole body pulsed with fear. The tears in her eyes that had seconds ago been from joy were now from regret. "Oh, what have I done?" she cried silently. Then her tiny frame pushed past a few people and slid before Jesus. Head bowed, bottom lip trembling, she fell to her knees and began to sob. The crowd backed away as someone asked, "Isn't that the unclean woman? What is she doing here?"

Then Jesus, living out the upside-down nature of the Author's Kingdom, slipped to His knees to hear the woman's story. She had a captive audience with the Rescuer. Through sobs she explained, "Oh Jesus, I'm sorry! I never should have done it, but I desperately wanted to be healed! For twelve years, I have been bleeding," she burst out in a cry of grief and shame. "For twelve long years, I have been kept at arm's length, unfit for marriage because I can't have children. I haven't even had a hug since I was a girl!" The poor woman sobbed uncontrollably as her heart confessed the relational pain she had carried all these years. She composed herself and continued, "I haven't been allowed in a synagogue, much less the Temple; my disease has made me unfit for worship. I tried everything! Every penny I earned I gave to doctors, but all of their medicines only increased my suffering!"

Minute after long minute the woman explained her plight, which had lasted as long as Jairus' daughter's whole life. Poor Jairus just stood there, heart aching for his daughter, knowing her life could slip away any moment, yet feeling powerless to do anything to make Jesus hurry. The disciples, too, felt the tension. Jesus had the opportunity to heal the daughter of a man of high status! Why was He bothering with this insignificant woman who had broken their law and made countless people unclean?

"Precious daughter, be encouraged!" Jesus spoke with familial love and great tenderness as He did for her what no one had done for so long: He touched her. He took her head in His hands and looked into her eyes, saying, "Your faith healed you. Your suffering is over!" Jesus would not let this woman slip away into anonymity when she could enjoy a greater healing than just a physical one. With bold words and a tender touch, He reinstated her into community, confirming her physical healing and honoring her as a model of faith.

But faith was what Jairus was struggling with right now. A cry of soul-deep pain escaped from his throat as a man arrived and whispered something into his ear. "No! We're too late!" he gasped.

"I'm sorry, sir," the man continued, "but it's no use bothering the Teacher."

Jesus stood, extended a hand to the healed woman, helping her to her feet. As He did, He turned to Jairus. Looking straight into his eyes, Jesus invited him to have the same faith the woman had just shown. "Don't give in to fear, Jairus; give in to faith."

Jairus winced. What could such words mean on the heels of such news?

When they arrived home, Jairus' heart sank. The professional mourners had already arrived to play flutes and wail for his daughter. His desperate attempt to secure her healing had only kept him away at her death. His heart wailed in remorse.

Jesus turned and quietly dismissed the crowd. Then He chose Peter, James, and John to follow Him into the house. As Jairus walked through the door with Jesus, his wife ran to him, collapsing into his arms, tears streaming down her face. Jairus' heart could take no more. He sank to his knees, sobbing uncontrollably. With such loss and sorrow as this, what could Jesus possibly do?

"Why such mourning and weeping?" Jesus sincerely asked those gathered in the house. "Their daughter is just sleeping; she isn't dead."

Jairus was shocked. Was Jesus being irreverent? The gathering of family members and professional mourners hardly knew how to respond. They nervously laughed at

Jesus, showing they fully believed the girl had died and leaving them no room to deny what was about happen.

"Come with Me," Jesus said. The little girl's parents, along with Peter, James, and John, slipped into the room where her body lay.

Jairus' throat shut with grief, seeing his little girl lying there, lifeless. Even the disciples' hearts were heavy with grief, feeling both awkward and powerless just standing there.

Jesus walked slowly toward the tiny corpse, knelt beside her with tenderness, and gently took hold of her limp hand. He leaned over her body and released her from death's clutches by whispering life back into her little frame. "Little daughter, it's time to wake up," He said as if it were simply the beginning of a new day, and He were waking her from sleep.

Her tiny hand, swallowed by His, twitched to life. Her small chest rose with breath as her eyelids fluttered open. She turned to Jesus, His kind eyes and inviting smile welcoming her back to life, and she smiled in return. When she saw her parents behind Him, she jumped up and ran into their arms.

Jairus was in absolute shock, immobilized by awe. His wife shrieked with joy, embracing their daughter, showering her with kisses. "*This* is what Jesus meant when He told me not to give in to fear but to give in to faith?" Jairus wondered incredulously.

Jesus embodied Always Love that day in a way few people would have expected. In a culture where women were less valuable than men, unmarried women and young girls were virtually insignificant. But in Jesus' Kingdom, all image-bearers are valuable and worth taking time to restore—physically, relationally, emotionally, and spiritually—with the Author's Always Love.

Unclean Hands & Unclean Hearts
Matthew 15:1-28
Mark 7:1-30

"It's so disgusting! Jesus claims to know so much about the Author, yet look at His disciples! They don't even wash their hands the right way before they eat!" A group of Pharisees had come from Jerusalem to keep an eye on Jesus and were not liking what they saw. "Shouldn't we do something about this?" asked a Pharisee in the group. "Jesus and His band of followers don't seem to keep any of our traditions. These traditions make us the true Israel; they make us right with the Author! Yet these men undermine everything we teach and model."

The Pharisees thought themselves to be special: having the right ethnicity, with the right education, living in the right neighborhoods, doing all the right things. They considered themselves the keepers of the Binding Promise, convinced that if their Jewish people would just keep it perfectly, they would be made right with the Author, and Israel would be restored to greatness. Jesus seemed to disagree, however, and they didn't like that.

The Pharisees were irritated, disgusted, and would not stand by silently. They approached Jesus and His disciples while they were sharing a meal.

"Teacher," began one of the Pharisees, "we noticed that your disciples…"

"Not to mention, You!" muttered another Pharisee under his breath.

"Your disciples don't really follow the hand-washing traditions our ancestors gave us. These traditions are meant to ensure we don't break the Binding Promise and that we stay acceptable in the Author's sight. Why do You let them disregard our traditions?"

Jesus, caught with His mouth full, kept chewing, as He pondered His response. He was amazed at how tenacious the Pharisees could be, both at making up rules and imposing them on others. Jesus swallowed and then opened His mouth to reply, "The very fact you ask such questions proves you don't understand the Story or Israel's place in it."

He paused, letting His rebuke sink in, then continued, "How easy it is for Israelites to miss the whole point of the Story. You think that if you wash the right way at the right time, you'll be clean in the Author's sight—as if doing the right thing can turn you into the right person. All the while, your hearts are dirty, and your traditions keep you from the Author's Always Love."

The disciples were wide-eyed, chewing slowly, swallowing discreetly, and not quite sure if they should take another bite with so many Pharisees breathing down their throats and their Teacher called into question.

"I wholeheartedly agree," affirmed Jesus, "that cleanliness before the Author is an issue that must be addressed. All image-bearers are stained, unclean in the Author's sight, completely unfit for His presence. But what I don't agree with is the way you teach people to become clean. The Author Himself has been telling you what it takes to become clean, yet you disregard His voice."

A Pharisee took offense, "I beg your pardon, Jesus, but that simply is not true. Moses told us how to stay clean before the

Author, and we take those laws very seriously, while you and your disciples do not!"

Jesus' tone grew serious, "You've missed the whole point of the cleanliness laws. You Pharisees try to hijack the Story as if you've created just the right soap to wash yourselves of your filth. That's not the point of the Story! No earthly soap can wash your dirty hearts and make them clean enough for the Author."

The Pharisees scowled, storming off angrily, while the disciples were full of questions. Jesus was turning upside-down something they had been taught all their lives: that doing the right things made an image-bearer right with the Author.

Jesus looked His disciples in their eyes, earnestly wanting them to understand, "You've been taught that what you touch or eat determines your cleanliness in the Author's sight. But I'm telling you that those ways of living served their purpose. They set you apart from the evil nations around you so that you could point them to His Always Love. They revealed your need for the Author's cleansing by showing you how pervasive sin is and then pointed to a time when the Rescuer would fulfill the cleanliness laws. That time is now."

The disciples turned to one another, wondering if they were alone in their confusion. Jesus could tell they weren't yet understanding, so He continued, "There's a deeper filth than dirt on hands. It's the filth on your heart where sin takes root. So the problem isn't keeping dirt out of your stomach but washing the filth from your heart."

The Pharisees refused to see it; the disciples struggled to understand it. But in a nearby town, a woman understood the Author's heart and her place in the Story better than the Pharisees did.

"This isn't my place," she thought to herself, pausing outside the door to take a deep breath. "He's a Jew; I'm a

Gentile. He's a well-known Teacher; I'm an unimportant, working-class woman. He is religiously clean, while I know enough about Jewish tradition to know that I am not. I'm unworthy, but I'm so desperate!'"

Her desperation drove her into Jesus' presence, invading His retreat from all the crowds and non-stop ministry opportunities in Israel. He and His disciples had sneaked away to Gentile territory to enjoy a bit of anonymity and reprieve; and yet even here He was sought and found and needed. She threw herself at His feet, her desperate heart begging through her lips, "Jesus, an evil, unclean spirit has my little girl captive and won't let her go. Only You can set her free."

Jesus looked at the woman begging at His feet. He could have either turned her away or snapped His finger to heal her daughter and be done with it quickly, but He did neither. Instead, He told a short story to draw out what He suspected was inside her, "Dear woman, the food on the table is for the children. They eat first, and then the puppies get the leftovers."

The woman, keeping her begging posture face down at Jesus' feet, didn't miss a beat. "I know I am not part of Israel's family, but the meal the Author has spread before Israel is not just for them, it's for puppies like me—and my daughter's life depends on it. I don't have any right to His Always Love, but if it's as extravagant as I've heard, then I know it will overflow from the table and fall to the floor for my family." Humbly she kept her posture before Jesus, waiting for His response.

Eyes twinkling, Jesus smiled. He thought He had seen something wonderful in her when she boldly entered the room, and He was right. He was glad He had mined for it and drawn it out. He shifted His gaze from the Gentile woman to His Jewish disciples and asked incredulously, "Can you believe her answer?"

He got no response for the disciples were struggling to understand.

He continued, "She knows her place in the Story of the Author's Always Love. Though born outside Israel, she wasn't born outside the Story! There is a place for her in the Author's Always Love, and she knows it!" Jesus shifted His gaze back to the woman at His feet and reached down to gently guide her to a posture where He could look into her eyes and affirm the incredible faith she had modeled. "Dear woman, the Author's Always Love *is* as extravagant as you have heard. Go on home; your daughter has been set free."

When the Pharisees refused to see it, when the disciples struggled to understand it, this Gentile woman embraced the Story more than most in Israel did. On the surface, she had no right to approach the Author. She didn't keep Jewish religious traditions. She didn't wash her hands the right way. She accepted her label of "unclean." But she knew the Author's heart went deeper than her ethnicity or religious traditions and knew His Story was for the whole world. She laid aside any attempts to be good enough for Him, and He rescued her daughter with His Always Love.

Chapter 42

Blindness & A Glimpse of Glory

Matthew 16:13-17:23
Mark 8:22-9:32
Luke 9:18-45

Gathering in Caesarea Philippi, near the mouth of the Jordan River, Jesus and His disciples were at one of the furthest points from Jerusalem in all Israel. As they walked along the road, Jesus asked them curiously, "Who do people say I am?"

"Some say You're John the Baptist come back to life," one disciple replied.

"Others think You're Elijah, You know, since Elijah will come before the Rescuer," chimed in another.

Another disciple added, "Most Jews don't think the Author is sending messengers anymore, but some think You might be a messenger from old, like Jeremiah, perhaps."

"Well, how do you see Me?" Jesus inquired.

Peter didn't need to think twice about his answer, "Jesus, I *know* You're the Rescuer! You are the promised Son of David!"

Jesus put His arm around Peter saying, "Peter, you are a 'rock,' just like the rock-solid statement you declared! The Author's Kingdom rests firmly on that rock-solid statement, and nothing can destroy it. Not even death can silence the truth you've just declared! In fact, that's the key to entering the Kingdom, Peter, and you hold that key, ready to enter."

But Jesus wondered if Peter's expectations of the Rescuer were accurate. So He continued, "Today we begin our final trip to Jerusalem. Once there, things will become very difficult for Me. I will suffer at the hands of the leading priests and teachers of the Binding Promise."

His disciples gasped in horror. What could He mean?

But Jesus wasn't finished, "In fact, they will kill Me. But listen, this is very important: on the third day, I will rise again."

Jesus' words angered Peter, and he rebuked his Teacher, "Jesus, You have to stop saying that! You're the Rescuer! You can't talk about things like suffering and martyrdom. The Rescuer is supposed to *rescue* us—how can You do that if You're dead?"

Jesus looked Peter in the eye. "You're not seeing clearly, Peter. You see I'm the Rescuer but you don't understand what that means. Do you want Me to wrest the pen from the Author's hand and rewrite the next chapter? I'm sure the Author's enemy would love that! You, 'the rock,' are a stumbling stone on the path I am walking. You need to get behind Me, Peter. Be a disciple who follows well!"

Then turning to His friends, He explained, "The path before Me leads through suffering. If you want to follow Me, you have to be willing to suffer, to walk past the ridiculing mob toward your execution. It will cost you everything, but you will get the Good Life in return! So follow Me, even if it's not to where you think I should be going."

As they made their way toward Jerusalem, Jesus used any teachable moment to help His disciples see who He really was. Recently, outside the village of Bethsaida, Jesus had taken a blind man by the hand and done a most peculiar thing. After spitting on his eyes and then laying His hands on him to heal him, He asked the blind man, "Can you see anything yet?"

The man's eyelids fluttered open, wet and sticky. "Well, I see something like trees walking around," he said squinting. The man was on his way to seeing clearly, but not quite there. Was Jesus struggling to heal the man or telling a story with His healing?

Jesus put His hands on the man's eyes one more time. "Now what do you see?"

Once again, the man's eyelids fluttered open. "Everything!" he exclaimed joyfully. "It's all so clear now!" Tears flowed freely from his once-blind eyes.

In stages the man saw clearly; and likewise, in stages the disciples were coming to see Jesus clearly. They had come to see Him as the Rescuer but didn't yet understand what that meant. So six days later Jesus invited Peter, James, and John to climb a mountain, giving them another chance to see what it meant to be the Rescuer.

The four men climbed and climbed while thinking of how often in the Story so many incredible things had happened on mountains. Elijah had led a showdown between good and evil on Mount Carmel. Moses had received the Binding Promise on Mount Sinai. Mountains were stable, immovable parts of the landscape and geography of not just Israel, but Israel's Story. And today's mountaintop experience would be just as powerful.

As the men reached the top of the mountain, suddenly something bizarre began to happen to Jesus. Right before their eyes, His form changed from the Jesus they knew well to one they hardly recognized. His face outshone the sun, light itself wrapped around Him like clothing! Then, out of nowhere, Moses and Elijah appeared to talk with Jesus about the next chapter of the Story.

Peter was awestruck! *This* was the Rescuer Peter wanted Jesus to be—the one who came in power and authority, who stood on mountains and shone with majesty! He wanted Jesus to always be like this and blurted out, bold as ever, "Jesus, it's so good we're here with You because we can make tents for you, Moses, and Elijah and stay here on this mountain together!"

What was meant to be a glimpse of what would come, Peter wanted now—without any suffering. But it couldn't be that way. The Author Himself descended in a thick, bright cloud to swallow up Peter's bright idea, and help heal his blindness. It was the same dense cloud that led Peter's people out of Egypt, filled the Tent in the desert, and interrupted all sacrifices in Solomon's Temple. Ezekiel saw the cloud of His presence go east to live among the exiles and knew one day it would dwell among His people again. Now His presence wrapped Jesus in a strong embrace, His voice streaming through the cloud to say, "My Son brings Me immeasurable joy! He is Mine, and I am His. Take to heart what He says!"

At the start of Jesus' ministry, the Author had publicly declared His Always Love for His Son, and now at the start of His journey toward suffering, He was declaring it again on this mountaintop. Always Love had been the hallmark of their relationship since before there was time. Come what may, neither Jesus' disciples nor Jesus Himself would have any reason to doubt the Author's Always Love.

But while such powerful expressions of Always Love were common between Jesus and His Father, the three disciples were overwhelmed with fear and fell to the ground in terror. Who could see such a presence and hear such a voice and live?

Jesus knelt and put a hand on them to tenderly calm their fears. "It's okay, My friends. Let Me help you up."

As they stood and looked around, they realized they were once again alone with Jesus. No more Moses, who had given them the laws of the Binding Promise. No more Elijah, who had exemplified the faithfulness of the messengers. They both had faded from view, and there was only their familiar Jesus, standing with them on the mountain.

But as they descended the mountain, Jesus once again explained the task before Him, "Suffering and death are about to come to the Rescuer, but that is essential to the Story. Remember, everything will change on the third day when the Rescuer rises to life again."

After seeing Jesus in power and majesty on the mountaintop, His disciples couldn't imagine Him suffering or dying. Like the man whom Jesus healed outside of Bethsaida, the disciples were still not seeing their Rescuer clearly. Yes, one day He would come in power and great glory—their mountaintop experience foreshadowed that. But they didn't want a suffering Rescuer. They wanted a Rescuer who would come in power and make their greatest hopes come true!

Grabbing for Power & Preparing for Death

Matthew 20:17-28; 26:6-16
Mark 10:32-45; 14:1-11
Luke 18:31-34
John 12:1-11

"Jesus, will You promise to say 'yes' to whatever we ask You?" requested James and John as they pulled Jesus aside.

"What do you have in mind?" Jesus asked the brothers.

"We know You will soon sit on Your throne as King, and we want to sit beside You. One on Your left, one on Your right." The brothers, proud of their idea and already envisioning themselves seated on thrones like royalty beside their King, waited for an answer.

But Jesus looked troubled, "Brothers, you don't know what you're asking. Intense suffering paves the road to glory. Do you really think you can walk that path with Me?"

Visions of fighting battles and overthrowing enemies flashed through their minds. Sure, there would be risks and no doubt injuries, but they were all in! "Of course, we can!" they both assured Him enthusiastically.

Jesus didn't share their enthusiasm. Instead, with deep compassion He said, "You both will walk through your share of suffering, but I'm not the one to decide who will sit where in the Kingdom."

"What are you all talking about?" Philip butted in, overhearing the last part of the conversation. "Who is sitting where in Jesus' Kingdom?"

James and John silently looked down at the ground.

"You didn't think *you two* would sit next to Jesus, did you?" Philip asked. "Oh, so you think you should be second in command? You think *you* deserve that honor?"

"What about the rest of us?" chimed in Andrew. "Why do you think you're so much better?"

Before long James and John had ten angry men around them arguing over who would be the greatest in Jesus' Kingdom.

"Friends," Jesus hushed them, "you're proving how poorly you understand the Author's Kingdom. Leaders of the world seek glory to flaunt it and seek power for personal gain. But in the Author's upside-down Kingdom, if you want to be first, then walk yourself to the back of the line. If you want to lead and rule, then become the servant of those around you. How often have I told you that the Rescuer goes to Jerusalem with a death sentence hanging over His head? He doesn't demand honor or expect to be waited on hand and foot; instead, He gives up His life to give life to others. That is the path to greatness in the Author's Kingdom."

Later that night, Jesus and His disciples were enjoying a banquet in a small town outside Jerusalem at the home of His dear friends Lazarus, Martha, and Mary. Many of Jesus' closest friends were gathered to celebrate life—Lazarus' life—and to honor Jesus who just days before had raised him back to life again! It was the Passover season, and their village, so near Jerusalem, was already swelling with pilgrims singing holiday songs. What a wonderful season to be celebrating life together!

But Mary's heart found it hard to celebrate. Her heart was full of gratitude—Jesus had raised her brother back to life! But she sensed that Jesus did it at great cost to Himself. She had sat at His feet for years, listening to Him explain the Story and talk of the Rescuer and His Always Love. She saw how much power He showed standing outside Lazarus' tomb, calling her brother back to life; and yet, she was not blind to the evil lurking in the shadows. She knew that not everyone was happy her brother was alive again. She feared Jesus had traded His life for her brother's.

Suddenly, it struck her, "This could be the last time we see Jesus!" Agony overwhelmed her, and she retreated to a quiet place to be alone. Lazarus' death was fresh on her mind. She remembered how hopeless she felt while she and Martha anointed Lazarus' body and wrapped him in strips of cloth. "Who will do that for Jesus should He die?" she wondered aloud, fighting back tears. She stood and reached for a smooth, white jar on a shelf and then carried it back to dinner.

Mary paused in the doorway of the room where the men were dining and looked down at the jar in her hands. It was beautiful—the most precious thing she owned in all the world. This precious heirloom had been in her family for generations and was worth more money than Mary could even imagine. Yet she could think of no better way to spend it than on Him. She looked up from the exquisitely carved jar in her hand to Jesus seated across the room. She knew He was her King, but deep down, she knew her King's path to the throne would cost Him everything.

She took slow, deliberate steps across the room and quietly knelt behind Jesus. She didn't know what Jesus would face in the coming days; but she would give everything she could to honor her King, anointing Him at the same time for both His coronation…and His burial. Gently she broke open the jar, arresting the attention of everyone in the room with the extravagant smell of perfume. Sadness welled up in her heart, tears brimmed up in her eyes as she poured the costly perfume onto Jesus' feet. Then she reached up to pull the covering from her head, letting her long, dark hair fall freely down her back. Taking her hair into her hands, she bent over, wiping the oil from Jesus' feet, mingling it with the tears that fell from her eyes.

The room was quiet. What could anyone say after such an extravagant display of devotion?

But then Judas Iscariot could stay quiet no longer. "Why didn't You stop her, Jesus?" he demanded indignantly. "Do you realize she just poured a *year's* salary on Your *feet?* What a waste! You could have sold it and given the money to the poor!"

Of the twelve disciples, Judas was the one in charge of their finances. Donations to their Teacher went into a bag he carried, and sometimes money slipped out for personal reasons. But now this extravagant gift would have no benefit to their money bag—or to him.

"Let her be," Jesus gently reprimanded Judas. "You'll have plenty of opportunities to care for the poor, but our time together is short, and she knows that."

Perhaps more clearly than all the other followers in the room, Mary understood the reality of Jesus' identity and mission and simply responded in love. Mary wasn't like Peter, trying to change Jesus' plan because it included suffering. She wasn't like James and John, grabbing for power in His Kingdom. And Mary wasn't like Judas, trying to profit financially from it all. Seeking nothing for herself, she sacrificed greatly to honor her King.

Chapter 44

Welcoming a Pilgrim & Cleansing the Temple

Matthew 21:1-17
Mark 11
Luke 19:28-48
John 2:13-25
Psalm 118:25-27
Isaiah 56:7
Jeremiah 7:11

Passover was a time for Israelites to remind themselves of one of the most dramatic chapters in the Author's Story. They remembered the pain of their people enslaved in Egypt and remembered with great joy how the Author set them free. Every year at Passover, hopes were high that the Author would do something similar; that He'd set them free from their Roman oppressors and restore their nation to greatness.

Passover songs were in the air, and Israelites from far and near flooded into Jerusalem to celebrate one of the most important Jewish holidays in the most important Jewish city. It was tradition for those already in Jerusalem to welcome the Passover pilgrims into the city with singing and great rejoicing.

As the crowd gathered along the road to Jerusalem caught a glimpse of the next arriving Pilgrim, shouts of immense joy rose from their lips. It was Jesus! So unassuming and yet so strong, He rode toward Jerusalem on a young donkey. Those welcoming Him had high expectations for Jesus and quickly took off their outer robes, laying them before Him in the street. Others waved leafy branches to hail His arrival, while some placed them on the road ahead. The young donkey's hooves walked over the robes, over the branches, carrying the hopes and dreams of the cheering crowd into the great city of Jerusalem. As Jesus rode past them, they sang the chorus of a popular Passover song,

Oh, save us, our King!
All Your praises we sing!
The Son of David is here,
Peace and glory brought near!

Hopes were soaring that perhaps this would be the weekend Jesus would prove He was the Rescuer and take the throne as their King. The people who recognized Jesus as He rode into Jerusalem that day saw in Him the fulfillment of all their hopes for a Rescuer. Perhaps *this* would be the Passover when the Author would finally hear their cries and rescue them!

"What's all the commotion?" many native to Jerusalem asked as Jesus rode through the gates of the city. Jesus had spent so much of His time away from Jerusalem that He didn't have as much of a following here as in Galilee.

Visitors from Galilee explained, "It's Jesus! The Author's great Messenger from Nazareth!"

Unsure how someone from such a small, insignificant town could create such a commotion, many from Jerusalem simply shrugged their shoulders and went on with their business, while their Rescuer rode right past them, peaceful and unassuming.

But what Jesus did next was neither peaceful nor unassuming. Rather than go straight to the palace to overthrow the government as everyone had hoped, He made His way to the Temple, to the center of power for the religious leaders of the day, to the one place on earth where sacrifices and offerings were made to wash away sins, where the Author Himself met with His people.

The outer court of the Gentiles was bursting at the seams with throngs of people and animals. People scurried here and there as the cacophony of bleating sheep, clucking birds, clanging coins, and the buzz of holiday busyness filled the air. It was more convenient to travel long distances with a simple coin purse than with an animal sacrifice in tow, so those arriving for the Passover had to first exchange the money they had brought in from outside Jerusalem and then use local coins to purchase an animal for their sacrifice. Thousands of people needed thousands of sacrifices for the holiday, so there was much business to attend to in the Temple.

But Jesus' heart was filled with grief and anger as He squeezed His way into the court of the Gentiles, weaving past merchants and pilgrims, past livestock and money changers. The Temple was bursting with business today, but not the business the Author had intended for His Temple.

Suddenly, a crash reverberated from the walls of the Temple court. Tables overturned sending money flying and coins clanging. The sudden noise sent birds squawking in fear, wings beating against their cages. Sheep jumped and kicked, breaking free from pens and ropes, running every which way. Merchants yelled angrily, watching their money scatter on the floor. The whole Temple court was in chaos.

The priests overseeing the business that day scanned the crowd for the perpetrator, eyes stopping on the one causing such chaos. Hair flying, eyes glaring, muscles straining, Jesus was forcefully interrupting one of the busiest, most profitable days in the Temple. But He wasn't just turning tables upside-down. More than that, He was turning the whole Temple system upside-down.

Jesus lifted His voice and cried out, "The messengers of old said the Author's Temple should be a place for prayer and worship—for Jews and Gentiles alike!" His chest heaved as He caught His breath, "But you, on this holiday to remember the greatest rescue in the Story so far, crowd out Gentiles from the one place in the Temple where they can meet with the Author! You crowd out the nations with your traditions and your business and benefit financially from it all. That is not how it's meant to be! *Everyone* should have access to the Author here!"

The religious leaders, enraged by Jesus' audacity, would not stand by silently and watch this happen. "Who do You think You are?" they challenged Him openly. "Who gave You the authority to do this in our Temple?" They glared at Him, hoping to make a mockery of Him in front of the crowds.

"I'll show you where I get My authority!" Jesus asserted. "Bring down this Temple, and in only three days I'll re-build it!"

Jesus' confidence was noteworthy, but what exactly could He mean?

"You're a lunatic!" the religious leaders laughed, grateful Jesus had so easily made a fool of Himself. "This Temple took forty-six long years to build, and You're going to rebuild it in three days? We'd like to see that!"

But as everyone turned to clean up the mess Jesus had made, and as the religious leaders turned to walk away, they were now more determined than ever to finish Him off once and for all. They only had to find an opportunity.

The perfect opportunity came in a way they least expected. Judas Iscariot, one of Jesus' own disciples, walked through their door with a plan. He had had enough. Nothing was going as he had hoped. The Author's enemy had slithered up to Judas and whispered an idea, a way to change the Story as it was unfolding.

"How much money will you give me if I turn Him over to you?" Judas asked.

The religious leaders turned to each other and smiled very sinister smiles. *Betrayal.* A perfect opportunity indeed.

A Glorious Temple & The Promise It Will Fall
Matthew 24
Mark 13
Luke 21:5-38

"Stop for a moment, Jesus. Turn around and take in this incredible view!" one of the disciples called to Him as they walked away from the Temple as a group. Sunlight danced on the gold of Herod's Temple, making it shimmer gloriously. The huge structure loomed above them, standing tall, wide, and strong, a sacred emblem of the richness of Jewish culture and religion. It seemed to them an invincible place of power, a permanent symbol of the Author's favor to His people.

"Isn't it breathtaking?" Thomas asked as he stood there in awe. The disciples had spent hours and hours with Jesus in the Temple courts but had never just stood back and reveled in the majesty of the impressive structure before them.

This was the week they were sure Jesus would take the throne and begin reigning as the rightful King, so the disciples were feeling proud, strong, and confident—like the Jewish people felt about their Temple.

"Friends, I know it looks impressive, but it will fall," Jesus said, shattering the confidence His disciples had felt just seconds ago.

"What could You possibly mean?" Peter asked, astonished.

"A page is turning in the Story, and the Author is writing a new chapter. This Temple has served its purpose in the Story, and its days are numbered," Jesus gently told His disciples, who were now more astonished by Jesus' words than by the Temple in whose shadow they stood.

Sure, the disciples had heard of such things happening in the Story. The Babylonians destroyed Solomon's Temple, but the Author restored His people from exile, and Zerubbabel rebuilt it. Then, although Antiochus Epiphanes had desecrated it, they got their Temple back, and now King Herod had built a more magnificent one, the wonder of all Israel. Why in the world would the Author allow their Temple—*His* Temple—to be destroyed *again*?

The quiet party walked silently out of Jerusalem to a nearby mountain, each trying to make sense of what Jesus said. When would this atrocity happen? Did the Temple's destruction have something to do with Jesus becoming King? Or would its fall bring about the end of the world? The men were devastated by such a heavy blow in what should've been a week of joy and victory.

Suddenly, their questions came pouring out one after another. Jesus smiled compassionately at His disciples, sitting them down to explain. "My friends, the fall of Jerusalem and the end of the world are two separate events. Let Me explain both, so that neither will surprise you," Jesus reassured them.

"Within this generation, Jerusalem and Herod's Temple will be destroyed. You've heard Me warn the Pharisees that their dead rules and traditions are sucking the life out of Israel. They stiff-arm the very one who could breathe fresh life back into them, and so their destruction is imminent."

Shocked, one disciple asked, "So, the Temple's fall will be a judgment against our people?"

"The transition from one chapter to the next will devastate Israel," Jesus continued, leaving the disciples unsure whether He had answered their question or not. "Persecution will be rampant; Jews will betray their own brothers and sisters, horrible things will happen—things worse than Israel has ever experienced. The enemy will come, taking the people of Israel as slaves, so pray that you will be left behind! If you're left, you'll have hope for survival. And here's how you'll know the Temple is about to fall." Jesus leaned forward so His friends wouldn't miss what He said. "When you see an army surround Jerusalem, run! When you see the Temple defiled, escape to the mountains! You'll be safer there! Get out of Jerusalem with urgency—don't even bother grabbing a coat, just run for your lives, for it will fall with barely one stone left on another. The vultures will gather to feast on the corpse of Israel."

"So that's how the world will end?" John asked with dismay the question everyone wanted answered. A defeated Israel didn't fit into anything they'd learned about the Rescuer restoring Israel's greatness and all Gentile nations surrendering to Jewish supremacy.

Jesus shook His head. "No, there will still be much more in the Story. Jerusalem's fall is the beginning of the end, like labor pains for a woman. Contractions begin slowly with much time in between. Birth is imminent, but the labor is just beginning. Before the end comes, you'll be handed over to government officials. Beaten and persecuted, you'll stand trial because you follow Me. This world's kingdom will wage war with the Author's Kingdom, and great will be the suffering of the Author's people. But endure faithfully to the end, for your rescue is sure!"

Jaws hung open; eyes were wide. It all felt like too much. The disciples had thought Jesus was about to establish His rightful reign in Jerusalem, and yet He was speaking once again of suffering and persecution, and even of the destruction of their own beloved country.

Jesus continued, His voice earnest and solemn. "This is all part of the enemy's desperate attempt to hijack the Author's Story. He knows his time is short, knows his doom is sure, so he will fight with all his might. But know this, My friends," Jesus said as He stood up, too animated to remain seated. He leaned toward His friends, His eyes shining with Always Love for them, "The Rescuer's coming is inevitable, and when He comes, everyone will see Him! A cosmic war is raging; heaven and earth are its battlefield. But never doubt it, My friends, the Rescuer will be victorious!"

"But You say Jerusalem will fall within this generation," began Bartholomew. "So, when will the Rescuer return? Will it be long after that?"

Jesus laughed lightheartedly as He answered, "Only the Author knows that detail of the Story. But I can assure you that even though you don't know exactly when the Rescuer will return, you'll be able to look around and tell His coming is near. Let that move you to awareness and preparation."

"Awareness and preparation? What do you mean by that?" asked another disciple.

"Well, look over there at that fig tree," Jesus pointed to a tree nearby. "When you begin to see fresh leaves sprouting on the branches, what does that tell you?"

"Summer is near!" called out Andrew. All of the men were smiling, for the sign of the fig tree had been a welcome one since boyhood.

"Exactly!" Jesus replied with enthusiasm. "The same kind of thing will happen when the Rescuer is about to return.

So watch closely for His coming, longing for it in the same way Noah and his family did. While everyone around him went on with their lives, rejecting the enormous invitation of Always Love taking shape before their eyes, Noah prepared himself and his family. Do the same. Don't live for the kingdom of this world and then be unprepared for the Rescuer's final coming. It's that simple."

But it didn't seem very "simple" to the disciples who heard such words that day. Their hearts ached to think that another kingdom would overtake their country once again, to think the most sacred expression of their religion and culture—their Temple—could be destroyed within their lifetime.

This week in Jerusalem was hardly going as they expected. But the Author still had His pen in His hand. Jerusalem and the Temple would soon fall; yet this weekend the Author would let an even better Temple fall, to write something more lasting in its place.

Chapter 46

A Garden & A Betrayal

Matthew 26:36-27:31
Mark 14:32-15:20
Luke 22:39-23:25
John 18-19:16

"Oh, Daddy! I just don't know if I can do this!" Jesus groaned, His prayers seeping out of His soul in the form of blood sweating out of His pores. Agony filled His mind. Grief overwhelmed His heart. Fear barraged Him from all sides. He trembled at the thought of what He was about to experience. Shaking, gasping for breath, He cried, "Oh Daddy, I *long* for the Story You've written to unfold, but isn't there another way to write this chapter?"

The Story had once again wound its way into a garden. Jesus, the new Adam, had fallen to His knees beneath a tree in a garden, but not in the same way the first Adam fell. Underneath garden trees they each had to make the same decision: try to secure the Good Life for themselves because the Author couldn't be trusted or entrust their lives to Him regardless of confusion or potential loss. The first Adam hadn't even put up a fight. But all through the night Jesus was fighting, wrestling, fully entering into the struggle of every image-bearer to trust the Author through confusion and overwhelming pain.

"The physical pain I can take," Jesus prayed. "The lies and mockery I can handle. I can stand the abandonment of My people Israel and My friends, but how will I bear it if *You* abandon Me? My life has been a beautiful dance of Always Loving You and being Always Loved by You. All I've ever known is that I am Yours, and You are Mine—since before there was time! But now, to rescue the world, I have to give that up!" His voice choked; His whole being repulsed by the thought. "How will I bear it?"

Then it was as if the Author came into the garden kneeling on one knee and taking the head of Jesus, His trusting Lamb, into His hands, whispering, "Today is a sad day. Life as We intended it unraveled long ago in a garden much like this one. We have known from the beginning how We would make all things right and good again, and now is the time. Everything in the Story has pointed to this. Are You willing to play Your role in this Story in the way We always knew You would? For there is no other way."

Jesus saw nothing but Always Love in the Author—no selfishness, no evil in the Author's heart for His Lamb. The Lamb knew He could trust His Father, so He said yes. His mind made up, He committed His broken heart to the Author with incredible determination.

"Daddy," Jesus cried out once again, "Your Story is good; I won't try to write My own. I will take on Myself all that is theirs, so everything I have can be given to them. I'll take their sin. I'll take their death. I'll be cut off from Your Always Love, so they never have to be. I'll be the one You abandon, rather than them. *It's My life for theirs!*" and He wept the most agonizing tears ever cried in this Story.

For you see, dear Reader, the Author was right; there was no other way. Our sin had created a deep chasm of darkness and death that broke our relationship with Him, that crushed our souls, deforming us as image-bearers. Sin, like a stain, leaves us filthy. Like a disease, it eats away at our lives, keeping us locked in death's grip. So His Always Wrath against sin must destroy everything that defames His Always Love.

But we love sin. Incapable of climbing out of the chasm of darkness and death, unable to cure our disease or wash away the stain, incompetent to restore ourselves to the image-bearers we were meant to be, we were *hopeless*. So Jesus resolved to do what was written in the Story at the beginning: He would dive head first into the deep chasm of darkness and take our place in death. He would do battle with sin and destroy it. He would Always Love us, even though His Always Love would cost Him everything.

Jesus struggled to His feet, wiping His face with His hands as He stood still for a moment, and took a deep breath in and slowly let it out. Then He turned to walk into the saddest, most unbelievable part of this Story.

Image-bearers had always struggled with the Author's Always Love—ignoring, doubting, abusing, rejecting, or even denying it. But on this night Judas, the image-bearer any of us could have been, did something unbelievable. Feigning friendship with Jesus, he walked into the garden and *betrayed* Always Love with a kiss. Yet Always Love proved to be more unbelievable still, as Jesus, standing quietly in the darkness of it all, let it all happen, for the Author's Spirit still hovered in dark places, and the Author Himself had *written His own death into the Story* to rescue those He Always Loved.

The darkest night of the Story unfolded as image-bearers had their way with their Rescuer. Spewing their hatred on Him hour after hour, Jewish religious leaders shamed Him, mocked Him, and lied about Him so they could hand Him over to the Romans.

The Romans flogged the one who never hurt anyone, lash after lash tearing deep grooves into His back. They crowned with thorns the King who came only to serve. They dressed in scarlet and mocked the one who only elevated the dignity of those around Him. Hatred, contempt, and violence were given to the one who had only Always Loved them. The next morning, their Rescuer stood before them dripping with blood, covered with open wounds, body racked with pain, hearing His image-bearers chant, "Crucify Him!" over and over until they had their way.

All the while the Author's enemy stood by watching and laughing with wicked delight. These last few days could not have unfolded more perfectly. "He has eluded me until now, but this time, I've caught Him in my trap!" the enemy gloated. "I cannot lose! Israel and Rome are working together beautifully to do my dirty work. Jesus' disciples have fled, leaving Him utterly alone and helpless, and Jesus Himself isn't even putting up a fight. In a matter of hours, the Rescuer will be dead, and the Story will be over for good!" Then he slithered into the darkness laughing a deep, wicked laugh.

Chapter 47

The Rescuer Falls & All Hope Seems Lost

Matthew 26:17-35; 27:32-66
Mark 14:12-31; 15:21-47
Luke 22:7-38; 23:26-56
John 19:17-42

"So is this what Simeon meant when Jesus was still in my arms?" Mary's heart wept her question at the foot of the cross. "Because a sword cutting deep into my heart is exactly how it feels to have birthed Him and now watch Him die. What of the angel's words that Jesus would sit on the throne and rule an endless Kingdom?" She cringed as the final nail pierced His flesh, and Jesus' cross was lifted high for all to see. The sword pierced her heart deeply.

John, Jesus' disciple, put his arm around Mary to give her strength. He alone of the twelve disciples had made it as far as the cross. Regretting his betrayal, Judas had taken his life. Having denied ever knowing Jesus, Peter was now off mourning bitterly. The others had fled, unwilling to risk suffering along with Jesus. But John was there, comforting Mary, and trying to make sense of it all.

"Is this what He meant last night when we celebrated the Passover together?" John wondered to himself. "I couldn't imagine then what Jesus meant by His body being broken and His blood being poured out, but now I guess I see."

So much of what Jesus had said and done the previous night hadn't made sense in the moment. Stripped down like a slave, Jesus had washed each of His disciples' dirty feet. Then tears welled up in Jesus' eyes as He said, "My friends, the Author is up to something very good, even if it doesn't make sense right now. You've grown to trust the Author so much. Keep trusting Him and trust Me, too! We'll soon be separated, but then I'll come for you, and we'll all be together forever!" He put His arms around His friends and continued, "It's actually better this way! If I go away, you'll receive the Author's Gift! The Rescuer's own Spirit will live inside you, teaching, guiding, comforting, and leading you in Always Love. Right now you're sad; but just wait! Soon, you'll be overwhelmed with joy! It will look like evil will triumph, but keep trusting the Author. Evil will not write this Story's final words."

"I guess this is what Jesus meant when He said we'd be separated," John's heart ached at such a realization. "Did He know all along it would end on a Roman cross?" Deep, deep sadness washed over John.

Others gathered at the cross not to mourn but to mock. Roman commanders jabbed at Him with their words, "Look at the sign above His head! *King of the Jews!* Some King You turned out to be!"

The religious leaders took their turn, "So much for Your plans to tear down the Temple and rebuild it in three days! The Temple still stands, but *You* have fallen!" They roared with laughter.

"He claims to be the Author's Son," scoffed another, "yet the Author is letting Him *die!*"

"Some Rescuer He is!" jeered another. "He rescued others from death but He can't rescue himself! Come on down from that cross, Jesus; then we'll believe You!"

They all broke out in evil laughter once again, because it was ridiculous, wasn't it, dear Reader? Who would have suspected that in spite of the normal instinct to flee pain and suffering, our Rescuer would run *toward* it instead?

Their laughter died out as deep darkness rolled in. It was an eerie, misplaced darkness cutting off the sunlight at the brightest time of day. Was the darkness the Author's deep sadness? Proof of His Always Wrath against sin like the dark plague in Egypt? Or was it the arrival of the hosts of evil coming to watch the demise of the Author's own Son? They had longed for this moment for millennia and wouldn't miss the chance for a front row seat. For three full hours, darkness ruled the day as Jesus simply hung there on the cross, suffering.

What an unexpected twist in the Story! The Rescuer had done no wrong, yet He was dying; the innocent once again giving His life for the guilty.

A soldier offered a sponge dipped in a special drink to relieve His suffering. But Jesus turned His head aside, refusing to dull the pain. He would feel the full weight of this sacrifice.

"Daddy!" Jesus cried out, hoarse, mouth dry from dehydration, "Daddy! Forgive them!" He gasped for breath as He looked at the crowd gathered to watch Him die. He blinked His eyes to clear away the blood streaming into them like tears. His heart felt more pain than His body did as words of grace dripped off His tongue, "They have no idea what they are doing."

But Jesus knew what He was doing. He was taking their place, the place of the mockers and scorners, those who beat Him and whipped Him, those who loved Him and mourned for Him.

He'd endured the violence, been beaten and whipped beyond recognition, and nailed to a cross. But this next part was the hardest as all the sin in the whole Story was placed on Him as if He Himself had done it all. Frantically, He searched the dark sky. Like a young child realizing the father he loves is nowhere to be found, He cried in agony, "Daddy?" His heart pounding, eyes searching the darkness but finding nothing. "Daddy, where are You? Where have You gone? Don't leave Me!"

But for the first time, Jesus received no answer. Instead, the hand that had held Jesus all His days let go of Him in His darkest hour of need. Jesus was utterly and completely forsaken.

"Daddy!" Jesus whispered as tears washed the blood from His cheeks, "You said I was Yours, and You were Mine! You've Always Loved Me! But where are You now? Even You have abandoned Me!" He winced with pain as He continued, "But I will always trust You. My life is in Your hands." Working hard for His next breath, pushing up on the nail that held His feet to the cross, He forced air into His lungs and back out again, His broken heart crying out His final breath, "It is finished!"

His body—battered, bloody, and bruised—went limp. The Author's Always Love had been Jesus' life-breath all His days, but now it ceased to be *always*. When Always Love for Him ended, so did Jesus' life. The Author had done the unthinkable. He let the Rescuer fall, reduced to ruins. The light that had pierced the darkness in the beginning was now swallowed up by darkness, exiled by the Author's Always Wrath against sin. *Jesus was dead.*

For a split second all was quiet, then a thunderous crack pierced the air! The Author's broken heart sent shock waves throughout creation, splitting rocks in two, shaking the ground beneath those who watched His Son die.

Then with His own mighty hands, the Author reached down into the Jerusalem Temple; and as one tearing his garment in grief and mourning, He tore the thick curtain before the Most Holy Place from top to bottom. Priests performing the afternoon sacrifice heard the ghastly sound and looked up, horror-stricken, to find they could see straight into the Most Holy Place! The final sacrifice had been made. It was finished indeed!

"Pilate, sir, may I request the body of Jesus who was crucified today? I'd like to honor Him with burial," a courageous man requested. His status as a prominent Jewish religious leader ushered him into the Roman governor's presence after business hours, but his status could only protect him so far. This man, Joseph, risked everything to make this request. He had followed Jesus secretly, afraid to admit he believed Jesus was the Rescuer. But he didn't care anymore. The religious leaders had gotten away with murder. The least Joseph could do was bury His body.

"He's dead already?" Pilate asked, surprised. "Normally it takes days for people to die on our crosses; He was crucified just hours ago! Well anyway, yes, take the body and bury it." Pilate was ready to be rid of this Man once and for all.

Joseph went straight to the cross, took Jesus' body down, and began wrapping it in burial cloth. So violently abused, His body was beyond recognition. "Can you believe it came to this?" Joseph asked his friend who'd come to help him. "Do you think," Joseph asked, his voice shaking with grief, "if we hadn't been afraid—if we'd stood up for Him—none of this would have happened?" He stopped wrapping to look at Nicodemus, hoping his friend knew the answer.

"I don't know," Nicodemus replied. "Perhaps. But I can't help remembering something Jesus once told me. I didn't understand it then, but now it might make sense." Nicodemus' voice drifted off as he thought back to that dark night years ago.

"What did He tell you?" Joseph asked, bringing Nicodemus back to the present.

"Well, He told me the story of Moses lifting up the bronze snake in the wilderness. He said that story points to the Rescuer—as if the snake had bitten the whole world, spreading its poison, creating a spiritual kingdom of darkness. But He said that one day the Rescuer would be lifted up so that anyone could look to Him with faith and be healed—birthed into the Author's Kingdom. Oddly, I suppose we could say Jesus was lifted up, just like Moses' bronze snake. Maybe Jesus *had* to die?" Nicodemus said, his voice trailing off again.

"Pass me the myrrh and aloes you brought," Joseph said. "Nightfall is quickly approaching and with it the Sabbath. We shouldn't let this take longer than necessary. And anyway, regret won't help us now. What's done is done. The best we can do is give Him a proper burial."

They finished wrapping Jesus' body, stuffing the cloths with spices to ward off the stench as the body decomposed. Then they carried Him to Joseph's own tomb, deep in the heart of a beautiful garden. As they carried His body, they couldn't help but feel they were carrying all the hopes and dreams of so many who thought Jesus would be their Rescuer. They laid His body inside the tomb and, with the help of many men, rolled a large stone in front of it while some women followers of Jesus stood nearby watching. All their hopes and dreams were now buried for good.

But Joseph and Nicodemus weren't the only religious leaders to make a request of Pilate. Those who wanted Jesus crucified approached him one more time, "Pilate, sir, there's one small detail needing attention." He'd given them what they wanted once already; surely Pilate would grant this small request as well.

Pilate sighed. "Will this Jesus business never end? What is it you want?"

"Dear Governor," one of them began, "when Jesus was alive, He said some odd things... particularly that three days after He died He would...well, it's ridiculous!" he stammered.

"Go on! What did He say?" Pilate asked, becoming impatient.

"Well, He said He would come back to life three days after dying! Now, of course, this won't happen, but we think His disciples might come up with a plan to steal His body and say He's alive again. That could be trouble—for us and for you!"

"Fine!" Pilate replied gruffly, "Take guards to the tomb. Secure it as best as you can."

And that's exactly what the religious leaders rushed off to do. They sealed the tomb, stood a guard of soldiers in front of it, and walked away to continue with their lives, patting themselves on the back for a job well done, relieved finally to be rid of Jesus.

Chapter 48

Back to Life & Back to Mission

Matthew 28
Mark 16
Luke 24
John 20

"Can you believe what happened this weekend?" Cleopas asked his wife, Mary, as they left Jerusalem to walk home. As followers of Jesus, they had come to Jerusalem a week ago with high hopes. Now they were heading home from the Passover holiday with their hearts a jumble of sadness, disappointment, and confusion.

"Three days ago our hopes for a Rescuer died," replied Mary, "and so did our hopes for our nation, but what the women said this morning was so surprising! What do you think it could mean? How could Jesus' tomb be *empty*?"

"Excuse me," Someone interrupted. "I couldn't help but overhear. What are you talking about?"

"Are You the only Passover pilgrim who hasn't heard what went on this weekend?" Cleopas asked as he and Mary slowed their pace, inviting the Stranger into their conversation.

"Was Passover this year different than other years?" the Man asked.

Cleopas and Mary looked at each other, wide-eyed. "Well, didn't You hear what happened to Jesus of Nazareth?"

But Mary didn't give Him time to respond. "He was an incredible Teacher of the Binding Promise. More than teaching it, He *lived* it. It was like He knew our Story so deeply that He *embodied* it in a way no one else had! But this weekend, the Romans crucified Him!"

"Now we're all disappointed," explained Cleopas. "We all had hoped He was the Rescuer—that He'd overthrow the Romans, become King, and restore Israel to greatness."

Mary interrupted again, "But this morning, when some women in our community went to the tomb to anoint Jesus' body with spices, they found that His body was gone!"

"Not only that," jumped in Cleopas, sharing what he hardly believed himself, "they said *angels* appeared to them saying Jesus is *alive*! Some of our friends ran to the tomb and couldn't find Jesus' body—or the angels. We don't know what to make of it all."

Their Traveling Companion's eyes twinkled, "Well, it sounds like this year's Passover was definitely different! But I suppose our whole Story pointed to this, didn't it?"

"What do you mean?" Cleopas asked, confused.

"Well, it goes back to the Garden," He began. "When disobedience brought death to all image-bearers, the Author spared Adam's life with a promise to send the Rescuer and then He sacrificed an innocent lamb. Death would wound the promised Rescuer, yes; but then, He'd crush death! It sounds like that happened this weekend when the Rescuer was wounded, and the innocent traded places with the guilty."

Cleopas and Mary hadn't seen the Story quite that way before.

Their new Friend continued, "Through Noah, we see the Author's Always Wrath against sin while His Always Love provided rescue for those who trusted Him. Like a boat in a flood, the Rescuer carries His people safely to life again. Then there was Abraham and Isaac," He continued. "When the whole world deserved Always Wrath against sin, the Author provided a sacrifice in their place."

Cleopas and Mary's eyes grew wide. They'd never understood the Story this way before!

The Man continued, "The Author invited Jacob's family to move the Story forward, but his family faltered greatly. They betrayed their brother Joseph, who suffered horribly but eventually rescued his family from death. The Rescuer started a new family and then was betrayed by that family, all so He could rescue the world from a death that plagued humanity since Adam.

"Next, Moses clearly pointed to the Rescuer when he led Israel out of slavery and into a Binding Promise of Always Love with the Author. Could it be that Jesus, dying during Passover, was giving Himself up like a perfect Passover lamb, His innocent blood giving life to His friends as death passed by, releasing them from a slave master more awful than Egypt?" the Man mused, His eyes twinkling again.

"Well," the couple stared blankly at each other, "we hadn't thought of that!"

"Next, think of Aaron, the priest, preparing for the most important sacrifice of the year. He spent all night in prayer with the Author before carrying innocent blood into the Author's presence—blood that would wash away Israel's sins for a whole year. The people watched closely to make sure no detail was forgotten and sighed with relief when they were right with the Author again. The Rescuer would do this, too, but He'd wash away *a whole history of sins!* Though it seems that rather than cheering on their Priest and Rescuer, His people mocked and spat on Him as He carried His own innocent blood into the Author's presence."

All three were silent for a moment.

Then the Man continued, "Next the Author raised up Joshua to lead Israel into the Promised Land. Joshua's obedience drove out the enemy, giving his people a home and rest. Could it be that the Rescuer did that this weekend as well? He drove away the enemy and brought His people into a home with Him, giving them rest more real than Israel has ever known!"

Excitement spilled out with every sentence as He connected dots for His friends. "Remember Deborah and Jael, two strong women who both pointed to the Rescuer?" He asked. "One led her people into battle; the other crushed her enemy's head to rescue Israel. The Rescuer has done both—but against an even worse enemy!"

"Need I mention David, the boy from Bethlehem with a heart to face any giant that defied the Author, to knock it down and cut off its head? Wasn't Jesus, also from Bethlehem, willing to go against the greatest giant—death itself—to knock it down and cut off its head because death defied His Always Love?

"Then Solomon built an extravagant house for the Author, yet the Rescuer built an even better house for Him—with His own body! An enemy tore down Jesus, the Author's temple, this weekend, but in three days it was rebuilt, never to be brought down again! Even our people's exile to Babylon pointed to the Rescuer! This weekend, He experienced the Author's Always Wrath against sin, going into exile for sin that wasn't His, so that image-bearers wouldn't have to."

"Messenger after messenger pointed to a Rescuer who would suffer, the innocent trading places with the guilty; yet, like Jonah, He would rise from the belly of death and live to tell about it!"

The three of them talked and talked, time passing quickly until they arrived seven miles later at their small town. Mary and Cleopas invited their Friend to stay for dinner. But when they served the meal, they were surprised that their Friend took the bread, becoming their Host. As He thanked the Author for the meal, they suddenly saw clearly the one who had broken bread with His followers so many times before. Then He vanished!

"I knew it was Jesus all along!" exclaimed Cleopas.

"I thought so, too!" burst out Mary, her heart full of joy. "The more He talked, the more my heart came alive!"

"This means...*He really is alive!*" Cleopas shouted.

"Even better," realized Mary, "it must mean *He really is the Rescuer!*"

The couple jumped up from their dinner to race back to Jerusalem as fast as they could. They couldn't wait to tell the other disciples the news! They burst into the room where the eleven disciples were staying.

"We've seen Him!" they panted. "We just spent the whole afternoon with Jesus!"

"I know!" exclaimed Peter, jumping up to greet his winded friends. "He appeared to me, too!"

Then gently a familiar voice greeted them. "Hello, dear friends!" said Jesus, His eyes twinkling, a huge smile on His face, and His heart overflowing with His Always Love for each person in the room. "You're surprised to see Me? But isn't this exactly what I told you would happen? The whole Story pointed to this weekend—to My suffering and death, yes, but also to My resurrection!"

The room was silent in disbelief as the disciples' minds and hearts caught up to what their eyes and ears were witnessing. Then the room burst to life as they gathered around, embracing Him. They saw His scars that told a Story of heartache that no one wanted in the Story and yet proved His Always Love for them. Standing in awe of their Friend Jesus, the Rescuer, the Author's own Son who had gone to such excruciating lengths to rescue them, they understood why it had to be this way.

"Always Love has won, My friends!" He said. "I was willing to lose the Author's Always Love, so you would never have to. In weakness, I took away death's power. Surely that doesn't surprise you after all I taught you of My upside-down Kingdom!" Jesus laughed from deep within His heart, and the whole room danced with joy. "Now the whole world needs to hear of My Always Love. Everything we did together in Israel, we'll do together among the nations. We'll start in Jerusalem and Judea, then in Samaria, and then in every corner of the world. I'll be going with you in a way you can't even imagine. But don't go yet! Wait together here in Jerusalem until the Author sends you a very special Gift that will empower you to be witnesses. And My dear friends, never forget that I am yours, and you are Mine!"

Chapter 49

Power & Persecution
Acts 1-8:3; 9:1-19

"What did the angels mean when they said Jesus would come back in the same way we saw Him leave?" asked Andrew as Jesus' followers were gathered together back in Jerusalem. "Remember how He disappeared into the clouds after promising to send a special Gift? Do you think it'll be much longer before He comes back? We've already waited ten days."

Waiting had filled so much of the Story. For millennia, the Author's people waited for the Rescuer. Now He had come, and ten days ago left them again. So His 120 followers in Jerusalem were *still* waiting. Though they didn't exactly know what they were waiting for, forty days of sharing meals, deep conversation, and friendship with the risen Jesus had dispelled all doubt and rooted them in His Always Love. So they waited—not in a boring, sit-around-and-do-nothing sort of way but an active, immersing-themselves-in-the-Story sort of way. They knew He'd come; they just didn't know when or how.

Then, on the most fitting day of the Story, He came. Jews streamed into Jerusalem to celebrate Pentecost, the next big holiday after Passover. With Passover celebrations of rescue from slavery fresh on their minds, Jews now celebrated Pentecost to remember the giving of the Binding Promise on Mount Sinai and to celebrate another successful grain harvest.

Suddenly, the same Spirit that had hovered over the deep darkness of both creation and Jesus' grave filled the room where Jesus' followers had gathered! The hope that blew like a breeze through each page of the Story now whipped through the room like a violent, rushing wind. The same fire of His presence that led Israel out of Egypt and gave Moses the Binding Promise was the Author's Gift to His followers.

Set free by Jesus from slavery to sin, baptized with fire by the Spirit, their hearts seared by a new Binding Promise, image-bearers could now house the very presence of the Author!

"What is that sound?" exclaimed a group of Egyptian pilgrims standing outside the house where Jesus' followers gathered. "How are they speaking my native language? I thought I knew all the Egyptians coming to Jerusalem for the holiday."

A group of Jewish travelers from another part of the world walked by and, surprised, said a similar thing. "How are these Galileans speaking my language? What's this they're saying about a Man named Jesus?"

Before long, a small but growing crowd had gathered in front of the house where Jesus' followers were staying. The first thing the Author's fiery presence did through His temples was open their mouths to proclaim the Story in other languages, so that each pilgrim gathered in Jerusalem could understand. Like Moses coming down Mount Sinai to share the Binding Promise with Israel, the followers took the news from their tiny upstairs room down into the streets. Peter explained to the shocked passersby what only moments before he hadn't understood himself. "Friends, don't be surprised by what you hear! Long ago, the Author promised to give a new Binding Promise, filling His image-bearers with His Spirit like temples, regardless of gender, age, or social status. He's doing that today! His Spirit is *here*!"

The more Peter talked, the more people joined the crowd.

"You all have heard about Jesus who lived among us and showed us the Author's Always Love," Peter continued. "Fifty days ago we responded to the Author's Always Love by nailing Him to a cross. Yet everything the enemy meant for evil, the Author turned into something extravagantly good! Death held us in its grip for so long that it seemed death would write the Story's final chapters. Yet death's strength was weak compared to the Author's power!"

The crowd grew to thousands, all gripped by Peter's words. Many had heard about the recent events concerning Jesus, and with shoulders shrugging and their hearts burdened and heavy, they cried out, "What do we do?"

"The Author's Kingdom is here and now, so change the way you live," Peter said, just as John the Baptist and Jesus had said before him. "Be baptized, letting your outer life reflect what has happened on the inside, and you'll receive the Author's Gift, too!"

Pentecost suddenly took on a whole new meaning. No longer about the anniversary of the old Binding Promise, it marked the day the Spirit seared the new Binding Promise on their hearts. No longer about a grain harvest, it was about the harvest of image-bearers as 3,000 entered the Author's Kingdom that day.

What started in a small room, quickly spread throughout Jerusalem as followers explained with words and embodied with actions the Author's Always Love. They healed the sick and lame, freed the captives, cared and provided for each other's needs with Always Love, and lived every day like Jesus would come back any moment. This was what it meant for Jesus' followers to be His witnesses—to gather together in Kingdom communities and live out everything He taught them.

But the birth and growth of this Kingdom community in Jerusalem led to great opposition, for it had an evil enemy. Tricked at the cross, robbed in the grave, the Author's enemy couldn't defeat the Rescuer, and now a dynamic movement of thousands who followed Jesus was overtaking Jerusalem.

Fear and jealousy slithered into the Jewish religious leaders' hearts. Before long, Jesus' followers buried the body of young Stephen, their first martyr. Condemned in a trial of lies, this temple of the Author's Spirit was pelted with stones until he breathed his last, showing that this, too, was what Jesus meant when He said His followers would become His witnesses.

On the sidelines stood a young Pharisee named Saul, lips pursed in disgust, eyes squinting with hatred—for now an accomplice but vowing he'd take the lead in stomping out this movement of Jesus followers. Fueled by Stephen's stoning, Saul went from house to house knocking down doors, grabbing Jesus' followers, and dragging them to prison.

"We have to take stronger measures to put an end to this rebellion!" Saul passionately implored the high priest. "These rebels worship a false god—a dead man!—tricking the masses into walking away from the Author! Our attempts to stop this madness have simply scattered His followers to further parts of Judea, into Samaria, and beyond. Wherever they go, they spread these infernal lies about this Jesus of Nazareth. We have to be more strategic—more covert. Give me authority to go to Damascus and bring them back to Jerusalem. This Jesus nonsense must stay in Jerusalem, or it will overtake the world!"

"Damascus!" exclaimed the high priest. "Saul, it takes a whole week to get there! You really want to travel that far to end this rebellion?"

"I will go as far as necessary to put an end to this!" Saul promised. "They disgrace the Author and threaten Judaism!"

Pacing the floor, the high priest stroked his beard. He admired Saul's tenacity; and to be sure, their attempts to extinguish the Kingdom community in Jerusalem had only fueled its growth. Perhaps Saul would be the one to end it. He could think of few Jews with better breeding or education than Saul. Few kept the Binding Promise with more vigor than he and few were more zealous about stomping out this rebellion.

"You may go, Saul," the high priest consented. "I'll prepare the paperwork. You may leave tomorrow morning."

"I will not disappoint you," Saul assured him.

As the high priest stood silently watching Saul walk away, he was confident it would take extreme measures to stop these Jesus followers. But that's the kind of man Saul was...extreme.

"No, Master Jesus, I could never do what You're asking!" Ananias trembled with fear. "Saul is insane, violent, bloodthirsty! He'll stop at nothing to kill Your followers. I heard he's on his way here to destroy us even now! If I go to him, it will cost me my life!"

But Jesus didn't hesitate as He appeared to Ananias, a follower in Damascus. "I've handpicked Saul to follow Me and spread My Kingdom beyond the Jewish world. It will cost him everything."

"Saul is going to…follow You?!" Ananias gasped in shock.

Within the hour, trusting Ananias walked into a dark corner of a house where he found the small figure of a man kneeling, bent over in defeat. Compassion flooded Ananias' heart. "Could this really be the man we're all so afraid of?" he wondered, crouching down beside Saul, putting his arm around him.

"Brother Saul," Ananias began, surprised by his own words, "Jesus appeared to you on the way here and then sent me to you."

Saul began to weep. "The light! It scared my horse and blinded my eyes! I fell to the ground! We were so close to Damascus. I would've hurt more people, but He stopped me!" Saul's blind eyes searched around him, his mind replaying the events of three days ago. But he could hardly go on, "I thought He was dead! I thought this whole thing was a hoax! I gave my all to end what He started…Oh, Ananias!" His confession flowed with tears from his blind eyes, "I wanted Stephen dead! I've murdered men, women, and innocent children!" Saul melted into a pool of grief.

Ananias gently laid his hands on Saul's shoulders. "Brother Saul, Jesus is yours, and you are His! His Love for you is Always, and He's giving you His Spirit!"

In an instant, the Spirit restored Saul's sight and transformed his heart, so that rather than destroy the Kingdom community in Damascus, Saul was baptized by them, becoming a part of the Author's Kingdom instead.

The Spirit had come with fire, resulting in explosive growth of the Kingdom, as well as explosive persecution. But Jesus' followers were not afraid. Jesus had conquered death, their greatest enemy, filled them with His Spirit, and promised to return bodily one day. More than that, He Always Loved them. He turned suffering into joy and turned Saul, a terrifying enemy, into Paul, a dynamic follower of Jesus. So they had nothing to lose—not even their lives!—and only stood to gain by giving everything to the one who gave everything for them. The Author's Spirit was on the move, and not even persecution could stop it.

Chapter 50

Two Friends & A Call to Go
Acts 9:20-31; 11:19-30; 13-14

"Paul, there you are!" Barnabas embraced his friend whom he hadn't seen for years. "I want you to come with me. There's something extraordinary happening in Antioch, and I think you should be a part of it."

"Antioch? That's so far from Jerusalem! What is going on there?" Paul asked in wonder.

"Peter sent me there because he heard the Author's Spirit was at work, and it's true! Jesus' followers, fleeing persecution in Jerusalem, started a Kingdom community in Antioch. The Author's Spirit is so active, and His followers are so bold that they even began sharing the news of Jesus' Kingdom with Gentiles and are seeing them begin to follow Jesus!" Excited to take part, Paul set out with Barnabas for Antioch.

Immediately after being baptized in Damascus, Paul had begun telling people about Jesus. He taught courageously in the synagogues in Damascus, showing people Jesus actually was Israel's long-awaited Rescuer. But before long, Paul was running for his life, fleeing a city full of Jews committed to killing him.

Paul then went to Jerusalem, but Jesus' followers in Jerusalem wanted nothing to do with him. He had shed their dear friends' blood; surely this was a nasty trick Paul was playing on them, and he'd soon betray them all. But

Barnabas intervened, sparing no details as he told Peter and the other disciples of Paul's dramatic encounter with Jesus and his bold witness in Damascus. Finally, the followers in Jerusalem welcomed Paul with open arms.

Paul had proven himself as zealous for Jesus' Kingdom as he had been in trying to destroy it. His presence in Jerusalem caused quite a stir. People on both sides could hardly believe Paul could have changed so radically. But it was true. What he had done in Damascus, he did in Jerusalem, boldly going from synagogue to synagogue, teaching that Jesus was the Rescuer.

Paul was fearless, but once again it got him into trouble. It wasn't long before another plot to kill him was underway, forcing Paul to leave the Kingdom community in Jerusalem and retreat to his hometown of Tarsus.

Now this Kingdom community in Antioch, birthed out of the persecution Paul previously was part of, welcomed their persecutor with open arms. The Author's Kingdom was upside-down indeed! Paul taught and served alongside Barnabas in the multiethnic Kingdom community in Antioch, until one day, as they were all gathered together, the Author's Spirit began whispering to them, "Barnabas and Paul have a specific role to play in the Story. Prepare them for what's next!"

So the Antioch community began fasting and praying, discerning together what role these men would play in the Story. Before long, Barnabas and Paul were boarding a boat, sailing away from the place where, over the last decade, the Author's Kingdom had taken deep root. They had been called to expand the Kingdom even farther. They would not be disappointed.

"Tell us all about it! We want to hear everything!" the Antioch community urged Paul and Barnabas as they welcomed them back from their long travels. Long into the night, Paul and Barnabas shared stories of how they courageously took the Story of Jesus' Always Love into new places, saw His Kingdom advance, but were also met with significant opposition.

"Our first stop was the island of Cyprus, where Barnabas is from," began Paul. "An important government leader heard about us and wanted to hear more about Jesus. But when we got to his home, a sorcerer, influenced by the Author's enemy, did everything he could to distract and interfere."

Barnabas jumped into the conversation, animatedly describing what happened next. "Then, Paul turned to the sorcerer, and with the Spirit's power, struck him blind, turning his opposition into the very thing the government leader needed to see to become a follower of Jesus. And he was a Gentile—without any background in Judaism!"

Applause and exclamations rippled through the gathering as people expressed their excitement.

Paul shared more, "We trekked over mountain ranges, moving throughout Galatia, always going straight to the synagogues to begin teaching our Jewish brothers and sisters about Jesus the Rescuer. Many times, the synagogue communities were open and willing to hear. Once, they invited us back the following Sabbath, and the whole city came out to listen! But some Jews were filled with jealousy when they saw the crowds coming to hear about Jesus, and they violently ran us out of the area. So we just moved on to the next!" Paul smiled as he reminisced. The trip had been so hard and yet so fulfilling!

Barnabas picked up where Paul left off, "In Iconium, the Author's Spirit came with power, healing people, setting them free from demons, confirming in tangible ways everything we were teaching. But the city was divided. Some began to believe and follow Jesus, while the Jews swayed others not to believe. In fact, they were plotting to kill us; but thankfully, we found out their plan and left for Lystra."

"Which is where the people tried to worship us, thinking we were their Greek gods, Zeus and Hermes!" Paul exclaimed.

Their friends could hardly believe it. "Why in the world would that happen?" they asked.

"Well, Paul saw a lame man who had never walked a day in his life," Barnabas explained. "Paul simply told the man to stand up. The Spirit healed him, and he jumped to his feet to the shock of everyone who saw him! They thought such power could only be the work of their Greek gods."

"Then the whole city erupted in chaos," Paul continued. "They put wreaths on our heads and brought bulls to sacrifice to us. It was heart-wrenching to see how deeply entrenched idolatry was in their hearts. We were barely able to keep them from sacrificing to us."

"But just as we were about to explain that Jesus was the one who had healed the man," Barnabas interjected, "the same group that tried to kill us in Iconium showed up. We didn't realize it in time; they grabbed Paul, stoned him, and dragged him out of the city thinking he was dead!"

Everyone gasped, wide-eyed, eyes fixed on Paul, who sat unmoved by the memory of it. Barnabas continued, "We thought he was gone and we'd have to bury him; but as we gathered around his body, the Author healed him! Before we knew it, we were all walking right back into the very city where Paul had just been stoned."

As Paul and Barnabas shared late into the night, it was now more evident than ever that the Author had always meant for people from every ethnicity and culture to be invited into the Author's Always Love—for the whole world to be His Temple! The Antioch Kingdom community, because of its diversity, was poised and ready, not only to celebrate, but to support this move of the Spirit. This is what Jesus meant when He said that His followers would become His witnesses! What had first happened in a small corner of the world had just one more challenge to overcome before it could take the world by storm.

Chapter 51

To Jews & To Gentiles
Acts 8:4-40; 10:1-11:8; 15
Galatians 2
Luke 9:51-56

"Of course, Gentiles can become followers of Jesus, but ultimately, they have to keep Moses' laws and customs. After all, the Binding Promise is from the Author, and Jesus Himself kept these customs too. We have to teach Gentiles how to live like Jews," a man said, articulating one side of the argument.

"No!" contradicted Paul, then he articulated the other side of the argument. "People do *not* need to change their culture to become a true follower of Jesus! Faith makes us Jesus' followers and brings us into the Author's Kingdom—and the Author's Kingdom isn't Jewish. Kingdom culture matters—not our ethnic or religious culture."

"What you all are doing in Antioch is fine," continued the opposing side. "We're glad so many people are hearing about Jesus and believing He's the Rescuer. But ultimately, their faith needs to be expressed by keeping the same laws and customs that we keep. That's why we sent people to Antioch to teach the Binding Promise."

"No!" said Paul, shaking his head. "It was wrong for you to send people to Antioch. Why would you meddle in what the Author's Spirit is doing there?" Paul was distraught. If this was the conclusion the Jerusalem Kingdom community came to, then more than just his ministry to the Gentiles was on the line. The Story itself was on the line!

Gentiles were joining the Kingdom every day, but they weren't becoming Jewish. So the leaders of the Jerusalem Kingdom community faced a dilemma: Could someone authentically follow Jesus yet not become Jewish? What is essential to following Jesus? The argument was heated, with no one on either side willing to yield.

Peter, who had sat back listening as both sides debated, now stood up, bringing the argument to a standstill. "My dear friends," he said, knowing close friends were on both sides. "Ten years ago, I met a Gentile man named Cornelius through whom the Author showed me that He doesn't choose anyone based on ethnicity. He makes temples out of Jews and Gentiles alike, putting His same Spirit in both. If the Author gives His Spirit to Gentiles before they prove they can follow the Binding Promise, what is the point in teaching them to follow it? We have to rethink this! The old Binding Promise is a heavy burden to bear—one we can't keep ourselves! Jesus has fulfilled the whole Binding Promise for us, yet we burden our Gentile friends with keeping it. If our own laws and customs were never able to rescue us, the same is true for our Gentile friends."

"You know," began John, taking the floor, "once my brother and I were so angry we wanted the Author's Always Wrath against sin to destroy a whole Samaritan village. Peter, do you remember that? We wanted to call fire down from heaven because they rejected Jesus."

Peter laughed out loud, "I remember that! You and your brother were truly sons of thunder!"

John laughed and then continued, "But Jesus simply embraced the inconvenience of rejection, and soon I saw why. Later when I visited Philip in Samaria, we saw the Author's Always Love fall on a Samaritan village instead. His Spirit filled people we grew up calling 'dogs.' The Spirit did that without any one of them becoming Jewish."

"It's happening in Africa too," Philip chimed in. "Once I was following the Spirit down a desert road when I met an Ethiopian man reading the scroll of Isaiah. By the end of the conversation, the man was baptized and taking the Author's Always Love—not any rules from the Binding Promise—back to Ethiopia! The Rescuer's Spirit knows no bounds! With His sights set on permeating every pocket of the globe with His presence, He is moving us, His Temples, to just the right places, whispering invitations of adventures down desert roads or whisking us from one place to the next to give everyone a chance to know His Always Love."

James, Jesus' brother, now a leader in Jerusalem's Kingdom community, stood up and continued, "Friends, the Author is at work in our midst, but it shouldn't surprise us. If we reflect on the Story, it's evident the Author always meant for His Kingdom to reflect all ethnicities and cultures. It seems His plan is for all nations to know His Always Love *through* Jews—not for all nations to *become* Jews."

James paused to consider what he would say next. Jesus' followers were at a crossroads. What they decided now would significantly impact what future Kingdom communities would look like. As leaders, they wanted to discern what the Author was writing for this chapter of the Story and then fully live into it, however uncomfortable or confusing it might seem. James moved them toward a decision.

"I believe we shouldn't meddle with what the Author is doing," James declared. "We should not make it harder for Gentiles to become Jesus followers. I say we write a letter to our sisters and brothers in Antioch, affirming their faith and freeing them to live out that faith in their own culture. The goal is not for them to become Jews, but the hope is that Jews and Gentiles will live peaceably together in the Author's Kingdom."

What James was saying was timely and true. They had been wrong to require more from Gentile followers than Jesus required of them. One by one the leaders' hearts changed, and one by one they agreed with James and together wrote a letter to the Kingdom community in Antioch.

James then put his hands on Paul's and Barnabas' shoulders and looked into their eyes and said, "Brothers, take this letter back to Antioch with you. Read it aloud, so our brothers and sisters there will know how deeply we love and support them."

With the letter in hand and their hearts full of joy, Paul and Barnabas said goodbye to James, Peter, and the others in the Jerusalem Kingdom community and set off to return to Antioch.

When Jesus' followers in Antioch heard the letter, they erupted in shouts and applause. The Kingdom community in Jerusalem had affirmed that following Jesus is not just for Jews, and more than that, following Jesus didn't even have to look Jewish! The Author's Kingdom was now free to look more like the multicultural, multiethnic Kingdom it was always meant to be.

Chapter 52

Suffering & A Life Well-Lived

Acts 16-28
Romans 15:17-23
2 Timothy

Timothy rolled the scroll back and forth in the palms of his hands. He had just received another letter from Paul and was mulling over it as he walked to his friends' house to share its contents. What could Paul have meant when he wrote that his departure was near? He'd been released from prison once before; maybe he thought he'd be released once again? Or did Paul suspect something far worse—that prison was where his life would end? Timothy sighed deeply.

Paul had mentored Timothy for more than a decade as they traveled, planted Kingdom communities throughout the Roman Empire, and wrote letters to those communities together. Timothy now oversaw the Kingdom community in Ephesus, a role for which Paul's intentional influence had shaped him profoundly.

As he arrived at his friends' house, Timothy walked through the door without offering much of a greeting, blurting out instead, "I'd like to make a trip to Rome. Paul asked me to get there before winter, so he'll have his cloak before it gets cold, and…" Timothy hesitated, "I think it may be my last chance to see him."

Priscilla and Aquila sat down with Timothy. All three had traveled around the Roman Empire with Paul, experiencing incredible victories and also overwhelming opposition as they shared Jesus' Always Love.

Timothy admired Priscilla and Aquila deeply. They had met and learned from Jesus personally. Kicked out of Rome, they moved here and there starting Kingdom communities. In a culture where men viewed their wives as possessions, Aquila saw his wife as his equal in every way, knew her to be a gifted teacher and trainer, and empowered her to live fully into her gifts to influence and grow the Kingdom. They were a dynamic couple who both lived out the unique ways the Spirit gifted them, and Timothy knew they would encourage him.

"What did he write to you?" asked Aquila, inviting Timothy to share what weighed heavily on his heart.

"It seems like this imprisonment is harder on Paul than the first one. He seems to think the end is near. He likened his life to a fight he has fought, a race he has finished running. Now he's ready to die and see Jesus," Timothy explained.

Both Priscilla and Aquila looked at each other and sighed. They could attest to Paul's faithfulness—his was a life well-lived! But they too were deeply saddened at the thought of their dear friend suffering in a prison cell, awaiting what seemed inevitable: martyrdom.

"Timothy, remember how the first Kingdom community started here in Ephesus, through hard work and suffering?" Priscilla began. "Every afternoon Paul taught and trained Jews and Gentiles in Tyrannus' lecture hall while the rest of the city slept through the heat. Paul labored, weaving the message of Jesus' Always Love into the very fabric of this city. You saw what happened!"

"I did!" replied Timothy. "The Author's Kingdom came to Ephesus with power, healing people and setting them free from evil spirits!"

"Exactly!" Priscilla said as she smiled, "and then what?"

"Well, before we knew it, people from all over Ephesus came confessing their sins, repenting of things like sorcery and magic. I even remember a group of them gathering all their scrolls of incantations and their amulets and burning them in a huge fire," replied Timothy.

Aquila added, "I heard the value of those scrolls was more than what forty people could earn in a lifetime!"

"Yes," affirmed Timothy. "The Author's Spirit was changing their hearts with His Always Love! His Kingdom was breaking into many parts of the city."

"And what happened after that?" asked Priscilla. "After Paul sent you and Erastus to Macedonia, did he tell you what happened?"

"Didn't a huge riot break out?" Timothy answered.

Priscilla nodded and continued, "As people began to see through the lies of the Artemis cult, they quit worshiping her and, of course, quit buying those little idols, those replicas of Artemis' temple. They say when you buy one, you can take it anywhere and bow before it, and it's the same as if you were here in Ephesus worshiping Artemis at her shrine. They sold thousands each year! When the money dried up, the silversmiths started a riot because we both know wealth, more than Artemis, is god here in Ephesus, a city in the wealthiest province in the Empire. The riot became violent, and Paul had to hide, while his friends were taken captive."

Priscilla paused to emphasize what she'd say next. "Timothy, you know that sooner or later, when the Author's Kingdom comes into a city, the authority of King Jesus will clash with the powers that hold the city in their clutches. When they clash, people are often set free, but sometimes followers of Jesus suffer for it. Suffering is what Jesus said it meant to become his witnesses."

Aquila picked up where his wife left off, "We've seen it happen all over the Roman Empire. The Author's Kingdom, no longer restricted to a certain geographical location, is spreading all over the world! What began in Jerusalem, the Jew's center of power and faith, has now spread to Rome, the center of power and faith for Gentiles. Jews opposed it in Israel; Gentiles oppose it all across the Empire. But the Author's Kingdom still spreads because Jesus is the rightful King, and His followers are faithful, even to death."

Timothy breathed deeply. "Paul said as much in his letter. He said, 'Even if we're in chains, the message of the Kingdom never will be.'"

"Timothy," Priscilla reminded him, "Paul wouldn't want you to fear suffering—yours or his. Remember the Author's Always Love. He's writing a very good Story and one day will make all things right again."

Timothy sighed, "In his letter, Paul told me not to be ashamed of his suffering because it's the calling of all who follow Jesus. Over and over I watched Paul suffer. Over and over I watched the Author rescue him from evil. And through it all, the Author enabled Paul to share His Always Love with more and more Gentiles!"

Priscilla laughed as she remembered something. "We used to joke with Paul that if he kept it up, he would run out of places to share the message of the Kingdom. Everyone in the world would hear of Jesus in his lifetime! Paul has shared the Good News with kings and queens, with soldiers and ship captains, in provinces all over the Empire."

"And you know, Timothy, it's happening," continued Aquila. "It's costing us everything we have, but the whole world is hearing. So let's not lose heart. Let's keep following the Spirit, sharing the message of His Always Love, teaching people who will teach other people, and let's suffer well. Let's give our all to the one who gave His all for us."

"Thank you," Timothy said, encouraged by his friends. "I'll be leaving for Rome in the morning."

The three friends said their goodbyes, and Timothy went home to pack his belongings and to retrieve the cloak, scrolls, and parchments Paul had requested in his letter. The next morning he set off for Rome, racing against the forces of darkness to arrive in time to encourage his friend in his final days.

The Author's Kingdom was indeed spreading powerfully throughout the Roman Empire. What began as a small Jewish sect in Jerusalem quickly spread like wildfire throughout the known world, carried like burning torches by people like Paul, Timothy, Priscilla, and Aquila. But the Author's Kingdom did not grow without opposition. Followers of Jesus suffered great persecution, and many of them gave up their lives. Emperor Nero would soon behead Paul. Emperor Nerva would later take Timothy's life. And Priscilla and Aquila would both be martyred as well. But as Paul had reminded Timothy, the message of the Kingdom was unstoppable.

The End of the Beginning of the Story
Revelation

Suffering. All followers of Jesus were experiencing it these days—even John. Exiled to the island of Patmos by Emperor Domitian, John now sat on the beach, the sound of the incoming waves soothing his weary soul. John was an exile—not in the Babylonian Empire like his people long ago but in the Roman Empire. Rome had become the new Babylon.

John's lonely exile gave him ample time to pray, but today he could only pray about suffering. Kingdom communities throughout the Empire were struggling, either giving in to the comforts, pleasures, and powers of Rome or valiantly trying not to. Many of John's friends had not succumbed to Rome's idolatrous ways and so were beheaded, crucified, torn apart limb by limb by wild beasts, were rotting away in dark dungeons, or denied jobs and access to resources.

"We need perseverance," John whispered to the sand and the waves, though they didn't say anything in return. "Oh, Author of All Life, how long will this Story last before You send the Rescuer again as You promised? We long for Your Kingdom to come in all of its power. We need perseverance until it does for we are suffering greatly!"

Suddenly, a voice called him. "Who could that be? I thought I was alone," John muttered as he turned. Nothing could have prepared John for what he saw.

"Jesus!" John cried as he fell on his face, thinking he must have died, for this Jesus standing before him was unlike any Jesus he had ever known! Dressed in royal robes, flowing white hair crowned His head, evoking a wisdom older than time. His eyes blazed with all-seeing sight; His feet glowed bronze and made every square inch He trod bow to Him in reverence. And His voice! It was like the sound of a deafening waterfall!

"Don't be afraid, John," Jesus said soothingly, bending down to help John to his feet. "I, the Author, am the Beginning and End of this Story. Come with Me; I'll give you a peek into the final chapter of My Story. Then tell My followers what you see so they can be faithful and endure."

John's island of exile suddenly became a portal into the very throne room of the Author! The soft sand beneath his feet became a vibrant rainbow of jewels around the throne. The sound of rushing waves became nothing short of a glorious roar of creatures all declaring their ceaseless praise. On the throne sat the King who had been on His throne since before the Story began. He has sat there through every chapter and will keep sitting there long after the final page is turned. He held within His hand a sealed scroll—the final chapter of the Story. All creation longed to know the Story's end, yet the scroll remained sealed. John wept, for no one was worthy to open it and bring this Story to its completion.

"John, don't weep," said a voice. "Look behind you! The Lion of the tribe of Judah has won the war! He is worthy to reveal the final chapter!"

John turned, afraid to come face to face with this Lion, but was surprised. "Where is He?" John asked, "I see only a Lamb who looks as if He died, yet lives!"

The slain Lamb approached the throne and took the scroll. As He did, the throne room erupted in thunderous praise, "Yes! The Lamb is worthy to open the final chapter because He gave His life to give life to Abraham's family, a family that speaks every language, wears every skin tone, and lives in every corner of the earth!"

"Come!" a booming voice invited John, "and you will see the Author's heart. One facet is His Always Love, another His Always Wrath against sin. Sin has corrupted image-bearers, diminishing the glory of this Story for a time but no longer. The Author's Always Wrath against sin will now be satisfied, and when it is, the beginning of the Story will end!"

Bewildered, John witnessed the unexpected: as the Lamb broke the seals, Always Wrath against sin poured out on earth, and worship broke out in the throne room! On the earth below, image-bearers devoured each other with swords, streets flowed with human blood, wars broke out between nations, famine swept across the earth. Everything that image-bearers had ever turned into an idol now revolted against such misplaced worship, rising in protest. Beasts ravaged image-bearers, the earth shook beneath their feet, stars fell from the sky, seas crashed upon the inhabitants of the land. Hail rained down, and fires broke out, racing to consume anything left. All image-bearers who had spent their lives trying to wrest the pen from the Author's hand to write their own stories of wealth and power, now found their arrogance catching up to them. For them, horror filled this final chapter.

"What are they doing?" John cried, squinting, doubting he was seeing clearly. For men and women, young and old, were running here and there, begging mountains and rocks to hide them from the Lamb's Always Wrath against sin. "Why don't they turn to the Lamb instead? Don't they know He is gracious and forgives?"

"John," an angel replied with sadness, "these image-bearers love their sin so much they prefer to be swept away with their idols into destruction rather than worship the Lamb. Stubbornly, they reject His Always Love."

Smoke began to rise from an open abyss, and rising with it was a beast—a dragon!—the same serpent that lives to fuel humanity's love affair with sin and has been trying to destroy the Story.

"What is the dragon doing?" asked John in horror as the beast ravaged the land, deceiving and devouring image-bearers.

"John, the dragon is furious because he knows he can never win the war he began with the Author long ago. He hears the Story's final pages turning and knows it's almost over. His destruction is sure, so frantically he tries to bring as many image-bearers with him to destruction as he can," the angel replied.

Another angel called to John, "Come, let me show you how the Lamb will pour out His wrath on Babylon."

"On Babylon?" asked John who turned to see a woman clothed in purple and scarlet, covered with sparkling jewels, trimmed with gold from head to toe. She was both stunning and hideous and held in her hand a golden goblet, overflowing with the blood of the Author's people. She rode into the vision on the scaly back of the dragon, bringing the goblet to her mouth to drink deeply. She threw back her head, laughing a wicked laugh, not even bothering to wipe away the blood that dripped from her mouth. "I am Queen Babylon!" she boasted. "I have nothing to fear! All nations look to *me* for the Good Life rather than to the Author!"

"This woman!" gasped John. "Who is she?!"

The angel accompanying him replied, "She is the Garden-rebellion gone global. She is every system and structure, every kingdom and empire that ever set itself against the Author. She is everything evil image-bearers have tried to do with the Story."

"Then how is this a good Story?" John protested in desperation. "She is winning—her dominance fueled by the blood of the Author's people! How much longer will the Author let His people suffer like this?"

The clouds rolled back like a scroll to answer John's question with another vision. A loud voice shouted, "Seal all 144,000 of the Author's people from the twelve tribes of Israel!"

Suddenly, John cried out, "But I see an army of far more than 144,000! They're uncountable! As far as the eye can see there are image-bearers of every ethnicity and nation, speaking every language ever spoken, all dressed in white, and their weapon is—*worship*!"

"John," the angel explained, "these are those kept by the Author's Always Love—an uncountable multitude, an unshakeable Kingdom, all the Author's fulfilled promises to Abraham. They've found their life in the slain Lamb, giving everything to follow His footsteps. Now their suffering is barely a distant memory because, John, they aren't being destroyed—they've become the Story's greatest army. They have experienced the wrath of the kingdom of darkness but they will *never* experience the Author's Always Wrath against sin."

Awestruck, John exclaimed, "So, as the Lamb breaks the seals, unleashing His Always Wrath against sin, He seals His people, unleashing them to worship! This is what it means for the Author's people to be His witnesses: to suffer and worship and bring the Story to its climax!"

"Yes, John," the angel affirmed, "now watch this!"

A white horse galloped into view, and on the steed was Faithfulness Himself, the same Jesus who had invited John to see the Story's ending. His eyes burned with Always Wrath against sin; His heart beat with Always Love for His image-bearers. He is the true King and crowned with many crowns! In one hand He holds a sickle to harvest the earth, in His other, an iron scepter to bring unruly nations to submission. In the beginning, this Word breathed life into the Story; and now, with the sword of His mouth, the Word will cut from the Story everything in rebellion to the Author. The first time He came, He quietly slipped into His own Story unnoticed, a helpless Babe born to die in weakness. But now, He rides gallantly, unmistakably back into the Story, the long-awaited Warrior-King! And behind Him is His army of martyrs, dressed in white, as He is. It is the beginning of the end, and His victory is sure!

"Come!" an angel's voice called all the earth to battle. Then every evil image-bearer, every beastly enemy that ever grasped for the Author's pen gathered themselves to wage war against the King. Battle lines were drawn.

But suddenly John cried out, "What just happened? Did I miss the battle? The enemy is already captured!"

"John," whispered an angel with a smile, "it was over before it began."

Then the King threw His captive enemy into eternal defeat, a lake burning with incessant fire, fueled by His Always Wrath against sin—all idolatry, fear, immorality, and injustice swallowed up in a grave that would never let them go. Every page of the Story had given image-bearers the chance to choose His Always Love; but many had rejected it, choosing His Always Wrath against sin instead. They too were swept away.

When His Always Wrath against sin had extinguished anything that would diminish His Always Love, a deafening victory cry arose from the Lamb's army, worshiping their King for His Always Wrath against sin and for His Always Love. Then, as if wiping the earth clean with a fresh cloth, the Story turned a page, showing John what was always in the Author's heart for His world—a glimpse of an eternity of all things made new.

And when the visions faded from view and John found himself alone on the beach once again, he finally knew how all followers would endure! He grabbed a scroll and pen and wrote what he saw to the Kingdom communities throughout the Roman Empire:

Dear friends, we're at war! So let me encourage you to endure suffering and live faithfully in exile. Here is what our Warrior-King says:

Enduring Ephesus, you've worked so hard but have forgotten I want you to be My working lovers, *not My loving* workers. *Come back to My Always Love; let it fuel our partnership together in this world.*

Suffering Smyrna, your earthly poverty is your Kingdom riches. You suffer greatly now, but eternal life with Me will be your crown.

Persecuted Pergamum, you've buried my slain faithful witnesses, yet you still haven't buried your false teaching. Rid yourself of what is false so that you can be faithful to Me!

Tolerant Thyatira, you mix your perseverance with tolerance of immorality as if lowering your standards is the only way to endure. Raise them, even if it means death!

Sleeping Sardis, wake up! I'm still at work among you, but you've fallen asleep on the job. Don't let this world lull you to sleep any longer.

Faltering Philadelphia, with little strength left, hold on! My Always Love will sustain you to the end!

Lukewarm Laodicea, why must I stand outside your gatherings and knock? Your self-sufficiency keeps you from Me and from having any lasting impact on the world around you. Let Me in. Find in Me all you need!

Remember, I am yours, and you are Mine—to the very end! One day all suffering and sorrow will fade from view when I take you as My Bride to live forever in My Always Love. Keep holding on; I'm coming for you!

John put down his pen. Looking up at the sand and waves stretching before him in his exile, he whispered a prayer all creation and a history of image-bearers have prayed, "Yes, Jesus, we long for your coming!"

Epilogue

Finding Your Place in the Story

"Just burn it down!" one Roman general sternly ordered.

"Yes, this Jewish revolt has gone on too long. I didn't come to Jerusalem to leave behind a single trace of hope for these insolent people!" another general agreed.

"But look at this place!" Commanding General Titus pushed back passionately. "It's immaculate! It seems a shame to destroy it."

The generals were at an impasse. Two days ago the Roman army, led by Emperor Vespasian's son Titus, had finally captured the Temple. He set up the Roman Emperor's divine image, defiling the Jewish Temple and sending a clear message to the people: this Temple belongs to a new god, the Author has been defeated.

All around the Temple lay the devastated city of Jerusalem. Caught unaware, the Jewish people quickly found themselves trapped inside their city, surrounded by an army, and left with few resources to survive. For three-and-a-half years they tried to hold out, believing they could throw off the wicked, power-mongering Roman government and be free at last. Fed up with Roman rule, Roman taxes, and Roman influence, in A.D. 66 the Jewish people lit their Roman representative's house on fire and began attacking Roman soldiers. Emperor Nero wasted no time sending the order, "Attack Jerusalem and burn it down!"

Year after year Jewish zealots fought General Vespasian and his army until Nero took his own life, and the army pulled back, unsure of whether to keep attacking or not. This gave the Jewish people a glimmer of hope and time to regroup until Vespasian became emperor and sent his son Titus to finish the job.

Now, famine had ravaged the city of Jerusalem, children had died from starvation, unburied corpses lay piled in the streets, and to their shame, mothers had even resorted to eating their children to stay alive. The end had come. Jerusalem had fallen.

Some people, believing Jesus' warning that Jerusalem would fall, were quick to flee to the mountains to save themselves. But those who either did not heed His warning or did not know about it were left to suffer miserably inside a city doomed to fall. The Romans had recently breached the walls of Jerusalem and occupied it. The last bastion of hope the Jerusalem zealots had was the Temple, until that fell also.

For two days the generals had been at a stalemate, arguing over what to do, until the faint cry of someone shouting, "It's going up in flames!" reached their ears. The smell of smoke and the sound of crackling fire began to reach them as well.

"What? Who did this? I gave no order to burn it down!" yelled Titus indignantly. "Put out the fire!"

But it was too late. A soldier had taken matters into his own hands, lighting a piece of wood and throwing it into the heart of the Temple. The sacred space was now going up in flames.

Gone was the Most Holy Place where high priests had entered with innocent blood to wash away the sins of their people. Gone were the altars for daily sacrifices and burning incense. Gone was the most tangible expression of everything it meant to be people of the old Binding Promise. Then stripped of even its melted silver and gold, the Temple was laid waste, barely one stone left on another.

Rome had its way. Rome had the final say.

Or did it?

The Jerusalem Temple is no more, and even the Roman Empire that destroyed it has fallen from the pages of history. But there was one more thing that John saw in his vision and shared with Jesus' followers to encourage them to live their chapter of the Story faithfully.

"Come," an angel invited John once more. "Let me show you the Author's Bride."

But as John turned, the Bride that he saw was a radiant City, a new Jerusalem—heaven coming to earth. "I can hardly believe it!" he exclaimed. "This City is radiant! It's bedazzled with jewels, paved with gold, and filled with the Author's presence! And there, flowing from the Author's throne, giving life to all nations, is the river Ezekiel saw so long ago. *This* is what the Author always had in mind for His image-bearers! It's the Good Life with Him gone global! But where is the Temple?"

"John, there is no need for a Temple in this new Jerusalem," explained the angel, "for the Author Himself is their Temple, and the new Jerusalem is the Most Holy Place where all nations live uninhibited and welcomed in His presence. This is the fulfillment of every promise the Author ever made to Abraham's family. Never again will His image-bearers experience exile, for sin is no more, and they have found their forever home in Him, in this City called, 'The Author is Always with Us!'"

Dear Reader, everything in the Story points to the day when those who find life in the Author's Always Love will live the Good Life forever with Him. Until the day He renovates this world and makes all things right again, He invites us, His image-bearers, to live our chapter of His Story with faithfulness and with the end of the Story in mind.

For thousands of years, the Author's people waited faithfully for Jesus' first coming. Now the Author's people have been faithfully waiting thousands of years for His second. Dear Reader, *how are you waiting?*

In every chapter, women and men, young and old, of every skin tone, language, and nation, have longed for the Good Life. Some chose to write their own broken stories for their lives trying to get what they wanted, while others believed the life they longed for could only be found in the Author. *What will this chapter of the Story say about you?*

Perhaps you've spent your life writing your own story, clinging to the false hope that if you have enough wealth, power, prestige, or religion, life will be the way you want it. You've been willing to make sacrifices small and great—people, resources, your very heart as an image-bearer—to create your own kingdom, thinking it will give you the life you think you deserve. But one day, sooner or later, dear Reader, you will find there is no Good Life apart from the Author's Always Love. Either way, the Author wins. No one can take His pen from His hand; *He has already written the end of the Story*. In light of His Always Love for you, will you surrender to His Story?

Others of us find ourselves disoriented in the waiting, unsure of our place in the Story. Tricked into thinking the Good Life is found here and now, we indulge ourselves in trivialities, taking Always Love for granted, while missing the Author's Kingdom around us.

Could courageously entering the Story mean that you follow your Rescuer into a desert experience, through suffering, or into a grave with only the assurance that He Always Loves? Or will entering the Story mean that you leave behind everything familiar to carry the Author's Always Love to a nation of image-bearers different from yours, who live every day with no chance to ever hear of Jesus and the Story of His Always Love? Will you give up grasping for the Good Life here and now so you can offer it to Abraham's lost family in every corner of the globe, and in so doing, speed His return?

And to those waiting and working faithfully: Keep persevering! Dear Reader, be a faithful witness, living in exile in a world empire doomed to fall. Will you resist its tantalizing invitations to compromise? Will you raise your voice to resist the beasts that wreak havoc on the earth? Will you do that, Reader, even if it means you suffer or give up your life?

Oh, to be found ready and waiting at His return! To have given our all to the one who gave His all for us, only to find that anything we gave up pales in comparison to the gift He would one day give us fully: *Himself.*

So today, dear Reader, whatever the pages of your personal story have said of you so far, will you be willing to be brave and to be part of His Story in a way you never expected? For remember—*He is yours, and you are His.*

Author's Note

Why I wrote *Always Love*

In May of 2018, I sat in a Starbucks south of Denver, Colorado, my heart a jumble of emotions. Just weeks before, on the heels of a miscarriage and a sudden move away from our life in Southeast Asia, we had packed up and returned to the US. I was grateful for a full day to simply be alone with God and hear His heart for this unexpected season I found myself in.

I opened my Bible to Nehemiah, the book I was studying that month, and as I read of Ezra reading his people their story, a dream was conceived in my heart: I knew I wanted to write a book that helped God's people reconnect with the Story of Scripture.

Little did I know, God had already been shaping my heart for this book in many ways. First, my oldest child had entered that liminal stage where she was beginning to out-grow picture Bibles yet was still learning to read the real Bible for herself. We had already given her an easy-to-read version of the full Bible, and being the eager reader she is, she started at the beginning and read every word until she got a few chapters into Leviticus. Then she stopped. "You don't have to read each book in order," I told her, so she jumped ahead to a different book and kept reading. But something about that experience stayed with me, because deep down, I don't want my daughter to skip Leviticus as if it's not important. Yet, every picture Bible I'd ever read to her skipped it entirely as if it weren't "story" material. I knew we needed a resource to help our family wade into what sometimes feels like the murky waters of the difficult but important passages of Scripture.

Second, my personal "method" for studying Scripture since January 2017 had been "A Book a Month." Each month, I take a different book of the Bible and study it deeply, both alone and in community. And while it will take five years to go through each book this way, I'm now more than halfway through and completely convinced that one of the best ways to study Scripture is to see the role that each book plays in telling the larger Story and to immerse myself in it for a while.

Third, grief and loss shaped my heart to long more deeply for the love and presence of God. While writing this manuscript, I experienced two more miscarriages, and as I grieved these losses, there were days I wrote these chapters through tears, rooting my soul in the message of this book: that I am His, and He is mine, and He *Always Loves* me—even when the Story is confusing and painful. It took nine months to write the manuscript of *Always Love,* and had this book been a real baby, she would've been born the day before her due date when I typed the final words. Then the editing and publishing process took another nine months. So while my arms feel so empty at times, longing for the babies I deeply wanted, my heart has been full of nurturing this "book baby" that was unexpectedly conceived in my heart and birthed into the world in a season of great personal loss. My hope and prayer is that the message of this book will meet you, dear Reader, in whatever season you find yourself and root you in the Always Love of God.

Let me say just one thing more, since some of my early readers raised questions about why I use a phrase like "Always Wrath" in a book called *Always Love.*

I've heard people say that "the God of the Old Testament" is a "God of wrath" and "the God of the New Testament" is a "God of love"—as if God had a change of heart between the Testaments.

But then I've also heard people say that the person who spoke most about hell and judgment in the Bible is actually Jesus. While I've never gone through the Gospels to tally up how often He mentions it, even a cursory reading of His teachings will reveal that Jesus did in fact speak *often* about God's wrath—and with more detail than He ever did about heaven. If we read on in the New Testament, we find Paul and Peter and others also clearly mentioning God's wrath, and then Revelation takes us face to face with vivid depictions of judgment.

So really, *both* Testaments present us with a God of wrath against sin and evil. But we tend not to talk about that today. In fact, the word *wrath* itself has become rather archaic, and I struggled with whether or not to use it in this book. "People either won't understand it or they will be turned off by it," I was told. And I knew that could be true. So I searched high and low for a better word to describe what God has for sin but could not find one. God's wrath, as both a word and a concept, has become something of a relic of a Christianity long past—as if we've become too modern to have use of such an antiquated concept. Broadly speaking, it seems that most Christians have moved on with life without it.

So, I had to make a decision about my book: *Would my language determine my theology, or would my theology determine my language?* If an integrated reading of the narrative of Scripture presents us with an unchanging God who outrageously loves people and also outrageously hates sin; of a God who goes to unfathomable lengths to rescue lost image-bearers and also goes to unfathomable lengths to obliterate every ounce of sin from His creation, then my book must reflect that. And until someone coins a new, succinct word or phrase for "wrath," this is the best word I can find, and that is the reason I use it in my book.

Some may question my combination of *always* with wrath, and the reason for it is simply this: an unchanging part of God's heart is that He will *never* be okay with sin. Even when sin is done away with, were it to ever creep back onto the pages of His Story (though I'm not at all implying that it could or would), He would *still* both hate it and do something about it (wrath). He is *always* against evil.

To always give us His love, He has to always have wrath against sin. There has to be the absolute and utmost hatred for anything and everything that would harm the objects of His love. Or He wouldn't really love us. So you see, God's wrath is more closely connected to His love than we might realize. We might even say that wrath is an expression of love. It is His love in action as He comes against anything that would detract from His love or hurt those He loves. Perhaps the reason we struggle with His wrath is because we struggle to fully grasp the ferocity of His love for us.

By using the word "wrath," I never mean to present God as having the fly-off-the-handle sort of anger that hurts relationships—the kind of anger we might show each other as sinful humans. His wrath is both *against sin* and is incredibly and mercifully *patient*, preferring that we would give up our sin and take His love instead. But when we cling to sin, refusing to let go of it, and He judges all sin and destroys it, then image-bearers get what they've chosen.

My hope is that we would either reintegrate the word "wrath" into our common vocabulary or create a new word that captures the same meaning, but let us not leave behind the theology of wrath. For if talking of God's wrath should ever make us uncomfortable let us remember this: the most shocking part of this Story is that God takes all responsibility for our sin and takes on Himself all the wrath we deserve for it, so that when He destroys sin with finality, He doesn't have to destroy us too. He gets us, and so very undeservedly, we get Him. *That* should be the only part about His wrath that makes us uncomfortable.

With that, dear Reader, may you go out into the world knowing and living like you are Always Loved by the Author.

Sara Lubbers
Sydney, Australia
July 2019

Printed in Great Britain
by Amazon